THERE'S POWER IN RELATIONSHIP

Working Toward a Christ Centered Relationship

Rupert & Glenette (Red) Hinds

Uriel Press

Copyright © 2023 Rupert & Glenette (Red) Hinds.

All rights reserved. No part of this book may be used or reproduced by any means, graphic, electronic, or mechanical, including photocopying, recording, taping or by any information storage retrieval system without the written permission of the author except in the case of brief quotations embodied in critical articles and reviews.

This book is a work of non-fiction. Unless otherwise noted, the author and the publisher make no explicit guarantees as to the accuracy of the information contained in this book and in some cases, names of people and places have been altered to protect their privacy.

Uriel Press books may be ordered through booksellers or by contacting:

Uriel Press
1663 Liberty Drive
Bloomington, IN 47403
www.urielpress.com
844-752-3114

Because of the dynamic nature of the Internet, any web addresses or links contained in this book may have changed since publication and may no longer be valid. The views expressed in this work are solely those of the author and do not necessarily reflect the views of the publisher, and the publisher hereby disclaims any responsibility for them.

Any people depicted in stock imagery provided by Getty Images are models, and such images are being used for illustrative purposes only.
Certain stock imagery © Getty Images.

ISBN: 979-8-8861-2028-8 (sc)
ISBN: 979-8-8861-2029-5 (hc)
ISBN: 979-8-8861-2030-1 (e)

Library of Congress Control Number: 2023920301

Print information available on the last page.

Urial Press rev. date: 01/09/2024

Scripture quotations marked KJV are taken from the Holy Bible, King James Version.

Scripture quotations marked NKJV are taken from the New King James Version. Copyright © 1982 by Thomas Nelson, Inc. Used by permission. All rights reserved.

Scripture quotations marked NLT are taken from the Holy Bible, New Living Translation, copyright © 1996, 2004, 2007 by Tyndale House Foundation. Used by permission of Tyndale House Publishers, Inc., Carol Stream, Illinois 60188. All rights reserved.

Scripture quotations marked HCSB®, are taken from the Holman Christian Standard Bible®, Copyright © 1999, 2000, 2002, 2003, 2009 by Holman Bible Publishers. Used by permission.

Scripture quotations marked MSG or The Message are taken from The Message. Copyright 1993, 1994, 1995, 1996, 2000, 2001, 2002. Used by permission of NavPress Publishing Group.

Scripture quotations marked CEB are taken from the Common English Bible, Copyright © 2011 by Common English Bible.

Scripture quotations marked ESV are from the ESV Bible® (The Holy Bible, English Standard Version®), copyright © 2001 by Crossway Bibles, a publishing ministry of Good News Publishers. Used by permission. All rights reserved.

Scripture quotations marked ASV are taken from the American Standard Version.

Scripture quotations marked AMP are taken from the Amplified® Bible, Copyright © 1954, 1958, 1962, 1964, 1965, 1987 by The Lockman Foundation. Used by permission.

Scripture quotations marked NIV are taken from the Holy Bible, New International Version®, NIV®. Copyright © 1973, 1978, 1984 by Biblica, Inc.™ Used by permission of Zondervan. All rights reserved worldwide.

JANUARY 1

HAPPY NEW YEAR!!

His Thoughts Are Of You!

Meditation Verse: Jeremiah 29:11 HCSB

For I know the thoughts that I think toward you, says the Lord, thoughts of peace and not of evil, to give you a future and a hope.

Scripture Reading: Jeremiah 29:1-13

We are parents! And not a day goes by when we don't at some point think about our children. And even though they are grown and leading their own lives, it does not mean that they ever leave our care and concern. God thinks about us in the same way, it is part of His divine order. He started it all, we just emulate His Love. God just doesn't think about us He directs His thoughts "toward" us. David said in Psalm 40:5, (NKJV), "Your thoughts toward us cannot be counted to You in order; if I would declare and speak of them, they are more than can be numbered." It is designed to give you a "future and a hope." God's heart is toward His people, the promise that His plan is perfect. As you begin to focus on this new year, don't take your eyes off God. Move toward His plan and purpose, He has already ordained it. You cannot be stopped!! We are praying for your future and hope. God started it; we love because He first loved us. The best is yet to come:

Happy, Healthy and Blessed New Year!

Blessings, Rupert & Red.

JANUARY 2

Be Encouraged

Mediation Verse: Psalms 71:15 NKJV

My mouth shall tell of Your righteousness and Your salvation all the day, For I do not know their limits.

Scripture Reading: Psalms 71

It is our firm and utmost desire, to uplift and inspire you. To challenge your thinking and cause you to look within. We will not call anyone out by name, we do not want to disparage any individual. Our assignment is to plant seed. We cannot save or deliver anyone it is only God that can provide that increase on and in your lives. We do what we do out of obedience and love. Our hope is that we can point you in the direction that causes you to begin or deepen your relationship with God. You are here for a reason, God has a purpose and plan for your life. We cannot keep this to ourselves, because that is what you do with good news, you share it with anyone who will listen. We do not claim to have all the answers, we just believe we know the One who does. So as the verse says, we plan to tell people about the goodness of God, His righteousness and salvation that has no limits. As we said before our assignment is to plant seed, you determine the soil it falls in, we pray for good ground.

Blessings, Rupert & Red.

JANUARY 3

Trust Makes The Marriage Secure

Meditation Verse: Proverbs 31:11 NLT

*Her husband can trust her, and she will greatly enrich his life.
She brings him good, not harm, all the days of her life.*

Scripture Reading: Proverbs 31

Some salient advice for the married couples, do you want to live a happy married life? A few things to remember: 1) God needs to be the center of your marriage. Everything that you said to each other when you took your vows, you said before God. He heard you, so keep your word! 2) Never demean your mate, when you do you demean yourself! It is extremely hard to come back, and repair hurtful words said to or about your mate. Someone once said, "Before you criticize your spouse's taste, stop and remember, they chose you!" Truth is we all have habits, struggles, weaknesses, fantasies, childhood memories, unspoken needs, and longings hidden deep inside. Our yearning for someone to trust is deep and non-negotiable. 3) Always have shared dreams and goals. Statistics state that couples are divorcing at an alarmingly high rate between the seventeenth and twenty-fifth year of marriage, because that is usually when the last child graduates from high school or college and leaves home. Years of living with and for your kids and work, and now it is just the two of you. You live separate lives forgetting that you are a team. Avoid that scenario by having lifetime goals that you both can work towards. Remember you are more than just parents and God has a plan for your lives as a couple. Talk about it, pray about it together and ask God to reveal His plan! He keeps His promises!!

Blessings, Rupert & Red.

JANUARY 4

God Loves You Enough To Wait For You

Meditation Verse: 2 Peter 3:9 HCSB

The Lord does not delay His promise, as some understand delay, but is patient with you, not wanting any to perish but all come to repentance.

Scripture Reading: 2 Peter 3:3-16

Sometimes waiting has its perks, instead of having entitlement issues, you develop patience, and the ability to see that only God can work things out for your good. Delayed is not denied, it is the window that God gives for you to repent and trust Him with your life. When you come to the realization that it is His will to save you, He will fulfill every promise to you. The blessing is a transformed life. Please don't let the delayed expectation of the promise cause you to miss God's perfect timing of the blessing...

Blessings, Rupert & Red.

JANUARY 5

Who's Your Daddy?

Meditation Verse: Romans 8:15 HCSB

For you did not receive a spirit of slavery to fall back into fear, but you received the Spirit of adoption, by whom we cry out, "Abba, Father!"

Scripture Reading: Romans 8:12-17

The general statement "We are all God's children," is a false one. Until you have been born again and receive the Spirit of adoption, you are a creation of God without any rights or privileges. The good news is you can change your status. Decide today to confess Jesus, join the family of God and enjoy the right and privilege to call out "Abba Father!" There's power in relationship!

Blessings, Rupert & Red.

JANUARY 6

God Took Care Of It In Advance

Meditation Verse: Romans 5:8 KJV

But God commendeth His love toward us, in that, while we were yet sinners, Christ died for us.

Scripture Reading: Romans 5:6-11

In a hotel room in Okinawa, Japan, after reading Romans 5:8 so many times over my life, this day, on November 8th, 1994, that verse completely overwhelmed me. I began to cry uncontrollably, and I did not know why at first, then the revelation hit me: God truly does love me and believed I was worth enough for Christ to give His life for me. Now, I had believed that most of my life and had confessed Jesus as my Lord and Savior. However, that day, that glorious day, was the beginning of a true relationship, one that has sustained me throughout the ups and downs, the good, bad and ugly in my life. I pray that you get to know God on a personal level. It is the only total surrender that guarantees victory and not defeat.

Blessings, Rupert & Red.

JANUARY 7

Believing Is Seeing

Meditation Verse: Psalms 8:3 NLT

*When I look at the night sky and see the work of Your fingers-
the moon and the stars You set in place.*

Scripture Reading: Psalms 8

We really cannot understand how people can reconcile creation to one random explosion, or even many random explosions. The argument is so compelling for intelligent design. My wife and I have had the opportunity to travel, and the beauty of this world is inescapable. The architecture of scenery is sometimes difficult to comprehend. How in the world can this be a fluke or happenstance??!! God has made His presence known in all of creation, so man is without excuse! Romans 1:20 (KJV paraphrased). You do not have to be a world traveler to fall in love with creation or the Creator; you need evidence? Just look up!! More on this later…

Blessings, Rupert & Red.

JANUARY 8

To Forgive & Forget

Meditation Verse: Psalms 103:12 HCSB

As far as the East is from the West, so far has He removed our transgressions from us.

Scripture Reading: Psalms 103:1-12

It has always been God's property to forgive. It is hard to fathom the grace and mercy that just seems to be a never-ending source from Him. Interesting the lengths that God goes to, to show His love for us. Consider that he did not say as far as the north is from the south, because north and south will eventually meet. East can never meet west, that is how thoroughly God has forgiven us. Let it go, forgive others and forgive yourself, God already has made a way...

Blessings, Rupert & Red.

JANUARY 9

Direction – Straight Ahead!!

Meditation Verse: Philippians 3:13 NLT

No, dear brothers and sisters, I have not achieved it, but I focus on this one thing; Forgetting the past and looking forward to what lies ahead.

Scripture Reading: Philippians 3:12-14

Sometimes leaving things in the past is difficult to do. Painful memories and regrets can hinder us from receiving what God has for us. But understand mistakes and regrets do not have to define you. There is a reason why the rearview mirror is smaller than your windshield, your focus should be on what is in front of you and not behind. Make the decision to live your life moving forward and put the past where it belongs, in the past…

Blessings, Rupert & Red.

JANUARY 10

A Life of Integrity

Meditation Verse: Proverbs 20:7 HCSB

The one who lives with integrity is righteous; his children who come after him will be happy.

Scripture Reading: Proverbs 20:7

This verse struck me as an admonishment. Integrity is a word that you don't hear much anymore. We ourselves have not always walked as such. Even though our past is under the blood, we have the obligation to keep integrity now as a character trait. A virtue that people will see, and hopefully our children and grandchildren will emulate. Conform to the image of Christ; make integrity a part of your character. Choose to live for truth. The world does not teach truth, because they don't teach Christ, who is the Truth…

Blessings, Rupert & Red.

JANUARY 11

I Need You Now!

Meditation Verse: Psalms 70:1 NKJV
Make haste, O God, to deliver me! Make haste to help me, O Lord!
Scripture Reading: Psalms 70

There is never a time when we don't need God. Every breath you take is dependent on Him. We take so much for granted, but trials and tribulations place God front and center. Thank God, He is full of compassion and mercy. When we call, He answers, trust His timing. He has already worked it out for our good. So, don't worry about how big your problems are, just know that God is bigger than any problem you may face…

Blessings, Rupert & Red.

JANUARY 12

Love Is All You Need

Meditation Verse: Galatians 5:14 HCSB

For the entire law is fulfilled in one statement: Love your neighbor as yourself.

Scripture Reading: Galatians 5:1-15

These words that were first spoken by Jesus, is the key to a just society. There is no law, statute, institute, government, or society that love cannot transcend and transform. It is the greatest attribute there is in its purest form. Love for love's sake, the pure agape love will turn everything around for your good. The challenge is for every person to understand this simple truth; EVERYTHING, works by love. We will be sharing this more and more in the weeks and months ahead.

Blessings, Rupert & Red.

JANUARY 13

Read The Signs

Meditation verses: 1 Corinthians 10:13 HCSB

No temptation has over overtaken you except what is common to humanity. God is faithful, and He will not allow you to be tempted beyond what you are able, but with the temptation He will also provide a way of escape so that you are able to bear it.

Scripture Reading: 1 Corinthians 10:9-13

Nobody is exempt from temptation, it comes to everyone in various forms and ways, normally in those areas where we tend to be the weakest. The adversary knows and attacks those areas with a vengeance. But God always shows us the way out. Our issue is not that we can't see it, but our choice sometimes, if we are honest, is not to take it. Don't confuse temptation with trials and tribulations, there are some things we must endure, discernment is the key, but if victory is ours, then the battle must already be won. Claim your victory and walk out of the escape hatch!!

Blessings, Rupert & Red.

JANUARY 14

Do Mercy

Meditation Verse: James 2:13 HCSB

For judgment is without mercy to the one who hasn't shown mercy. Mercy triumphs over judgment.

Scripture Reading: James 2:1-13

In the life of the Christian, the walk is more important than the talk. Because it is what you do that will gain favor with God. We talk about love, and faith, but you MUST DO love and faith. Just like a child is more likely to do what he or she sees you do rather than what they hear you say, your actions will always speak louder than your words. Sometimes you will have to do the hard part for others, not just because its noble, but because it's right. Christ did the hard part for us. Judging is easy but brings no blessing. "Blessed are the merciful for they shall obtain mercy." Matthew 5:7(NKJV). These are among the many things we will talk about that are important to God. So, go, Do Mercy…

Blessings, Rupert & Red.

JANUARY 15

Come Together

Meditation Verse: Psalms 133:1 NKJV
Behold, how good and how pleasant it is for brethren to dwell together in unity!
Scripture Reading: Psalms 133

When the purpose of a thing is not known or understood, abuse is inevitable. To live in harmony with one another creates the purpose for unity. We seem to fight for everything but a unifying result. God always intended for us to live as family. It is part of the Divine construct. The bedrock of unity is selflessness. Without it, unity cannot be achieved. When we learn to esteem each other higher than ourselves, our purpose to dwell together begins to take shape. Instead of fighting for first place, let's fight to arrive at the finish line together.

Blessings, Rupert & Red.

JANUARY 16

A Firm Foundation

Meditation Verse: Psalms 127:1 HCSB

Unless the Lord builds a house, its builders labor over it in vain; unless the Lord watches over a city, the watchman stays alert in vain.

Scripture Reading: Psalms 127

Safety and security are primary in the days that we now live in. There are some who can choose to live anywhere they want, for many though, that choice is not an option. But can we share with you that it is more important how you live than where you live? This verse is more about where your priorities lie than the placement of mere bricks and mortar. God demands first place in your life, second or third place is a waste of your time. It gets deep but it is not complicated. Simply put, there's power in relationship! If God is not your foundation, then your living will be in vain…

Blessings, Rupert & Red

JANUARY 17

Lifelong Praise

Meditation Verse: Psalms 146:2 NLT

I will praise the Lord as long as I live. I will sing praises to my God with my dying breath.

Scripture Reading: Psalms 146

"I will." Those two words are important in our attitude towards praise. It shows intent, our actions are deliberate. I mean to praise Him, no ifs, ands, or buts! The goodness of God can be so overwhelming that even in trying times, praise should be a natural reaction. He is so deserving no matter how we feel. Everything belongs to Him, so be intentional, and should you ever need incentive, just listen to your heartbeat, that alone makes Him worthy!!

Blessings, Rupert & Red.

JANUARY 18

Possess The Land

Meditation Verse: Joshua 6:2 NLT

But the Lord said to Joshua, "I have given you Jericho, its king, and all its strong warriors.

Scripture Reading: Joshua 6:1-16

I remember the feeling of anticipation as a kid knowing that I was going to get a gift on Christmas. It was already mine, it was wrapped with a bow with my name on it! I was just waiting on that day to receive it! God's promises are Yes and Amen. He told Joshua that He had given them Jericho, but there was a timetable with instructions in order to receive the land. We believe that God wants to bless us beyond what we even ask or imagine! In fact, the blessing is already ours, we just have to be ready to receive it. God's timing will prove His favor and grace, just be ready to take Jericho without a fight.

Blessings, Rupert & Red.

JANUARY 19

A Prayer For The Day

Scripture Reading: 1 Kings 8:49 MSG

Listen from Heaven to what they pray and ask for and do what's right for them.

Father we give You praise! Your love for us is unconditional, Your grace and mercy inexhaustible. There is no one like You!! You alone are worthy of all glory and honor. Our lives are Yours and our hearts seek to please You, because without You we are nothing, but with You all things are possible. Order our steps as we desire to do Your will. Thank You for all You have done, are doing, and will continue to do in our lives. You, Lord, get the glory from our lives as we continue to live as You would have us live. You are our refuge and strength, and we wholly lean on Your name. Bless, comfort, touch, heal and deliver, all those who read this prayer. Do what only You can do in the lives of your people, meet them all at the point of their needs. Grant strength, peace and faith where it is needed. Give us a love for one another, so that we may dwell in safety, free from hurt, harm or danger seen and unseen, and a consideration for everyone that fosters community and togetherness. In Jesus name we pray, Amen and Amen. Have the best of days!!

Blessings, Rupert & Red.

JANUARY 20

Choose To Forgive

Meditation Verse: Matthew 18:32-33 NLT

Then the king called in the man he had forgiven and said, "You evil servant! I forgave you that tremendous debt because you pleaded with me. Shouldn't you have mercy on your fellow servant, just as I had mercy on you?"

Scripture Reading: Matthew 18:21-35

Forgiveness is a huge problem in not only the body of Christ, but in society at large. The main reason? You are offended. You are upset with the Pastor, the church, your wife, husband, your neighbor, co-worker, even the dog! You say, "but you don't you know what they did to me." It does not matter, forgiveness is not for them, it is for you! Nine times out of ten the person who offended you does not even realize it. While you are stewing and fuming and losing sleep, the offender is oblivious to your condition. For the Christian, forgiveness is not a two- way street. It is one of the stops along the narrow path, that you must deal with in order to free yourself of the baggage that keeps you from God's best. You, like that wicked servant, have been forgiven a debt that you can never repay. When God forgave, it was for you, and the burden was lifted. When you forgive, you experience the same benefits, so forgive and get your rest.

Blessings, Rupert & Red.

JANUARY 21

Eternity Lasts Forever

Meditation Verse: Isaiah 40:8 NLT
The grass withers and the flowers fade, but the word of God stands forever.
Scripture Reading: Isaiah 40:1-8

It may not be something we like to talk about, but our mortality is sure and unavoidable. Just like the flower we will all eventually fade from the scene. God's Word, however, is eternal and stands to exceed the test of time. Why? Because God esteems His Word above His very name, and He has already guaranteed The Word's future at His right hand. What if we told you there was a way that you could guarantee a future in the presence of Almighty God? That He loves you so much that He provided a way for you to get that forever Word in you, and if you abide in that Word, forever with Him is guaranteed? We double dog dare you to consider attaching yourself to the Word of God, after all; Forever is a long, long, time…

Blessings, Rupert & Red.

JANUARY 22

Walk Of Life

Mediation Verses: Galatians 5:22-23 KJV

But the fruit of the Spirit is love, joy, peace, longsuffering, gentleness, goodness, faith, meekness, temperance: against such there is no law.

Scripture Reading: Galatians 5:16-26

This world is so fast paced and full of distractions that many times the attention to detail gets lost in the fray. When the mind is racing beyond the point of real contemplation, it becomes easier to compromise than deal with truth. And the truth is, none of this will produce real peace. We seldom, if at all, make time for what is real anymore. Why do we spend so much time focusing on what is temporal with no thought of the eternal implications? It is not mere walking that determines our destination, it is how and where we walk that does. When we commit to walking in the Spirit, our lives take on the true meaning of purpose; to affect lives for Christ; Being blessed to be a blessing. All the things that walking in the Spirit produces are meant to have a profound effect in the transformation of our lives and others. This is the responsibility of the disciple. Whatever we do in life, whatever our profession, never forget our true walk of life. The walk that makes eternity our destination.

Blessings, Rupert & Red.

JANUARY 23

Created For A Purpose

Mediation Verse: Psalms 139:13 HCSB

For it was You who created my inward parts; You knit me together in my mother's womb.

Scripture Reading: Psalms 139:1-18

We were created on purpose, you may have been an accident, a surprise, or maybe even an inconvenience to your parents, but not to God. He designed you and formed you for relationship and with a plan for your life. People have made this plan some mysterious and deep mission that you must somehow navigate on your own and discover. It is not! God desires that we begin a relationship with Him that will create intimacy, draw us closer to Him, so that He can get glory out of our lives. Our gifts, or God given abilities become the springboard or catalyst that over the course of our lives proves to be the blessing that people see that inspires them to want and desire relationship with God. You are the epistle that people see that brings light to dark places and illuminates the purpose for which you were formed in the first place. You just need to rise, shine and give God the glory on purpose…

Blessings, Rupert & Red.

JANUARY 24

Image Conformity

Mediation Verse: Daniel 1:7 HCSB

The chief official gave them other names Belteshazzar to Daniel, Shadrach to Hananiah, Meshach to Mishael, and Abednego to Azariah.

Scripture Reading: Daniel 1:3-15

Image is everything!! Daniel, Hananiah, Mishael, and Azariah, were in captivity in Babylon. Although their captors tried to strip them of their culture and language and forced them to assimilate to a completely new way of life, they never lost sight of their identity and the God that they served. It seems as if our culture is always changing, searching for the next best thing, the new flavor of the month, the coolest people to emulate! It is a plan of the enemy to draw you away from who and what you were designed to be. The Bible warns us not to be conformed to this world, but to be transformed by constantly renewing our minds. Romans 12:2a (paraphrased). People talk about keeping it real or being 100%! But we are not loyal to truth! Reality shows are not based on reality!! Don't let culture strip you of who you are! We are made in the image of Christ, when you get ahold of who you truly belong to, you will conform to the proper image! Do not allow the culture of the day to become your captors! You cannot afford to lose your identity; your future depends on it...

Blessings, Rupert & Red.

JANUARY 25

From Level To Higher Ground

Mediation Verse: Psalms 143:10 HCSB

Teach me to do Your will, for You are my God. May Your gracious Spirit lead me on level ground.

Scripture Reading: Psalms 143

The fact that God has given us free will can be a blessing and a curse. Free will is given to everyone but not everyone can handle it. The spirit world works opposite to the physical. In the physical you cannot surrender to be free, but in the spirit, it is the only way to be free. In this world, most people know the difference between right and wrong, but few understand the difference. What the world calls right, the spirit world understands as wrong, because the world lacks the wisdom to know the difference. Wisdom is the correct application of knowledge, without wisdom you will never fully grasp what you know. Confused? Let me help you, the will of God is what you need to know and comprehend, because without it you will not trust God. It's His will that leads us to level and higher ground. We will rather believe for God to change our situations instead of our hearts. We don't want to be taught; we just want results. The Psalmist believes that the will of God is the road to freedom. The next level is to surrender to His will in order to be free.

Blessings, Rupert & Red.

JANUARY 26

God Can Use You

Mediation Verse: Ezra 1:2 HCSB

This is what King Cyrus of Persia says: "The Lord, the God of Heaven, has given me all the kingdoms of the earth and has appointed me to build Him a house at Jerusalem in Judah".

Scripture Reading: Ezra 1:1-4

The prophetic books of the Bible can at times be a little difficult to grasp, but what is amazing is how astonishingly accurate they are! Cyrus, the king of Persia, had been prophesied about in Isaiah, one hundred and fifty years before his birth! It was said that he will allow the Israeli people to return to Jerusalem and rebuild the house of God. We see in Ezra 1:1, that God placed in Cyrus' heart that fulfilment of prophecy. God can use anyone to accomplish His purpose. Cyrus was able to see his role in the fulfilment of the prophets. We were created for purpose as well. All through the Bible we can see our role in meeting that purpose. God has placed it in our hearts. It is our mission if we choose to accept it! The truth is, it will be accomplished with or without us! I want to accept my mission and be part of the kingdom. Do not lose out, answer God's call! His word will not return to Him void it will accomplish what He pleases and prosper in the thing for which He sent it. Isaiah 55:11b (NKJV). If God can use anyone, it might as well be you.

Blessings, Rupert & Red.

JANUARY 27

Examine Your Motives

Mediation Verse: 1 Timothy 6:5 NLT

These people always cause trouble. Their minds are corrupt, and they have turned their backs on the truth. To them, a show of godliness is just a way to become wealthy.

Scripture Reading: 1 Timothy 6:3-10

This scripture leaped out at us in light of the greed and selfishness that seems to be everywhere lately. While we have always known, we now deeply understand that people's actions are always a consequence from what resides in their heart. Unless the heart changes and seeks pure motives, right behavior can never be the result. As long as money is our god, we will continue down the path of destruction. Do not be fooled by the insincere chatter of people who profit from the misery of others. God will deal with them. We appeal to all of us who know and understand the true worth of prayer. Pray for the change of hearts that govern this country, and every country for that matter. We know how helpless we feel when an unspeakable atrocity is forced upon us. But we can never give up, evil will triumph when good men do nothing. We need to examine our own hearts and make sure that our motives mean a stand for righteousness, a change of heart moves the kingdom closer.

Blessings, Rupert & Red.

JANUARY 28

Be A Giver

Mediation Verse: Psalms 146:3 NLT

Don't put your confidence in powerful people; there is no help for you there.

Scripture Reading: Psalms 146

People who put their trust in riches are the most likely to misuse their wealth. They do not understand what the blessing is for, in fact they do not even see it as a blessing. They are like the man who stored his crops in his barns till they were full to overflowing and decided to build bigger barns, retire and keep his food to himself. He put his trust in the wrong thing and was called a fool and died that very same night. Luke 12:16-21 (NLT). We cannot see our fellow man suffer and if we are able to help, refuse. God is well able to give you a return on your giving. You need to be a giver, not because God needs your money, but because in your giving God blesses you to be a blessing to someone else. It does not always have to be money, but time and talent count as well. Trust only in God and not in what you have, it is far better to give than it is to receive. Acts 20:35b (NLT paraphrased). God is in the multiplication business; you can never beat His returns…

Blessings, Rupert & Red.

JANUARY 29

There's Strength In Prayer

Meditation Verse: Luke 22:32 HCSB
But I have prayed for you that your faith may not fail. And you, when you have turned back, strengthen your brothers.

Scripture Reading: John 17

Although this particular scripture was directed to the apostle Peter, it is relevant to all of us who call ourselves Christians. We are convinced that, after the word of God, prayer is the most powerful weapon we have. Whether it is intercessory, consecration, or petition, it has the power and potential to change any situation. Most of us can testify that change has been the result of many a sincere prayer. Although, if we are honest, sometimes it may not always yield the result that we are expecting. Even so, it is so important that we pray for one another. It causes us to see the stumbling blocks, regain focus, and renews determination. As the seasoned saints would say, "It encourages me to go on and see what the end will be." There are so many benefits to prayer that they are too numerous to mention. Jesus prayed for us specifically in John 17, He desires that we do the same; want to increase your faith and strengthen your brother or sister? Pray!! It avails much…

Blessings, Rupert & Red.

JANUARY 30

Blessing By Trial

Mediation Verse: Luke 6:22 HCSB

You are blessed when people hate you, when they exclude you, insult you, and slander your name as evil because of the Son of Man.

Scripture Reading: Luke 6:20-23

When you read the verse above, it seems like an awful lot to go through in order to be blessed. We need to realize, though, that whenever you make a stand for Christ, you are going to have problems with some people. Everybody wants to be down with being blessed and talk the spiritual talk, but don't mention Jesus, can't get with that Jesus thing, that's much too deep!! See, when you talk Jesus, now you are talking about the Word, and we can't handle the Word, because that means handling truth!! The mirror is full length and that is too much exposure! What becomes problematic, is our future is determined solely on what we do with Jesus. You have to carry the cross if you want to wear the crown. Being popular won't get you eternal life, relationship is key, take the stand now, because sooner or later you will have to kneel, let it be by faith and not by force.

Blessings, Rupert & Red.

JANUARY 31

Awesome Praise!

Mediation Verse: Psalms 147:1 HCSB

Hallelujah! How good it is to sing to our God, for praise is pleasant and lovely.

Scripture Reading: Psalms 147

Praise Break!!

Today, we just want to praise our God!! We want to extol and exalt His tender mercy, loving kindness, amazing grace, unconditional love and endless blessings. We want to bless His name and honor His sovereignty!! He is truly better to us than we could ever be to ourselves, and our lives are totally in His hands. Our desire is to grow ever closer to Him, be more in love with Him, strengthen and deepen our relationship with Him. We pray that you too, man and woman of God, realize the richness of right relationship with the Father. Pursue God with all your heart, there is nothing that compares to the joy that will be yours, not just in this life, but in the life to come…

Blessings, Rupert & Red.

FEBRUARY 1

How is Your Vision?

Mediation Verse: Genesis 22:13 HCSB

Abraham looked up and saw a ram caught in the thicket by its horns. So, Abraham went and took the ram and offered it as a burnt offering in place of his son.

Scripture Reading: Genesis 22:7-14

For the physical man, vision is a function of the eyes, but for the spirit man vision is a function of the heart. Vision is required in order to believe that God will provide. In the spiritual world seeing is not believing but believing is seeing. A heart that is established toward God, need not fear what he cannot see but believes that the unseen is possible. What are we saying? It is not important that you see how God will provide, your heart's vision tells you He will. Before you even saw the need, God knew it. He previsioned it! How long do you think that ram was caught in that thicket of bushes? We believe it was before Abraham was about to sacrifice his son! God is in the pre-seeing business! Abraham believed that God would provide. He did not see how, but his faith and obedience were rewarded. Seek the vision and God will provide the pro!! Believe us it works!!

Blessings, Rupert & Red.

FEBRUARY 2

Bloom Where God Plants You

Mediation Verse: Genesis 12:1 HCSB

The Lord said to Abram: Go out from your land, your relatives, and your father's house to the land that I will show you.

Scripture Reading: Genesis 12:1-9

We do not like moving! It is not that we are lazy, well ok, maybe a little, but who wants to do all the work that comes with relocation??!! We are comfortable where we are! The problem with comfortable is, that it sometimes turns to complacent, and that can stunt your growth. Now don't get me wrong, we are all for comfort, it is one of our favorite things, but when God calls you to another level, He is more concerned with the development of your character, than your comfort. Leaving the comfort zone is often necessary for your growth. When God says it is time to move, it may not be to a different physical geographic location. It may be just a mindset, a concept, or a paradigm shift. God needs you to move to accomplish His will and your good. Everyone does not thrive in the same environment. So, the next time God calls you to move, pack your bags and be wise, even the sunflower knows to turn its face toward the sun.

Blessings, Rupert & Red.

FEBRUARY 3

Contend For The Faith

Mediation Verse: 1 Timothy 6:12 HCSB

Fight the good fight for the faith; take hold of eternal life that you were called to and have made a good confession about in the presence of many witnesses.

Scripture Reading: 1 Timothy 6:11-14

In the proper context of this verse, Timothy was charged with pursuing those things which were valuable to God. Of all these things that he was to pursue; righteousness, godliness, love, patience, gentleness, his faith was the only thing he had to fight for. Why? Because the devil is after your faith!! If he can cause you to doubt your calling, your mission, your purpose, everything that you are in pursuit of loses meaning. Your faith must be intact so that you can stay committed and to lay hold of eternal life. Remember, "Now without faith it is impossible to please God," Hebrews 11:6a (HSCB) so with all that you have, fight for your faith! It is the only battle that God requires of you, until that which is perfect is come…

Blessings, Rupert & Red.

FEBRUARY 4

Nobody Greater

Mediation Verse: 1 John 4:4 KJV

Ye are of God, little children, and have overcome them: because greater is He that is in you, than he that is in the world.

Scripture Reading: 1 John 4:1-6

We all have had overwhelming situations, circumstances and struggles that seem to be a companion in this life. No one is exempt. It saps our strength, our will and sometimes our faith. It is in our nature to be able to control every aspect of our lives. It is hard not to concern ourselves with the things that are beyond our control. Consider one of the greatest declarations made in the New Testament. "Greater is He that is in you, than he that is in the world!!" 1 John 4:4b (KJV). That is good news! We know it is hard and we know that it hurts, but God can make a way out of no way! We are writing this to encourage somebody. Don't give in to the spirit of fear, with God you are the majority, so declare victory in the name of Jesus! There is light at the end of that tunnel, just believe, and remember the condition though; The Greater One has to reside on the inside of you. The power is in the relationship!

Blessings, Rupert & Red.

FEBRUARY 5

In God We Trust

Mediation Verses: Psalms 33:20-21 NLT

We put our hope in the Lord. He is our help and our shield. In Him our hearts rejoice, for we trust in His holy name.

Scripture Reading: Psalms 33:12-22

It is difficult to put any trust in man when God has proven himself to be more trustworthy than anyone. The biblical meaning of trust is literally a bold, confident and sure security. It is by trust that we have peace. "You will keep him in perfect peace, whose mind is stayed on You because he trusts in You." Isaiah 26:3 (NKJV). No matter what the circumstance we choose to trust God, even when the evidence seems to be contrary. Our hearts can rejoice because our praise confounds the enemy. Don't expect people to understand your story, it is only yours to tell. God will protect you. He is your shield, His arms surround you, with a love that is immeasurable. God has your back in any and every situation. He will not falter, flake out or fail. Our heart's desire is that you will put your trust in God completely, He knows you better than anyone, and He has a plan for you that will blow your mind! You will never value a relationship more; He is just that kind of Friend.

Blessings, Rupert & Red.

FEBRUARY 6

Omniscient God

Mediation Verse: Psalms 33:14-15 NLT

From His throne He observes all who live on the earth. He made their hearts, so he understands everything they do.

Scripture Reading: Psalms 33:1-15

Because of The Almighty, we live, move and have our being. We were created for His pleasure, and our lives were meant to bring glory to His name. It was never about you! It was God who placed our gifting and eternity in our hearts. He gave us free will so that we would have the choice to place Him on our hearts, or another god. What we often lose in the human translation is that our choice comes with a promise. You cannot say you choose God and then live any way you want. Remember God knows the intent of your heart. It is impossible to claim truth with a deceptive heart, that is a place of bondage. Freedom comes with knowing and acknowledging the Truth. Because anything else becomes an idol in your life. Your best friend, neighbor, even your spouse may be convinced that you have a relationship with them, but God knows and understands everything you do. Truth won't enter your heart by osmosis, you must intentionally let Him in.

Blessings, Rupert & Red.

FEBRUARY 7

Pray For Prosperity

Mediation Verse: Jeremiah 29:7 HCSB

"Seek the welfare of the city I have deported you to. Pray to the Lord on its behalf, for when it has prosperity, you will prosper."

Scripture Reading: Jeremiah 29:4-10

God has always promoted relationship. It is the hallmark of our existence. Our prayer life determines our limits. Even in the midst of exile, God planned for relationship with His people. Wherever God places you or tells you to go, don't go and live in isolation, establish your prayer life and develop relationships. Pray that God prospers you where you are and even those around you. There is a need like never before that we pray for one another. God says when you pray for others it benefits you. Your prayers can move mountains and turn the hearts of kings and rulers! Be the prayer ambassador in the city where you live and affect the atmosphere…there is someone waiting on you.

Blessings, Rupert & Red.

FEBRUARY 8

The Beauty Of Surrender

Mediation Verse: Ephesians 3:16 HCSB

I pray that He may grant you, according to the riches of His glory, to be strengthened with power in the inner man through His Spirit.

Scripture Reading: Ephesians 3:14-18

We talk a lot about surrender, what does it mean to surrender and why is it necessary to be willing to give all? Surrender means to give oneself up to the power of another. In our case, the One who has All Power, because it is what He requires. For us to give our all, especially the parts that went bad and need fixing. He wants to make us new by placing His Spirit within us and re-birthing us. Why wouldn't you want to give up a shaky, fickle, temporary life, for a power filled eternal one? Not only is your inner man regenerated but you are strengthened and empowered by the eternal Spirit of God, according to His riches in glory! Where else are you going to get a deal like that!! God is offering the ultimate do-over, the true chance of a lifetime, and all you have to do, is give Him everything you got.

Blessings, Rupert & Red.

FEBRUARY 9

He Knows Your Name

Mediation Verses: Psalms 8:3-4 HCSB

When I observe Your heavens, the work of Your fingers, the moon and the stars, which You set in place, what is man that You remember him, the son of man that You look after him?

Scripture Reading: Psalms 8

We touched on psalm 8 last month, however, when we mediate on this Psalm, the world around us feels very small. Just to contemplate the vastness of this universe, creation on a whole, it is overwhelming. We do not apologize for not buying into the Big Bang Theory, we believe that it is just as funny as the television show! There are those who are desperate to keep God out of the equation, but the universe screams intelligent design! But to know that through all of this is a loving God who created us, sees us, knows our names, and cares about our lives so much so that He desires relationship with us, is truly wonderful to comprehend! When you truly realize the love God has for you, then no entity, institution, church, club, foreign or domestic can take that away from you!! We have been blessed to travel this world, but you don't have to go further than your front door to feel and know what is in your heart. Just gaze at the night sky.

Blessings, Rupert & Red.

FEBRUARY 10

The Blessing In Giving

Mediation Verse: Acts 20:35 HCSB

In every way I've shown you that by laboring like this, it is necessary to help the weak and to keep in mind the words of the Lord Jesus, for He said, "It is more blessed to give than to receive."

Scripture Reading: Acts 20: 32-38

We just want to say that if you are in a position to be a blessing to someone today, please don't hesitate. The blessing does not always have to be monetary but give of your time and talent as well. This is a hurting world, and the more we move to do the little things that matter, the more we will see healing take place. You know it is usually those that don't have much that do the most giving, but you will be surprised at how much you have when you start to give it away!! So, do something nice for someone today, and strive to make it a habit. God sees, and He knows, and He will reward you openly for the things you do in secret.

Blessings, Rupert & Red.

FEBRUARY 11

Obedience: The Catalyst For Blessings

Mediation Verse: Deuteronomy 28:2 HCSB
All these blessings will come and overtake you, because you obey the Lord your God.
Scripture Reading: Deuteronomy 28:1-14

Who is like our God? He has called His people to the criteria for blessings, Obedience. God will honor His people with an abundance of blessings, cause the weapon that is formed not to prosper, and provide protection overall. He does not sleep or slumber, and in His presence are the everlasting arms. We are witnesses that it does not matter where you are in life. If God says go, go, if He says stay, stay. It makes absolutely no difference what it looks like, God is bigger than every situation you face, and He has already planned before time an expected end for your good. Yes, we have bad days, and sometimes we can't see our way through, but choose to let God order your steps. He knows better than we do, and He does all things well. Trust in the Lord with all your heart and lean not on your own understanding; In all your ways acknowledge Him, and He shall direct your paths. Proverbs 3:5-6 (NKJV). When we can't see or trace Him, He is still better than a GPS. For He knows the way that we take, and He will lead us to the everlasting, where the blessings live. Walk therefore on the path that He shows you; Listen! Obedience is better than sacrifice. 1Samuel 15:22b (NLT).

Blessings, Rupert & Red.

FEBRUARY 12

Daily Renewal

Mediation Verse: Romans 12:2 HCSB

Do not be conformed to this age, but be transformed by the renewing of your mind, so that you may discern what is the good, pleasing, and perfect will of God.

Scripture Reading: Romans 12:1-2

I can remember vividly being disciplined by my parents, it seemed as if they had super hearing and x-ray vision! There were six of us, so they had their hands full, and they did not play! Strangely enough, as I look back on those days of creative punishments and yes, the dreaded "whippings", I am filled with a sense of gratitude for the days when they were not exactly my favorite people! Because I understand now that the discipline was necessary for my transformation into a responsible adult. There are things now that as a grown man, I would not do because it would dishonor what I had been taught by my parents as a child. This world is not after your growth or the development of your character, they care only about your cooperation and to that end the fulfillment of their agenda. God does not want you to walk into that trap. It is only possible to avoid it, by the daily renewal of your mind. Trust God, and you will be able to look back with gratitude for the discipline that freed you from the evils of this world. God's Word will lead you to the ultimate transformation, a life designed for eternity.

Blessings, Rupert & Red.

FEBRUARY 13

Everything Comes From His Hands

Mediation Verse: Psalms 90:2 HCSB

Before the mountains were born, before You gave birth to the earth and the world, from eternity to eternity, You are God.

Scripture Reading: Psalms 90:1-6

It is hard to grasp the concept that God has always been, no beginning and no end! How do you wrap that around your intellect? You can hurt yourself trying to reconcile His sovereignty with His eternity. The answer is faith, you just have to believe it and never doubt that God is who He says He is. "In the beginning God…" Genesis 1:1a (NKJV). When God moves on your behalf in a miraculous way, there is a deposit of victory that makes you understand that nothing is impossible. Seek to grow your faith for big things, not just because you want stuff, but because the kingdom demands it. God has done the hard part…it speaks for itself, now we must establish His kingdom here on earth. Jesus said it this way; "According to your faith, be it unto you." Matthew 9:29b (KJV).

Blessings, Rupert & Red.

FEBRUARY 14

God's Love Never Fails

Mediation Verse: 1 Corinthians 13:6-7 HCSB

Love finds no joy in unrighteousness but rejoices in the truth. It bears all things, believes all things, hopes all things, endures all things.

Scripture Reading: 1 Corinthians 13

When we read verses 6 & 7, if we are honest, we will have to admit to ourselves; we have failed miserably at love. Love, according to 1 Corinthians 13, is far from easy, in fact you can say that it is darn near impossible to love at that level. The level that we love at is amateurish at best. We hang out at the fringe benefits of love, the touchy feely, gushing, giddy headed, emotions that tickle the physical. It is all based on how we feel. Guess what! Sorry to burst your bubble, but that does not even scratch the surface! Chocolates, flowers and candy do not say, I love you!! They say I feel you!! Love is not an act of emotion, but an act of the will. To love at the level of 1 Corinthians 13, has nothing to do with how you feel and everything to do with intent. You can't fall into this type of love you have to make the decision to love. You must give up everything to love at this level, because it can never be about you. This type of love is a journey that you have to want to take and aspire to. It is the greatest attribute you will ever have and the best character builder you will ever experience. And why is this type of love the greatest above all? Because it is the only currency you will need in eternity! Now that is worth living for!!

Blessings, Rupert & Red.

FEBRUARY 15

Our Help Is In God

Mediation Verse: Psalms 3:3 HCSB

But You, Lord, are a shield around me, my glory, and the One who lifts up my head.

Scripture Reading: Psalms 3

Anyone who says there is no help for them in God, lacks relationship. God is a shield for those who belong to Him! David did not request this from God, he knew and had confidence that God was this for him. "But You, Lord, are my shield!" Psalms 3:3 (paraphrased). It was a declaration of truth! Men find glory in a lot of things, fame, prestige, money, but David found his glory in the Lord. The whole purpose of your life should be for God to get glory from it. Otherwise, as Solomon said, "all is vanity!" Ecclesiastes 12:8b (KJV). All the problems in your life will seem insurmountable if your trust is in anything but God! He alone can take you to the next level of glory and be the lifter of your head. Once we experience that there is nothing too hard for God, then we cannot be turned around. He will always be more than the whole world against us. It is not wise to put your full confidence in men!! Men will always fail you sooner or later. God never fails!! Do not worry if there is nothing glorious to find in your circumstances, God will work things out for your good. When you put your trust in Him, that's His promise to you.

Blessings, Rupert & Red.

FEBRUARY 16

God's Got This

> Mediation Verse: Psalms 46:10 NKJV
>
> *Be still and know that I am God; I will be exalted among the nations I will be exalted in the earth!*
>
> Scripture Reading: Psalms 46

Have you ever relaxed at the beach or poolside or on your porch or patio, able to just revive and reflect? It is a calming and at the same time exhilarating feeling. To for a moment experience no problems, issues or worries. Moments like that are precious to us. Our trust in God should take us to that place of calm. He wants us to experience His peace, however, relationship is key. Acknowledging who God is and recognizing His power to have your back in any and every situation, releases a whole lot of unnecessary stress and worry. Problems will come, but it is good to know that the problem solver is bigger than any situation or circumstance we may face! So be still, exhale, and know that God's got you. He wants you to depend on Him. Relationship has its privileges!!

Blessings, Rupert & Red.

FEBRUARY 17

There Is A Purpose For Your Wealth

Mediation Verse: Deuteronomy 8:18 HCSB

But remember that the Lord your God gives you the power to gain wealth, in order to confirm His covenant He swore to your fathers, as it is today.

Scripture Reading: Deuteronomy 8:11-20

One of the hardest issues to discern and overcome is the issue of money. It is one of the issues that we will continue to talk about because it hinders a relationship with God. Most people who have wealth in abundance fail to realize two things; 1) God has caused your prosperity. 2) The purpose for your wealth. Let me be the first to say, I have no problem with money or people who possess it. But when you miss the purpose, selfishness becomes evident. The more money people make the harder it is to trust Almighty God, and the easier it becomes to trust the almighty dollar. Isn't it ironic that our money says, "In God we trust?!" We who are blessed financially, are to be a blessing to others. God wants you to come to the place where you find identity in whose you are rather than who you are. Because if you base your identity on anything temporal, the degrees you've earned or the money you make, your identity becomes a house of cards. There is only one solid foundation: Jesus Christ. So, what feeds your ego? Where or what do you put your security in outside of Christ? That is what you need to surrender on the altar today.

Blessings, Rupert & Red.

FEBRUARY 18

Designed Before Time

Mediation Verse: Ephesians 2:10 HCSB

For we are His creation, created in Christ Jesus for good works, which God prepared ahead of time so that we should walk in them.

Scripture Reading: Ephesians 2:1-10

Did you know that God never intended us to depend solely on our senses? The spirit man is far more powerful than the natural man. But until we are regenerated spiritually, we will never develop that important sixth sense which is our connection to God. You see Adam was connected to God until he decided to forfeit his spirit man for his senses. His good works and walk before God were prepared before he was created. And we were designed and assigned before time as well. In order for us to carry out the original assignment we must now be reborn to hear what the Spirit of the Lord says. Our good works will then come into focus, and we can walk as God intended. Use your senses, but not to the detriment of your faith, "For we walk by faith, not by sight." 2Corinthians 5:7 (KJV).

Blessings, Rupert & Red.

FEBRUARY 19

Where Are You Living?

Mediation Verse: Psalms 91:1 KJV

He that dwelleth in the secret place of the Most High shall abide under the shadow of the Almighty.

Scripture Reading: Psalms 91

This is my favorite Psalm, but the first verse is the condition to the promise of the next 15 verses. God's promises are incredible, however, He is all about obedience. We can only be obedient if we believe God, that is why it is impossible to please God if you don't have faith to obey. Why have faith in someone if you don't believe they can do what they say! The Word of God says that; "He is a rewarder of those who diligently seek Him." Hebrews 11:6b (NKJV). That is a promise and condition right there! You cannot be rewarded if you casually seek God, you must be diligent and intentional in your effort. The secret place is His will, His will is His Word! You have to dwell in His Word, in order for the Word to dwell in you. The absolute best place to be is under the shadow of the Almighty! His promises are always Yes! and Amen! So, the next question for you is, where are you living?

Blessings, Rupert & Red.

FEBRUARY 20

We Are Close To God's Heart

Mediation Verse: Romans 15:4 HCSB

For whatsoever was written in the past was written for our instruction, so that we may have hope through endurance and through the encouragement from the scriptures.

Scripture Reading: Romans 15:1-6

Because for so many years I travelled for my job, I kept in touch with my wife and family through letters, emails and phone calls. It was tough on all of us, but I always tried to encourage them throughout our separations. And they in turn would encourage me so that we would be able to endure until we could be reunited again. Their words meant so much to me, they gave me life and hope. That is exactly what God does through His Word. He brings us to the place of life, expectation and hope so we will not only just endure but be encouraged through this journey called life. When you read His words, you will come to realize His faithfulness, mercy and grace in a way that will sustain you throughout the vicissitudes, trials and tribulations of living. But He will also give you peace, joy and a sense of belonging in the family of God and the Body of Christ. You will be renewed and revived, because He has the words of eternal life. So, read and live by His Word, so that when you speak, you will speak encouragement and hope, because words matter. Make sure yours bring life.

Blessings, Rupert & Red.

FEBRUARY 21

His Love Conquers All

Mediation Verse: Deuteronomy 6:5 HCSB

Love the Lord your God with all your heart, with all your soul, and with all your strength.

Scripture Reading: Deuteronomy 6:1-9

There is a premise that underlines this verse: There is nothing that you can do in your own strength to quantify or qualify God's goodness. Nor can you begin to understand the way He cares for you without relationship. To think that the God of all creation believes that you are worthy of relationship with Him is mind blowing. But God is sovereign, and you cannot approach Him any old way. This verse is a command and not a suggestion. This is the criteria for true relationship with God. He must come first in your life, He demands it. Then your life must be surrendered to Him. Our love for God pales in comparison with His love for us. Even though we will fall short at times, He will uphold us with His right hand. The best we can do is rise every day thankful for a new opportunity to love and serve Him, one day at a time. He will give you the strength. There's power in relationship!

Blessings, Rupert & Red.

FEBRUARY 22

God: Creator Of Everything

Mediation Verse: Colossians 1:16 CEB

Because all things were created by Him: both in the heavens and on the earth, the things that are visible and the things that are invisible. Whether they are thrones or powers, or rulers or authorities, all things were created through Him and for Him.

Scripture Reading: Colossians 1:15-23

Just because you cannot see certain things does not mean that they do not exist. We benefit more from the unseen than the seen. It is really narrow minded to say, "I'll believe it when I see it." A lot of what we see in the physical is actually unreliable in the long run, because quite frankly, it does not last, or it is managed by people who are fallible. God created everything that you see and what you can't see. There are powers, dominions, and thrones that you cannot see. However, some of them influence the way that we think and behave. Character is formed by the things you don't see, though they become manifest by our own choices and actions. Your very life and being is managed by the unseen. It is God who created the atmosphere in which you live and breathe the very air you cannot see. You have a choice, depend on Creator God, or His creation. We pray you choose the Creator, the truth is it is better to know that believing is seeing.

Blessings, Rupert & Red.

FEBRUARY 23

God Wants To Hear From You

Mediation Verse: Psalms 27:8 NLT

*My heart has heard you say, "Come and talk with me."
And my heart responds, "Lord, I am coming."*

Scripture Reading: Psalms 27: 7-10

We can say without fear of contradiction that everyone that we have ever been in contact with has called out to God in one way or another. Whether they were a believer or not, trouble seems to bring out the revelation that God can help. The problem is when the crisis has passed, the lines of communication are severed until trouble rears its ugly head again. God has said time and time again, "You will seek Me and find Me when you search for Me with all your heart." Jeremiah 29:13 (HCSB). Too often we treat God like a get out of jail free card, instead of developing the true relationship He desires. Prayer is so much more than a weapon. It is the very lifeline to any and everything that has ever been important to you. And it is God who delights and desires to give you the things that you need. Stop living your life in temporal crisis mode. God created you for eternal relationship, listen to your heart, it is longing to say, "Lord I am coming." Psalm 27:8b (NLT).

Blessings, Rupert & Red.

FEBRUARY 24

Whom Will You Serve?

Mediation Verse: Daniel 3:1 NLT

King Nebuchadnezzar made a gold statue ninety feet tall and nine feet wide and set it up on the plain of Dura in the province of Babylon.

Scripture Reading: Daniel 3:1-5

Red and I have come to the agreement that anyone who must build a ninety-foot- tall monument to themselves is probably a bit delusional to put it mildly. What an ego!! This act was the epitome of pride!! Truth be told, though, we all have a little Nebuchadnezzar in us. We seek worship in subtle ways, we exaggerate on our resume, put people down behind their back, and try to hide the gray areas in our lives. We all try to fight our own battles, create our own opportunities, and establish our own reputations. And if our plans succeed, we think we did it all ourselves. Guess what! You were not created to bring glory to yourself, but to God! Are we saying you should not work hard, take care of your family and enjoy the fruits of your labor? Of course not! We are challenging your motivation. If you don't find your identity in Christ and what He accomplished on the cross for you, you will hide your insecurities in the monuments you set up for yourselves. People who do that think little of themselves and forget where their help comes from. There is a difference between Thy kingdom come and my kingdom come, and when you cross that line your relationship with God becomes self-serving. You are not serving God; you are attempting to use Him. When you think you are a self-made man or woman you are building monuments to yourself and that is idolatry… Don't be like Nebuchadnezzar. Never forget where your help comes from.

Blessings, Rupert & Red.

FEBRUARY 25

Your Heart's Desire

Mediation Verse: Psalms 37:4 NLT

Take delight in the Lord, and He will give you your heart's desires.

Scripture Reading: Psalms 37: 1-7

Wow! That seems like a dream come true! All we have to do is delight in the Lord and we can get what we want. But do you know what that word delight means? Most people forget that the original text is Hebrew and Greek, so words had several translations and multiple meanings. Some of the words that describe delight in the Greek are, pliable, amenable, and agreeable, also to be able to bend, surrender and be in agreement. When you delight in the Lord according to those criteria, you are allowing the Word of God to shape you into conforming to His image, so your heart then wants only what He wants, which is infinitely better for you anyway. His desires become yours because your heart desires His will and His heart. So, the next time you read this verse, whisper this prayer; "Not my will, but Yours, be done," Luke 22:42b (HCSB), in my life. God never disappoints.

Blessings, Rupert & Red.

FEBRUARY 26

Do You Have Your Ears On?

Mediation Verse: Hebrews 1:2 HCSB

In these last days, He has spoken to us by His Son. God has appointed Him heir of all things and made the universe through Him.

Scripture Reading: Hebrews 1: 1-4

When I was very young, the words of my father were paramount. I was in awe of my father's ability to speak to people and influence their lives. I thought it was the greatest thing ever! Who would disagree with my Dad? As I grew older, however, I realized that not everyone agreed with my dad. Preaching is not easy to people who don't have ears to hear. Conviction does not come to every heart. Opinions, logic, worldviews, all seem to trump belief and faith. The world today seems to be more and more anti-biblical truth. Everyone wants to speak their own truth, because then they can decide what truth is. What validates them. The problem with that reasoning is that truth needs nothing to validate it. Truth stands on its own. God has always spoken, but He sent His son to speak to us in human form. His every Word is Truth, it framed the worlds and universe. He sent it to heal, deliver and save. Only God can do this, man cannot. We can only have the Truth when we have Jesus. We are not just talking about the difference between the truth and a lie, we are also talking about the difference between life and death. Choose life, listen to the Truth, and you and your descendants will live, you who have ears to hear, your heart will discern.

Blessings, Rupert & Red.

FEBRUARY 27

Heaven! Wanna Go?

Mediation Verse: Revelation 22:1 HCSB

Then He showed me the river of living water, sparkling like crystal, flowing from the throne of God and of the Lamb.

Scripture Reading: Revelation 22:1-6

"Everybody wants to go to Heaven, but nobody wants to die!"

There is a fear of death, that is both rational and irrational. The Bible says that God has put eternity in our hearts. Everyone would like to live forever, depending upon their quality of life. Nobody wants to live suffering, in pain, or in poverty. The fear is that we don't know what happens after we die. Every civilization known to man has pictured and talked about life after death and what it would be like. We were made for more than this life. For the Christian, the Bible has a lot to say about heaven, but nobody really wants to talk about it anymore. We should live our best life here on earth, but life is brief and fleeting on this side. Why are we talking about this? Because we want to encourage you to embrace your citizenship in Heaven, God has taken the sting out of death, so we don't mourn as those who have no hope. Christ said, "If I go away and prepare a place for you, I will come back and receive you to Myself so that where I am you may be also." John 14:3 (HCSB). Heaven will be glorious! We want to be ready! We want to go! We don't believe it will be boring, strumming harps and sitting on clouds with wings, that is not what our Bible tells us. It will be beyond anything we can think or imagine, and we have vivid imaginations! But God says it will be far above what we can even envision! Just to see Him face to face will be joy unspeakable!

1 Corinthians 2:9 (KJV) says: "Eye has not seen, nor ear heard, neither have entered into the heart of man, the things which God has prepared for them that love Him." Let's talk about Heaven!! Don't you want to go?

Blessings, Rupert & Red.

FEBRUARY 28

The Choice For Repentance

Mediation Verse: Nehemiah 9:33 NLT

Every time You punished us You were being just. We have sinned greatly, and You gave us only what we deserved.

Scripture Reading: Nehemiah 9:1-37

Lessons from the past, even very painful ones, can help to prepare us for the future. The exile to Babylon was a painful experience for the people of God. The exiles took time to reflect on their past and seek guidance for the future. All of us can point to some time or episode in our lives, that was a reminder of a painful experience. Maybe it could have been avoided had we not determined to go our own way. It is a rewarding and tremendous moment in a Christian's life when he or she can honestly confess to God and say, "Yes Lord, You are right and I am wrong. I brought this all on myself, put myself in this situation and I got what I deserved." But beyond that must come the true face of repentance. No more arguing and bargaining with God, just turn away from your sin and live for what He desires for you. Not only will He forgive you, but He will give you a heart of flesh for the stony heart of self-centeredness. It is amazing how His desires become our own and His grace, His awesome, amazing, phenomenal grace, becomes sufficient.

Blessings, Rupert & Red.

FEBRUARY 29

Let Mount Zion Rejoice!

Mediation Verse: Hebrews 12:22 NLT

No, you have come to Mount Zion, to the city of the living God, the Heavenly Jerusalem, and to countless thousands of angels in a joyful gathering.

Scripture Reading: Hebrews 12:14-29

"No, you have come to Mt. Zion." Hebrews 12:22a (NLT). Just that phrase alone should give you cause to rejoice!! God has decided to spare you from the rigors of the law and endow you with grace to endure. You no longer have to live a performance-based life, filled with impossible ritualistic tasks, plagued with fear of making mistakes and failing, feeling miserable because of unattainable standards. God has provided the way for us to live an abundant life in a kingdom that cannot be shaken. Jesus went to the cross so that the perfect sacrifice once and for all could be given. Now He is our High Priest who forever makes intercession on our behalf. Mt. Zion is everything Mt. Sinai is not. We need not tremble and fear at its base. In fact, we are to come boldly to God and worship Him in spirit and in truth! Christ has paved the way for total access to the Throne. As mediator of the New Covenant, we can lay our concerns and desires at His feet, and they will be brought before the Father without fear of death. So, pay attention to what you have heard so that you don't drift away or slip.

Blessings, Rupert & Red.

MARCH 1

Know The Sound!!

Mediation Verse: John 10:14-15 HCSB

"I am the good shepherd. I know My own sheep, and they know Me, as the Father knows Me, and I know the Father. I lay down My life for the sheep."

Scripture Reading: John 10:1-16

We had always resisted the biblical comparison of people to sheep, after all they were considered dumb animals, right? But the more we lived and observed the behaviors of those who should know better, the more we realized how lost and hopeless we are. We are indeed like sheep who have gone astray, each to his own way, and to what we thought was right in our own eyes. If anyone needed a shepherd, yeah, that would be us, the smart ones! The Bible says that the sheep know the voice of the shepherd. They are not without understanding! They follow the one whom they know. We may never have a complete knowledge of our circumstances or all the answers to the questions of life, but we should understand the love of God and the importance of following Him to green pastures and living water. The shepherd can lead the sheep from the front or the back, because they know his voice. The shepherd calls and they come. Our response to Jesus must be the same. All we need is the sound of His voice. Now in order to know that voice, we must be ready to hear. His voice is that Word, the source of all life. Heed that voice! No other shepherd will do.

Blessings, Rupert & Red.

MARCH 2

Miracles Present Opportunities!

Mediation Verse: Acts 3:16 NKJV

And His name, through faith in His name, has made this man strong, whom you see and know. Yes, the faith which comes through Him has given him this perfect soundness in the presence of you all.

Scripture Reading: Acts 3

The healing of the paralytic man through Peter is well known as a miracle in the Acts of the apostles. Yet the healing was merely a means to an end. In verse 12 of the text, it states "Peter saw his opportunity." Acts 3:12a (NLT). The opportunity for the gospel to be preached and for God to be glorified was just as important. Yes, the faith that the man had was evident in his expectation to receive something from Peter, and he received much more than the monetary donation that he would have been satisfied with. (We encourage you to read the entire chapter of Acts 3). Peter made the man's life more bearable by the gift of faith that wrought a miracle of God through him. But isn't it our task to release the redemptive work of Christ on the earth? How do we seize the opportunity in our lives to minister to those who need the gospel more than silver or gold? We need like the paralytic man to get to a place where we expect to receive from God. This is faith, plain and simple. Placing that faith in Jesus Christ must be the priority. God is pleased to move on our behalf when we place our faith in His Son. This also means that there needs to be a paradigm shift in our thinking, to make a bold stand in witnessing the gospel. To believe in the "greater things" that Christ said we would and should experience as His disciples. It is a challenge that is not for the faint of heart. To boldly step out and say that we identify with the crucified and risen One, and that our lives are forever changed by Him. It is time for us to take some people by the hand and declare and decree that they "RISE UP AND WALK!!"

Blessings, Rupert & Red.

MARCH 3

Seek God While He May Yet Be Found

Mediation Verse: Psalms 53:2 NKJV

God looks down from Heaven upon the children of men, to see if there are any who understand, who seek God.

Scripture Reading: Psalms 53

There were six of us who grew up together in the Hinds' household, not including our parents. We had a wonderful childhood. Our parents provided for us, and we basically wanted for nothing. At that time, we did not understand the depth of their love for us. Oh, we knew we were loved and cared for, but we did not realize or fathom just how much, until we were grown and looked back on our lives growing up. Then we were aware that not everyone had the same experience. We were blessed in a way beyond our understanding, growth and reflection had taught us that. But regardless of the way you may have grown up, there is One who loves you more than you realize or understand, who can exponentially improve on your memories of childhood, especially if they were not the best. Someone who loves you, way beyond your expectations and gives you a future and a hope that does not disappoint. His arms are open wide to those who seek Him and are willing to come. He sees you and knows what you need, and His desire is to give you a better life, a more abundant life, a life filled with the promise of eternity. Your day is today, your time is now, do not delay, Jesus is waiting. You will look back over your life and understand the depth of the love the Father has for you, growth and reflection will teach you that.

Blessings, Rupert & Red.

MARCH 4

Joy In His Presence

Mediation Verse: Psalms 16:11 NKJV

You will show me the path of life; In Your presence is fullness of joy; At Your right hand are pleasures forevermore.

Scripture Reading: Psalms 16

I can sometimes be a creature of habit. I like to walk but lately I have not been able to walk as much as I should. I even liked the treadmill because the new ones you can program to be walking in different scenes, so I could be walking in San Francisco or Seattle on any given day. The path I choose determines whether I have the benefit of beach access, rain forest, country walks, or just walking on the city sidewalk. The scenes move to give the illusion that I am actually walking in those particular scenarios. In the same way the path we take in life often determines how we live in the future. His presence is a benefit that we can never take lightly. We are alive because of His presence, it shapes your mind, develops your attitudes, and increases your faith. Your commitment to God is received both in this life and the life beyond. The Psalmist said that "You will show me," Psalms 16:11a (NKJV), and because we are prone to get lost, He will keep us on the right path. His path, His presence, His pleasures, the trifecta for the well lived life. Get connected to the God who knows all about you anyway. He made you with a plan in mind. We need to set out on the path that God has ordained for us to walk, for only then will we enjoy the pleasures forevermore. So, get out and walk the walk!!

Blessings, Rupert & Red.

MARCH 5

Words Do Matter

Mediation Verse: Colossians 4:6 HCSB

Your speech should always be gracious, seasoned with salt, so that you may know how you should answer each person.

Scripture Reading: Colossians 4:2-6

"Sticks and stones may break my bones, but words can never hurt me." One of the biggest lies perpetrated on society. Words can have a devastating effect on people. It does not matter who you are, no one likes to get their feelings hurt. Sometimes the hurt goes way beyond feelings. People have been known to go into deep depression, lose their sanity, commit crimes and even suicide over hurtful words. It is so important that we treat people with kindness and dignity and speak in a way that shows love, caring and concern. Speak words that build others up, never tear down, and don't speak negative things over anyone's life. Speak healing and blessing, be a constant source of love and truth. Remember, "Death and life are in the power of the tongue," Proverbs 18:21a (NKJV), so don't kill anyone with your words! Let your prayer every day be: "Let the words of my mouth and the meditation of my heart be acceptable in Your sight." Psalms 19:14a (NKJV). Then go out and make it a priority to make someone's day brighter. In that way you will bring God glory and honor. It is always nice to be nice.

Blessings, Rupert & Red.

MARCH 6

The Attitude Is Gratitude

Mediation Verse: Psalms 50:23 NLT

"But giving thanks is a sacrifice that truly honors Me. If you keep to My path, I will reveal to you the salvation of God."

Scripture Reading: Psalms 50

How do you say thank you to someone who has saved your life? The words fail to measure up to the gratitude one must feel to have been given a second chance! What would you give if you could, to repay such an incredible debt? I do believe there would be nothing you could do, or give, that would make you feel that that person was adequately compensated. Being thankful would be an understatement!! Yet God sees thankfulness as sufficient. To praise God for His goodness and loving kindness is what He is looking for. The Bible says, "From the rising of the sun unto the going down of the same, the Lord's name is to be praised." Psalm 113:3 (KJV). God is honored by those who would give thanks and praise. Why would you not give thanks to the One who saved your life?! Who gave you a second chance? It is a debt you can never repay, yet it cost you nothing, a free gift from the King of Kings and Lord of Lords. He only asks that you receive it and follow the path that leads to salvation. It is something that we are thankful for everyday of our lives. New life!! A precious promise that only God can give. Be thankful today, your life is worth saving.

Blessings, Rupert & Red.

MARCH 7

Have Mercy!

Mediation Verse: James 2:13 NLT

There will be no mercy for those who have not shown mercy to others. But if you have been merciful, God will be merciful when He judges you.

Scripture Reading: James 2:8-13

It seems to be within the nature of the human psyche to criticize. It is always easier to find fault than to find the good in people. They say haters are going to hate, no matter what you do. Jesus said that in this life you will have persecution, and anyone who has lived long enough has surely found this to be true. That is why we find the best road to walk is in love, humility and with a forgiving heart. Now we are in no way suggesting that you allow people to disrespect you or take advantage of you, but you must learn to pick your battles, and then let God be the One to fight. Just vow to show mercy to those who wish to have unflattering or disparaging conversations about you. My mother always said, "You can't control what people say bad about you, just don't let it be true." 1 Peter 3:16b (NLT) says it this way; "Keep your conscience clear. Then when people speak against you, they will be ashamed when they see what a good life you live because you belong to Christ." People will always assume, but remember, assumption is the lowest form of knowledge. We must show mercy because we have been shown mercy. Allow your haters to be confused by your positive attitude. By doing so you will heap coals of fire on their heads! Romans 12:20 (NKJV). Love and mercy always win.

Blessings, Rupert & Red.

MARCH 8

Knowledge Is Not The Principal Thing

Mediation Verse: Matthew 7:24 NLT

Anyone who listens to my teachings and follows it is wise, like a person who builds a house on solid rock.

Scripture Reading: Matthew 7:24-29

Knowledge is wonderful, but it is not the principal thing. Application is what counts, and it is the hard part! Hear this: God does not bless you because you know the truth, but because you obey it. Jesus said, "Now that you know these things, God will bless you for doing them." John 13:17 (NLT). Application is hard and sometimes painful!! The truth will set you free, but first it may make you uncomfortable. God's Word reveals our motives, exposes our flaws, rebukes our sin and demands change. Don't be so busy going to the next church meeting that you forget to put in practice what you have learned at the last one. The conviction of your spirit man or woman is profitable only if you contain the flesh as a result. Treasure God's Word and be blessed because of it. His will is that "everyone who believes in Him will not perish but have eternal life." John 3:16b (NLT). Be doers not just hearers, trust me, that's wisdom. Apply it.

Blessings, Rupert & Red.

MARCH 9

Are You A Sheep Or A Goat?

Mediation Verse: Matthew 25:32 NLT

All the nations will be gathered in His presence, and He will separate the people as a shepherd separates the sheep from the goats.

Scripture Reading: Matthew 25:31-46

Christ is coming back, whether you believe it or not. Judgement day is happening contrary to all who oppose His truth, no one will escape or be able to hide on that day. What is God looking for? People who have compassion and the desire to love their neighbor as themselves, who have humanity on their side and in their hearts. "For I was hungry, and you fed me, I was thirsty and you gave me a drink, I was a stranger and you invited me into your home, I was naked and you gave me clothing, I was sick and you cared for me, I was in prison and you visited me." Matthew 25:35-36. (NLT). Social justice is important to God, He will determine where you spend eternity based on what you have done with His Son, and how you treat people. The sign of the saved is their concern for those in need. Compassion is a consequence of salvation. When you choose to treat those who have less, with dignity and respect, then you have captured the heart of the Master. Love will lift you to the place where your needs become secondary to the needs of others. Keep this in mind as you go through your day, every time that you feed, clothe, visit or comfort, the least of these, you extend that same courtesy to God. He receives it as an act of worship directed to Him. So, don't be the goat. Be the sheep, it will seal your destination. We will be talking about social justice quite a bit in the days, weeks, and months ahead, because we believe it is truly important to God and so it should be to us as well.

Blessings, Rupert & Red.

MARCH 10

The Benefits Of Relationship

Mediation Verse: Jeremiah 4:2 NLT

Then when you swear by my name, saying, "As surely as the Lord lives, you could do so with truth, justice, and righteousness. Then you will be a blessing to the nations of the world, and all people would come and praise My Name."

Scripture Reading: Jeremiah 4:1-2

Can a man have a relationship with God and still befriend the unsaved? We believe with all our hearts that God expects us to love the unregenerate. That is simply a term for those who have not accepted Christ. If we don't show justice, truth, and mercy to those who we consider lost, then how can we be a blessing to any nation? Hating the things that God hates does not mean hating the people who commit them, it means loving them the same way that God loves you. When the Word says to "hate evil," we are to avoid evil acts, that can block your blessings and remove the hedge of protection needed for every day. So, hating evil does not mean being intolerant, judgmental, or uncaring. In fact, loving people is a command! You don't have to pretend to approve of their actions, just show the love, understanding, the justice and tolerance that would afford people everywhere dignity and respect. We absolutely must live our lives in a way that brings glory to God and causes people to examine their lives and the way they live. Not just because you will be blessed, but because it is important to God.

Blessings, Rupert & Red.

MARCH 11

Get Your Rest!!

Mediation Verse: Matthew 11:28 HCSB

Come to Me, all of you who are weary and burdened, and I will give you rest.

Scripture Reading: Matthew 11:28-30

My twin brother and I are insomniacs. Sleep is something that we desire, but rarely achieve in the amounts that are healthy for us. We do fall asleep at odd times, but never sleep long. It is a very frustrating and draining condition. "Sleeping in," is foreign to us unless we are medicated. I will admit that my brother has it worse than I do. But rest is important, and we have learned that resting our bodies helps to compensate for the lack of deep sleep. This world system is designed to drain you, frustrate you and wear you down. It will drive you to a place that is unhealthy for you. The cares and worries and injustices of this world are enough to bring anyone to their knees. It is because we try to do it alone. God has offered "rest" in Him. His rest is guaranteed to give you the strength you need to face the task of daily living. It comes with "the peace of God which passeth all understanding," Philippians 4:7a (KJV), and a refreshing that will revive your soul. Let the burden bearer and heavy load sharer be your portion today. I guarantee that you will have joy that no man can take away. Despite what the world does, with God in control, you will get your rest. Take it, it is excellent advice.

Blessings, Rupert & Red.

MARCH 12

Emulate The Father's Example

Mediation Verse: Psalms 45:4 NLT

In your majesty ride out to victory, defending truth, humility and justice. Go forth to perform awe-inspiring deeds!

Scripture Reading: Psalms 45:1-7

When truth, humility and justice get together, victory is guaranteed. We live from day to day, never thinking that truth and justice are possible. For a lot of people, it is the unfortunate reality of everyday life. We believe that we were meant to do more than just survive. We believe that we were created with destiny and purpose, and for us to live so, truth and justice must prevail. The treatment of people will shine the light on our character. It will also determine our love walk. You cannot have awe inspiring deeds without love. It serves humanity's basic needs. When the love of God is shed abroad in our hearts, our purpose instantly becomes manifest. Truth and justice become our fruit, and next level living becomes possible. These are not lofty ideals or impossible standards. It is borne out of decency and respect. When the world was created God designed an order that would bring Him glory. We seem to forget why we are here in the first place. We cannot honor God if we are constantly trying to thwart His purpose. God tells us and warns us in His Word that what He sets out to do, will be accomplished in spite of what selfish desires become our agenda. If you want victory in your life emulate the love of the Father.

Blessings, Rupert & Red.

MARCH 13

The Prophetic Voice Rings True Today

Mediation Verse: Isaiah 59:14 NLT

Our courts oppose the righteous, and justice is nowhere to be found. Truth stumbles in the streets and honesty has been outlawed.

Scripture Reading: Isaiah 59

The Prophet Isaiah recorded a scathing indictment against the people of Israel who had lost sight of the true meaning of justice and righteousness. Their system was corrupt, and they were in denial that they were at fault. Fast forward to today and we are facing the same corrupt system. The words of Isaiah ring sadly true for the courts today that are not designed for justice, but partiality and inequality. The lack of integrity is obvious in the actions of those who are supposed to be the servants of the people. From the courthouse to the jailhouse, almost everyone is void of the compassion and commitment to improve the lives of others. We are so quick to throw away the lives of the less fortunate. The war is not on poverty, it never has been. It is on the poor, the widows, the orphans, the very ones God wants us to protect. So where did we go wrong? Because we have no interest in justice, God will not bless us. Because we have no interest in righteousness, God will not bless us. The blessings of God are inextricably tied to our obedience. I know we have heard this before, but it bears repetition, so many people call on God because they are in trouble but unlike God we refuse to forgive and show mercy. Allow justice to be found, don't oppress the poor or less fortunate. Make honesty the hallmark of your existence. Let His truth be your path to freedom.

Blessings, Rupert & Red.

MARCH 14

Believe The Resurrection

Mediation Verse: 2 Peter 1:16 NKJV

For we did not follow cunningly devised fables when we made known to you the power and coming of our Lord Jesus Christ but were eyewitnesses of His majesty.

Scripture Reading: 2 Peter 1:16-21

We believe the holiest of days on the Christian calendar are: Good Friday and Resurrection Sunday. The case of Christ is always and probably will always be in dispute, as long as we live on this side of eternity. Peter is one of our favorite apostles. His defense and explanation of the gospel is passionate, heartfelt and very practical. His sermons persuaded many thousands of Jews and Gentiles to accept The Messiah as Lord. Even though he stumbled, he was restored and became not only a great preacher, but a staunch advocate for the faith. Even though he was an eyewitness to the life and miracles of Jesus Christ for three and a half years, he cites the Old Testament as an even greater witness of Jesus Christ. The Old Testament contains over 300 prophecies of the details of the birth, life, death and resurrection of The Messiah. Jesus Christ fulfilled every prophecy. So, Peter is saying, "Look we can't make this up, Jesus is alive, and He is alive forevermore." We have come to know Him through faith, and the more we know, the more we understand that Jesus is real, and our lives are forever changed because of that fact. He died for you and me. The courts accept two or three witnesses to establish evidence. The Bible records hundreds of witnesses who had seen the risen Savior. The world's timetable acknowledges His birth and death. We are more than two thousand years in since the crucifixion. When you accept His life and resurrection then yours will be secured forever. This is not a cunning fable; it is good news. Read all about it!

Blessings, Rupert & Red.

MARCH 15

Sweet Freedom

Mediation Verse: Romans 7:24 NLT

Oh, what a miserable person I am! Who will free me from this life that is dominated by sin and death?

Scripture Reading: Romans 7:14-25

What would it take for you to truly feel free? To know that whatever you wanted to do was never an issue, the ability and resources to see any project to fruition, and live the good life, knowing that your future is secure. I am sure we all have pictures in our minds as to what that would look like. But in order to get to that incredible future, there are some things and some people that you must leave behind. Know that everyone cannot walk the same road as you, and everyone that is with you is not necessarily for you. That includes the habits that you have cultivated in your lifetime which may not have your best interest at heart. No one is exempt, we all have issues. So how do we get disentangled from the sin that so easily besets us? Or as Paul aptly called it, "the body of this death?" Romans 7:24b (KJV). If we wanted someone to fight for us, it would be one who has been in this fight before and has experience. Someone who has conquered death, hell and the grave and has put thousands of demons to flight! How about someone to whom nothing is impossible and has tens of thousands of legions of angels at their disposal. Or better yet has created everything for His own pleasure and has never been defeated! To know that victory in your own life is guaranteed along with life eternal. Ladies and gentlemen, we give you Jesus, the Christ, the author and finisher of our faith, and the only One who can deliver you from this life dominated by sin. Freedom and relationship come with the acceptance of the gift.

Blessings, Rupert & Red.

MARCH 16

Underserved Grace

Mediation Verse: Ephesians 2:9 NLT

Salvation is not a reward for the good things we have done, so none of us can boast about it.

Scripture Reading: Ephesians 2:1-10

There are many words that come to mind when mediating on this beautiful verse; however, we will only touch on a few. The first is it should produce humility in us. God is so awesome, He provided us with the gift of salvation, not just because He knew we needed saving, but also because He deemed us worthy of it. The next word is grace, it is entirely because of His grace, His free undeserved favor to us, not because of anything we have done. This grace produces the power to believe, another word that causes us to accept salvation as an accomplished fact. Without grace or the power to believe salvation is not possible, God can't believe for us, this is something that we must do. Belief is in fact a requirement for salvation, Romans 10:9-10 (NLT). We can never repay what God has graciously bestowed on us. While salvation should produce good works in us, there is no way we can boast about it. God and God alone deserve the glory. He did it all for us and besides, He considers us His masterpiece, Ephesians 2:10a (NLT), and we are good with that.

Blessings, Rupert & Red.

MARCH 17

God Is Love

Mediation Verse: 1 Peter 4:8 NLT

Most important of all continue to show deep love for each other, for love covers a multitude of sins.

Scripture Reading: 1 Peter 4:1-11

There is an element to our society past and present that is often overlooked or understated. And it is because people genuinely do not know how to respond to it. We talk about it, write plays and poems about it, sing about it, fight over it, cry over it, hurt and even kill over it. Yet the majority of the world has no real understanding of it. And that is because we treat it as an emotion and not a virtue, a feeling and not a fruit of the spirit. We see it as something to possess and not something to give away. It is the most misused and abused word in any language. That word is love. The enemy has been very successful in causing confusion over love, for every real thing there is a counterfeit, for every physical trait, there is a spiritual trait. When you don't discern the difference misuse and abuse is the result. Where there is genuine Godly love, many small offences, and even some large ones are overlooked and forgotten. But where that love is lacking in action and is viewed with suspicion, then conflict abounds, much to the enemy's delight. Love is what you do, not what you feel, you can't tie your emotions to love, for then you restrict its flow, free to saturate the homes, families, communities, cities, countries and eventually the universe. Sounds impossible? God specializes in the impossible, we were created, live and move, by love. It is the Alpha and Omega, and worthy of the highest praise. When you give love away everything changes for the better. Hear with your spiritual ears, don't just say it, believe it and walk in it. God is love.

Blessings, Rupert & Red.

MARCH 18

Seek Your Real Life

Mediation Verse: Colossians 3:3 NLT
For you died to this life, and your real life is hidden with Christ in God.
Scripture Reading: Colossians 3:1-10

Every one of us has a purpose and a calling. This is one of the many things that we cannot stress enough. And while some of us believe that they indeed are living their purpose, working at that dream job, teaching and educating children, treating and caring for the sick and disabled, protecting and championing for the less fortunate, preaching the gospel and helping to transform and change lives. Honorable pursuits all, noble and at times sacrificial in nature, but all temporary. This life we live on earth while precious is all too brief. Most of us, if not all can attest to how quickly time flies, and the older you get, the faster time seems to move. I have marveled at the fact that it seems like only yesterday I was seventeen and now we have grandchildren, whom we love dearly, but they are a sobering reminder that we have more of our earthly life behind us than we have before us. That is why it is so important to seek your real life before the temporary one ends. Therein lies your true purpose. You were not created to live on borrowed time, because there will come a time when time is no more. Usually, things that are temporary are in place until the permanent things are available. This is just my starter house, or secondhand car, or even a temporary job. Everything in this life is temporary, so why settle for a temporary life? Your real life is with Christ, He holds the keys to life eternal. No one else can offer you real life and no one can receive it for you. You must seek your real life, your best life, your forever life. Honor your true purpose by honoring the One who created you for it.

Blessings, Rupert & Red.

MARCH 19

Spend Time With God

Mediation Verse: Psalms 5:3 NKJV

My voice You shall hear in the morning, O Lord; In the morning I will direct it to You, and I will look up.

Scripture Reading: Psalms 5:1-3

I am a morning person, and I am also a night owl. I know that sounds a little oxymoronic, but I can function on both sides of the spectrum. I am not a typical musician, sleeping in is not always an option for me. I love mornings, to be up just before the sun comes up, usually very quiet except for the sounds of nature. It speaks to me about divine order and how God masterfully created the universe, and the things that we depend on and enjoy. It fills my heart with gratitude and praise. While I try to practice the presence of God throughout the day, it is at this time that I truly feel His presence and I begin to talk to God about any and everything, and in listening and watching I can hear His voice. Whatever time of the day is quiet for you, we urge you to spend time with God, read His Word and hear what He has to say about you. Jesus always took time to pray, in a culture that is becoming more and more prayerless we need to make prayer a priority in our lives. Jesus left an excellent example to follow, and it is one that we should follow faithfully. Lift your hearts and yield to the practice of prayer, your life will be so much richer for it.

Blessings, Rupert & Red.

MARCH 20

Trust God's Timing

Mediation Verse: Psalms 77:8 HCSB

Has His faithful love ceased forever? Is His promise at an end for all generations?

Scripture Reading: Psalms 77

In the grand scheme of things, patience is a virtue seldom practiced. We live in a microwave society and waiting is not our forte. Most of us live with the urgency of having to get things done. There are times when we have prayed over something and waiting on the manifestation of it, and it seems as if God has packed up and gone on vacation. We are used to getting our prayers through but now they seem to be bouncing off the ceiling so hard we develop a headache. Where is God when you need Him? What have I done to lose His favor and blessings? It is in times like these when we have to recall God's benevolence toward us. Has He been faithful so far? As you look back do you see His Hand providing your needs and making a way out of no way? One thing to remember and think about; God's promises never fail! They are yes and amen! He has not forgotten you, no matter what it looks like, God's got you! This is a word for someone who is feeling discouraged, tired, and yes impatient. "And let us not be weary in well doing for in due season we shall reap, if we faint not." Galatians 6:9 (KJV). Take heart, due season always comes.

Blessings, Rupert & Red.

MARCH 21

Share The Good News

Mediation Verse: Psalms 75:9 NLT

*But as for me, I will always proclaim what God has done;
I will sing praises to the God of Jacob.*

Scripture Reading: Psalms 75

Whenever we get good news, the first thing we want to do usually is tell it! Because it brings you joy, you want others to share in that joy you feel and celebrate with you. I mean what good is it if you keep it to yourself? Especially if others can benefit from it, even if just to bring temporary happiness, and good feelings. You may even want to shout it from the mountain top! Sharing Jesus seems to be a burden for the Christian. We receive the good news of salvation and God's redemptive plan for our lives and future, but we tend to keep it under wraps for fear of rejection. Can we encourage you to tell others the good news of what God has done for you and how He loves them and has the desire to do the same for them? Did you know that as part of the family of God, we are given the commission to share the good news with others? It is counterproductive to keep the news to yourself and not give others the opportunity to make a decision for Christ. No, you don't have to be a preacher, teacher, you just have to simply share the love of God, that can be done in numerous ways, by word, and or actions. It is a form of praise to share and show the good news that God is love. Kingdom building is the responsibility of every Christian. Share the good news, it has eternal benefits, and someone's life is depending on it.

Blessings, Rupert & Red.

MARCH 22

False Judgement

Mediation Verse: Matthew 7:4 NLT

How can you think of saying to your friend, "Let me help you get rid of that speck in your eye," when you can't see pass the log in your own eye?

Scripture Reading: Matthew 7:1-5

Can you picture a man with a log in his own eye trying to help another remove a speck from his own eye? It is kind of funny, but it is a sobering reminder about the standard by which we judge. Our hypocrisy in these instances is always more evident to others than to ourselves. We are called to show unconditional love, not conditional approval. We have to learn to love people who do things that would not be approved of. No one should condone sin and that is why we should not be so quick to pass judgement. We all are guilty of sin at one time or another, so a self-righteous attitude never sets an honest example. It is wrong to only speak to others about their faults, it is wrong to judge an entire life by the worst moments, and it is wrong to judge others, when there but for the grace of God go you or I. Jesus did not prohibit the judgement of others, but He requires that our judgement be completely fair. We cannot judge others by one standard and ourselves by another. God says in His Word, that "with the measure you use, it will be measured back to you." Matthew 7:2b (NKJV). This should motivate us to be generous with forgiveness, love and mercy to others. There is something to be said for balancing love with discernment. A good example of this is the woman that was caught in adultery, she had certainly sinned, but the men who brought her to Jesus were not really looking for justice, they were trying to trap Jesus. He exposed their motives with the statement: "He who is without sin among you, let him throw a stone at her first." John 8:7b (NKJV).

It is said that love covers a multitude of sin. Let's take care of that log in our own eye, and show love and mercy, and maybe then we can help that brother or sister with that speck. We don't have the right to throw a single stone.

Blessings, Rupert & Red.

MARCH 23

Spiritual Nourishment!!

Mediation Verse: Job 23:12 HCSB

I have not departed from the commands of His lips; I have treasured the words of His mouth more than my daily food.

Scripture Reading: Job 23:1-14

Want the Word to come alive in you? Only by reading it will that happen! Jesus said, "The words that I have spoken to you, are spirit, and are life." John 6:63b. (HCSB). The studying of the scriptures causes mind illumination, and the truth comes to life in you. The Bible is more than just a guidebook; it creates faith, produces change, causes miracles, heals hurts, builds character, transforms circumstances, imparts joy, overcomes adversity, defeats temptation, builds hope, releases power, cleanses minds, brings things into being and guarantees your future. You can't live without it! It is as essential to your life as food. God's Word is spiritual nourishment. The Bible is described as milk, bread, solid food and sweet dessert. That is a very appetizing meal. Let God's Word be on your to do list every day. It's time we grew up, we can't keep bypassing our time with God. Peter says it this way; "Like newborn infants, desire the pure spiritual milk, so that you may grow by it for your salvation." 1Peter 2:2 (HCSB)

Blessings, Rupert & Red.

MARCH 24

A Sound Mind Is A Blessing

Mediation Verse: Luke 8:35 HCSB

Then people went out to see what had happened. They came to Jesus and found the man the demons had departed from, sitting at Jesus' feet, dressed and in his right mind. And they were afraid.

Scripture Reading: Luke 8:26-39

The stigma of mental illness is a hard habit to break in this society. People tend to discount and destroy what they don't understand. We believe it is important for the Christian to understand that demons and demonic activity are at work in this world. The Word of God is clear in Ephesians 6:12b, (NIV), where it says, "We wrestle against powers of this dark world and against spiritual forces of evil in heavenly realms." However, if we have on the armor of God we can discern between satanic forces and the mental illness that plague our society. If we do not understand the wiles of the enemy, we may give in to the fear that sometimes accompanies a lack of knowledge. We cannot afford to lose the compassion, care and concern that is needed to deal with those who are afflicted, and at the same time recognize what strategy is needed to make the wounded whole. As the body of Christ, we have to develop ways to be able to help those who find themselves in dark places, be that through prayer, counsel or helps ministries. If those are your gifts, why not make yourself available to be a conduit through which those in need can be delivered. We can do this! We are not bound by the spirit of fear, ask God for a heart of discernment. He will give you what you need and then some. Who would not want to serve a God like that!!

Blessings, Rupert & Red.

MARCH 25

His Grace Is Sufficient!!

Meditation Verse: Acts 15:8-9 KJV

And God, which knoweth the hearts, bare them witness, giving them the Holy Ghost, even as He did unto us; And put no difference between us and them, purifying their hearts by faith.

Scripture Reading: Acts 15:6-12

In a recent devotion we talked about salvation being for everyone, another scripture grabbed us, and we would like to reaffirm that thought. The beauty of this text is that it confirms that God desires us to be heirs of the precious promise of salvation. Salvation, that is, by the shed blood and saving grace of Jesus Christ, and not a "legalistic religion," that was bound in tradition and impossible to keep laws. The doctrine of "Law versus Grace" was important then and it is now!

We all tend to have a little bit of "Pharisee" in us, be careful that we don't let tradition be a legal structure for obeying God. Make sure that the Gospel brings freedom and life to you and those who you are trying to reach. Jesus Himself said, "making the word of God of no effect by the tradition which you have handed down." Mark 7:13a (NKJV). We need not be guilty of this mistake. We need to accept the grace of salvation, continue to read and study God's Word, and "stand fast therefore in the liberty by which Christ has made us free, and do not be entangled again with a yoke of bondage! Galatians 5:1 (NKJV). Aren't you glad that grace overcomes legalism? Our Father thinks of everything!!

Blessings, Rupert & Red.

MARCH 26

To Whom Do You Answer?

Meditation Scripture: Acts 5:29 NLT

But Peter and the apostles replied, we must obey God rather than any human authority.

Scripture Reading: Acts 5:22-32

It is certainly surprising how much we take for granted. Truth is not a priority and being selfless for a greater good seems almost obsolete. There are people who would give their all and most who could not care less. Jesus came to prove that religion will never replace relationship. Relationship is everything and the reason why we serve. What are you willing to sacrifice in your service to God? Are you willing to suffer persecution and possibly death in obedience to the cause of Christ? This may sound extreme in the 21st Century, but the truth is that people in other countries around the globe, are tortured, beaten, maimed, imprisoned, and yes killed daily, simply because they name the name of Jesus. Here in the Western hemisphere, that is a rare occurrence. For the most part we are not called upon to give up our lives in the physical sense for the sake of Christ, so why not do the next best thing? Why not give your lives *to* Christ and LIVE *for* Him? Every day that we rise is another opportunity to offer ourselves as a "living sacrifice" so that we can be witnesses for the Truth!! So, to whom do you answer? Somebody is waiting for you to talk to them about Jesus!! Let's Go!!

Blessings, Rupert & Red.

MARCH 27

Intentional God!!

Meditation Verse: Acts 9:15 NLT

But the Lord said to him, "Go! For this man is My chosen instrument to take My Name to Gentiles, kings, and the Israelites."

Scripture Reading: Acts 9:10-16

God is so awesome!! A little history: When Alexander the Great conquered the then known world, he left pockets of Greek culture throughout. And even when the Roman Empire had conquered the Grecian Empire, the Grecian culture became dominant. Grecian culture at that time was more towards the music, philosophy, and arts, in contrast, the Hebrew culture of the day was very legalistic. The Pharisees who were representatives of the Jewish culture were very strict. This caused a real contrast between the two. Israel was divided between the Hellenistic and Grecian cultures. The religious hierarchy were Hellenistic except for the Sadducees, they were materialists, whereas the Pharisees were legalists. Paul, (Saul), was born in the city of Tarsus, which was one of the centers of Greek culture. So, although they were strict Pharisees, Paul was acquainted with both the Hellenistic and the Grecian cultures. His parents chose to send him to the Hebrew University in Jerusalem where he might sit at the feet of Gamaliel to become a Pharisee. So, Paul was the perfect blend of knowledge in both cultures, and the instrument God would use to bring the gospel to the Gentiles! Nothing just happens with God!! Long story short, our God is intentional!!

Blessings, Rupert & Red.

MARCH 28

The Power Of Prayer

Meditation Verse: James 5:16 NLT

Confess your sins to each other and pray for each other so that you may be healed. The earnest prayer of a righteous person has great power and produces wonderful results.

Scripture Reading: James 5:13-18

We believe that the Christian's most powerful resource is communion with God through prayer. It is never wisdom to wait until all else fails and use prayer as a last resort. Who has more power? You or God? Does it not make more sense to rely on the Greater Power? It is not only a privilege, but a Christian's duty to pray, and to pray for one another. And before prayer can change a situation, prayer ought to change you! Praying earnestly is praying with power, God is not looking only for the erudite and scholarly prayer. He is looking for the heartfelt, passionate and straight to the point prayer where you know that He hears you. It is not how many words you say, it is the heart that you pray with; JESUS!! Is a prayer, why? Because "at the Name of Jesus, every knee shall bow, of those in heaven, and of those on earth, and of those under the earth, and that every tongue should confess that Jesus Christ is Lord, to the glory of God the Father!" Philippians 2:10-11 (NKJV). Pray for one another regularly, and God will give you the words to say. And if you come to the point where "you don't know what else to pray, when you can't find the words to say, when you can't make it through one more day, SAY THE NAME!!" JESUS!! There is power in the Name!!

Blessings, Rupert & Red.

Foot note: "Say the Name" – written by Martha Munizzi/Clint Brown

MARCH 29

Stay The Course...

Meditation Verse: 2 John 1:8 NLT

Watch out that you do not lose what we have worked so hard to achieve. Be diligent so that you receive your full reward.

Scripture Reading: 2 John 1:4-9

There will always be those that will bring you a new "revelation" or "word" from God. It really is a result borne out of control and not love. As we have seen in the Word we must "look to ourselves" in the sense that we share in the responsibility of watching out for deceivers. We are often defined by what we reject as much as by what we accept. It may be wise to keep an open mind on many things, but one would not keep an open mind on what poisons a person might try. Discernment is an important key, but it is also important that we don't lean to our own understanding, when God is directing our path then our "walk" takes on purpose. Hearts that are established towards God will know how to reject what is false and evil, and our lives will be grounded in truth that can withstand the onslaught of any enemy... Don't fall for the "okey doke." Deception is the biggest tool of the enemy.

Blessings, Rupert & Red.

MARCH 30

Obedience; Not An Option...

Meditation Verse: Zephaniah 3:7 NLT

I thought, "Surely they will have reverence for me now! Surely they will listen to my warnings. Then I won't need to strike again, destroying their homes," But no, they get up early to continue their evil deeds.

Scripture Reading: Zephaniah 3:1-9

The prophet Zephaniah was called "The Royal Prophet" because he was of the royal line of Judah, the house of David. He dealt with God's judgement upon his own people and the surrounding nations. There is something to be said about the saying: "The definition of insanity is doing the same thing over and over again yet expecting a different result." Why do we persist on doing things that will never bring us life? Are we that complacent in our thinking that we just don't expect consequences for our actions? The fact is that we are the sum total of our decisions. If you don't like where you are going, change your direction!! While we contemplate the righteous indignation of an angry God, His love and mercy are still evident in His Word, in fact they are prevalent and paramount!! The Bible says however, "Therefore, to him who knows to do good and does not do it, to him it is sin." James 4:17 (NKJV). Just because you know the difference between right and wrong, does nothing to negate sin. There must be a paradigm shift, not just in what you know, but in what you do. Mental assent is an insult to God if there is no follow through! God requires obedience, it is the only way to receive His blessings and the way to eternal life. Make the change!!

Blessings, Rupert & Red.

MARCH 31

Courage To Face Adversity

Meditation Verse: Mark 14:30 NLT

Jesus replied, "I tell you the truth, Peter, this very night, before the rooster crows twice, you will deny three times that you even know me."

Scripture Reading: Mark 14:27-31

The spotlight on Peter's failure could have been on any one of us. It is always easy to fashion an answer when you already know the outcome. False bravado has been the downfall of many a person. There is so much to say about how Peter's betrayal mirrors our own. The strength to endure can only show up when we need it if we watch and pray. Not coincidentally it was Peter who penned these words; "Be sober, be vigilant; because your adversary, the devil, walks about like a roaring lion, seeking whom he may devour. 1Peter 5:8. (NKJV). The enemy has our number, and he knows exactly which fear and or weakness in our lives to exploit. We all have been guilty of denying Christ in our lives at some point. The good news is He stands waiting to redeem us, to make us whole, to reconcile us back to himself. Jesus knows that from time to time we will struggle with our faith, no one is exempt from these struggles. But we have to get honest with ourselves and realize that a lot of times when we find ourselves in trouble, it is because we allow trouble to find us, and we think that no one is paying attention. So, we try to bury our selfish motives under a rock, until our agenda calls for a shovel! God is looking for people who can be transparent. Issues, yes even yours are nothing new to God. Paul said it best when he stated, "Therefore let him who thinks he stands, take heed lest he fall." 1 Corinthians: 10:12 (NKJV).

Blessings, Rupert & Red.

APRIL 1

Who Is My Neighbor?

Meditation Verse: Luke 10:36-37 NLT

"Now which of these three would you say was a neighbor to the man who was attacked by bandits?" Jesus asked. The man replied, "the one who showed him mercy." Then Jesus said, "yes now go and do the same."

Scripture Reading: Luke 10:30-37

Jesus in telling the parable of the Good Samaritan, asks this important question. You know the story, a man (Jewish) was set upon by thieves, robbed, beaten, and left for dead. Two of his contemporaries pass him by but do nothing to help. A Samaritan man considered unclean and a half breed by the Jews, stops and has compassion and takes care of him, even paying for his expenses at a hotel. So, what is really in our hearts? Are we desirous of motives that are pure? Do our actions correspond with what we know to be true? Or do our attitudes betray the lack of the very things that Jesus commanded us to display, Love and Compassion. God's plan is to accept all those who desire relationship into the kingdom without regard to our selfish prejudices. The Samaritan showed "compassion" he was moved in his heart to show love to a stranger, and one, who if the roles were reversed, may have quite possibly been loathed to help him, not being a Jew. Love humanizes both the giver and the receiver, that is what it takes to be a neighbor. Whom do you love? Are you willing to risk eternal life in order to pick, choose, and refuse your neighbors? Pray for a heart of compassion, it is all a part of conforming to His image. Remember Jesus said, "Assuredly I say to you, inasmuch as you did it to one of the least of these My brethren, you did it to Me." Matthew 25:40b (NKJV).

Blessings, Rupert & Red.

APRIL 2

It All Belongs To Him

Meditation Verse: Psalms 24:1 NLT
The earth is the Lord's, and everything in it. The world and all its people belong to Him.
Scripture Reading: Psalms 24

"Our Daddy owns Everything!!" The words in this first verse of Psalm 24 will either comfort you or disquiet you. There is maybe something to be said about having the ability to own a thing, there is usually a sense of satisfaction, but with that comes a certain set of anxieties, that may or may not be anticipated. The ability to own does not always guarantee the ability to maintain. It is true that ownership of certain things brings independence to some but for others a shackled existence. Completing a thirty-year mortgage turns into another fifteen year mortgage, for renovations, a seven year car note turns into a new car at terms end and another chattel mortgage. The illusion of ownership is as fleeting as the next breath. The truth, the hard truth is that we own nothing. "When God gave the earth to the children of men, He reserved to Himself the property and allowed us tenancy. The riches in the center of the earth, the fruit it produces, the cattle on a thousand hills, and all the improvements made by the industry and skill of man, all His. No matter where you go in this vast world or beyond, you will never go off the Lord's ground. Whatever is considered our share of this earth and its productions is only on loan to us. That which is far away and hidden from our view, is not hidden from the Lord for He knows where to find it." Matthew Henry. Source: (Blue Letter Bible, blueletterbible.org). Even to ourselves, our bodies and our souls belong to God. "All souls are mine," Ezekiel 18:4a (NKJV), says God, "it is He who has made us and not we ourselves." Psalm 100:3a (NKJV). Even those that know Him not, or deny Him, are His. Our Father owns everything, and we own nothing. "God made it, formed it, and fixed it for our use." Matthew Henry, commentator. Source: (Blue Letter Bible, blueletterbible.org). So, you can cling to your worldly possessions and independence," but if I were you, I'd declare my dependence solely on Daddy…

Blessings, Rupert & Red.

APRIL 3

The Faith Fight

Meditation Verse: 1 Timothy 6:12 NLT

Fight the good fight for the true faith. Hold tightly to the eternal life to which God has called you, which you have declared so well before many witnesses.

Scripture Reading: 1 Timothy 6:11-16

We have said previously that this verse describes the only fight that God has called us to fight. Why is this fight so important that we are expected to do battle for ourselves? It is because the enemy is after your faith. If he can put you in bondage, fear, or doubt, then he has you. We need to realize that we are in a battle to keep something that God has already given us. The measure of faith. If we do not develop it, mature it and grow it, then Satan has an opportunity to gain a foothold in your life and wreak havoc. As Paul told Timothy, we should, "guard that which has been committed to our trust." 1 Timothy 6:20 (NKJV paraphrased). This fight God has called us to is not easily won if we don't have the proper equipment. In order to defeat the enemy, our thinking must be strategic because this is not a physical fight, but the battle is in our mind and will. Paul knew that Timothy would face challenges and so will we. If we keep our mind stayed on Jesus, we need not fear what man can do. It was Paul who said: "If God be for us who can be against us?" Romans 8:31b (KJV) Commit to changing attitudes and personal actions that need to be gone from our lives. We are in a fight, but we don't have to fight alone. So, face the enemy with courage and boldness, run at him or it like David ran towards Goliath, knowing that you have been ordained to fight the good fight of faith!!

Blessings, Rupert & Red.

APRIL 4

The Lord's Purposes Will Prevail

Meditation Verse: Amos 5:24 NKJV
But let justice run down like water, and righteousness like a mighty stream.
Scripture Reading: Amos 5:1-27

Today marks the anniversary of the assassination of Rev.Dr. Martin Luther King Jr. He was cut down in the prime of his life by hate. It was a wicked and desperate attempt to silence not just a man but a movement. It was an agenda to vilify a man because he believed in justice and dignity for an oppressed people. There will always be those who will oppose and deny the right for people to live free just because they look different. We, like the psalmist will sing of the mercies of the Lord forever, but we will also extol His judgement. God sees you and He knows your name. You who seek to crush the spirit of a man because of the color of his skin. You who pretend to love God, but harbor hatred for His creation. The hypocrites who profess to love Jesus but ignore and twist His word. You think you have your reward, but it is temporary and worthless. In the end the purposes of the Lord will stand. He is merciful but He will not reward sin. The light will shine bright as the noon day, and your deeds will be exposed. We know this devotional is a little different from the rest, but judgement is real. And those who oppose God will come to nothing. We say this to encourage and resist. Love can find you, but you have to stop the killing and the hate. We refuse to live in fear! Water is the most powerful natural force on earth, so when justice and righteousness begins to run down, you had better be on the right side, because you won't be able to get out of its way.

Blessings, Rupert & Red.

APRIL 5

One Hundred Sixty-Eight Hours...

Meditation Verse: Psalms 1:3 NKJV

He shall be like a tree planted by the rivers of water, that brings forth its fruit in its season, whose leaf shall not wither, and whatever he does shall prosper.

Scripture Reading: Psalms 1

We all get 168 hours in a week. How much of that time is spent developing your spiritual life? We know we all get busy, and life gets in the way, but, if we wait until Sunday morning to get it all in, we won't be able to mature in our walk. Just like a baby needs to grow, be disciplined and trained, so should we be moving beyond the infancy stages in our spiritual lives. The Bible says in Hebrews 6:1 (NLT), "So, let us stop going over the basic teachings about Christ again and again. Let us go on instead and become mature in our understanding." It is up to us to take that personal journey and discover God's plan for our lives. We can't survive on just milk; it is time to eat some solid food. Our walk will be so much closer, our prayer life will thrive, and we will become like that tree that is planted by the river, their leaves never wither, and they prosper in all they do!!

Blessings, Rupert & Red.

APRIL 6

We Cry Hosanna!!

Meditation Verse: Mark 11:9 NKJV

Then those who went before and those who followed cried out, saying, Hosanna! Blessed is He who comes in the name of the LORD!!

Scripture Reading: Mark 11:1-11

Jesus… The One who came triumphantly into Jerusalem, is now interceding for us in Heaven. He is fulfilling His role as Prophet, Priest, and King, for all who will confess and believe. Residing in us through His precious Holy Spirit, guiding, and confirming His Word in our lives. Our responsibility is to live a life of praise and thanksgiving, giving all the glory to God for what He has done and is doing in our lives. Not just for what He has done, but for who He is! Always being mindful of our motives as we worship; for true worship can only come from an intimate and spiritual relationship. Then, and only then, can we gain discernment for why we cry Hosanna!! Then we can come into true focus of who Jesus is!! It is all about the Kingdom! Don't mistake the Kingdom of God, for the kingdom of this world!! Blessings, Rupert & Red.

APRIL 7

Necessary Interference!

Meditation Verse: Jonah 1:3 NKJV

But Jonah arose to flee to Tarshish from the presence of the Lord. He went down to Joppa, and found a ship going to Tarshish; so, he paid the fare, went down into it, to go with them to Tarshish from the presence of the Lord.

Scripture Reading: Jonah 1:1-3

I do not like to have my flow interfered with! Whether I am reading, writing, studying, practicing, or even watching television, I need to focus on the task at hand without interference... that almost never happens!! Something or someone (I love you Red!!) always needs my attention on seemingly more important matters! I can relate to how Jonah felt, he was minding his own business when the Lord told him to go down to Ninevah to preach to his sworn enemies! When you think you have problems, someone else has it worse than you! Aren't we like Jonah though? We say we want to serve God, if it is convenient. We say that we desire to do His will; until it becomes uncomfortable. We want to hear his Word, if it does not convict us. Just as long as it does not interfere with our plans. Wow! Jonah ran away from God, yet I cannot get mad with him. When my plans are interrupted, I want to rebel against it. We often forget that God's love and grace can sustain us through whatever He may ask us to do. You do know that God does not need us to complete His plan! God's purposes will be fulfilled with or without us. However, we should count it a privilege to be co-laborers with God. It is part of the relationship He desires with His children. We encourage you to read the story of Jonah. It is about much more than a man and a great fish; it is a profound illustration of God's mercy and grace. His love and compassion prove that no one is beyond redemption. Learn the story of the reluctant prophet and realize that making yourself available to God is more important than the temporal inconvenience of an interruption.

Blessings, Rupert & Red.

APRIL 8

Our Personal Provider

Meditation Verse: Psalms 23:1 NKJV
The Lord is my shepherd, I shall not want.
Scripture Reading: Psalms 23

If, and only if, you understand and believe that the earth is the Lord's, then you can relate to the statement that no one can provide for us like God. This world system, which is different from the earth, has never intended to provide for you, only for themselves. There may have been a time when labor was respected and people took pride and joy in their chosen fields and even the employers, and the services they provided, but from conversations with many people, and even personal experience, it is now a rarity that precious few enjoy. With every buy out of major corporations by other major corporations, there seems to have emerged a heartless and cruel culture that values profits over people. Workers are disenfranchised, marginalized, overworked and paid less and less, so that one or even two jobs are not sufficient to live on. A climate of fear lingers over places of employment, where at any moment the proverbial hammer may fall that leads to joblessness and hopelessness. Sounds horrible right? It is, however, the sad truth of the times we live in and maybe has always been in some perverse form or another. Our trust is in the owner of everything!! In the midst of the storm and the dry places He sees to it that we are safe. He provides us comfort, rest, food, clothing and shelter. We may not possess all the things that trap society, but we always have what we need. Because when you know whose you are, everything that you need, God is. He is the reason why we are on solid ground in spite of what is storming in our lives.... All other ground is sinking sand.

Blessings, Rupert & Red.

APRIL 9

We Believe In The Resurrection!

Meditation Verse: Romans 4:25 NLT

He was handed over to die because of our sins, and He was raised to life to make us right with God.

Scripture Reading: Romans 4:13-25

I was reading that the Great Houdini promised he'd come back from the dead and talk to his friends. Some actually consulted mediums to see if there was any word from beyond the grave. There was not! Only one man who promised to rise from the dead kept His promise. Jesus! He did it to make us right with God. On Good Friday Jesus laid down His life, and on Resurrection Sunday, He got up and your salvation was paid for. But the greatest proof of the resurrection is in the transformed lives all over the world, including yours truly!! You ask us how we know He lives? He lives within our hearts!! Jesus announced: "I am He that lives and was dead; and behold I am alive forevermore; whosoever lives and believes in Me shall never die." Rev.1:18a, (NKJV), John 11:26b, (NKJV). Here is the truth: Unless you know Christ as your personal Savior, you are without hope in this world, and the world to come. No hope means nothing to look forward to. So today, repent of your sin and place your trust in the One who died and rose again for you. Guarantee your life to come, so you won't have to live eternity in regret!

Blessings, Rupert & Red.

APRIL 10

There Is Hope In This Life

Meditation Verse: Psalms 27:13 NKJV

I would have lost heart, unless I had believed that I would see the goodness of the Lord in the land of the living.

Scripture Reading: Psalms 27

You don't have to wait till you die to experience the goodness of God! David realized that to lose heart is to lose hope; but God intervened in his circumstances and became the lifter of his head! The trials are never meant to kill you, God's intent is to grow you. The decisions we make very often are the things that bring us harm. Until you put your trust in God and not man, you will always be going around the same mountain. It is a hard lesson to learn because we always want to believe that people will do what they say or promise, but sadly most do not. There is a difference between having good intentions and being intentional. God does not change, people do, the instability is real and will usually put us at risk. Let the love and wisdom of God guide you in the steps that you take. You can experience His grace and goodness in the land of the living! And if You lose heart? God is the only one who can give you a new one...

Blessings, Rupert & Red.

APRIL 11

Let Go And Let God

Meditation Verse: 1 Peter 5:7 NKJV

Casting all your care upon Him, for He cares for you.

Scripture Reading: 1 Peter 5:1-11

It is hard for us to yield control over the things that seem important to us. Even the things that are beyond our control can be a source of endless frustration and cause feelings of helplessness and hopelessness. No one is exempt from problems, and life at times will seem to throw at us more than our fair share. Stress is the dangerous animal that we give life to, knowing that it will slowly kill us. So, what is the solution? We must learn to let go and let God!! Now there will always be storms, but it does not have to take us out of the game. Casting your care is yielding control. It is doing what you can do and allowing God to do what you cannot. You need to know when something is beyond your control. Peace in the midst of the storm is satisfying! It does not mean that we are not concerned or pro- active, there is an indescribable calm that transcends our issues. When the problems of life overwhelm you and you feel like you are losing your mind, cast your cares on the One who cares for you, He will bring you through. Relationship has its privileges!

Blessings, Rupert & Red.

APRIL 12

The True Purpose For Wealth

Meditation Verse: Deuteronomy 15:11 HCSB

For there will never cease to be poor people in the land; that is why I am commanding you, "You must willingly open your hand to your afflicted and poor brothers in your land."

Scripture Reading: Deuteronomy 15:1-11

Why are we so indifferent to the suffering of others? Why do we treat people as "less than" if they don't quite measure up to our standards? Why are we as a society unable to find the love and compassion for the less fortunate? These are questions that hit the very heart of who we claim to be but fail to become. There are literally thousands of references in the word of God that speak to helping the poor. It is because of those scriptures we believe that God deemed this subject to be important to Him. So why, body of Christ, you who say you are followers of God, is this not important to you? We are more judgmental than ever these days and choose to castigate people because they are poor. We don't see humanity anymore. We have become mean spirited and callous. In this age of classism, we now have; "The working poor." God has commanded us to open our hand to the poor, but society has kept those who work and struggle in an untenable position. We will never have a just society while we have such an inequitable mentality. The Bible talks so much about helping, supporting and giving to the poor, yet we fail miserably over this mandate, and quite possibly to our own peril. We all will have to answer to God. Whatever God has blessed you with, be a blessing to someone. You will be better for it, society will be better for it, and the God who sees and knows all will bless you for it. Christian! If you say you love God then you must show your love, again; "inasmuch as you did it to one of the least of these My brethren, you did it to Me." Matthew 25:40b, (NKJV). We will revisit this issue again and again, It is that important to God!!

Blessings, Rupert & Red.

APRIL 13

What's Your Motivation?

Meditation Verse: 2 Corinthians 5:14 NLT

Either way Christ's love controls us. Since we believed that Christ died for all, we also believe that we have died to our old life.

Scripture Reading: 2 Corinthians 5:11-21

What's my motivation? A question usually asked by an actor looking for a reason to bring a particular scene to life. Usually posed to the director by the prima donna of the film or stage play. Motivation should be present in order for you to do anything well. There are, however, some good reasons with which to be motivated. Hope, kindness, joy, sorrow or even anger are good motivators. In the text it says that Christ's love controls us, other translations say, compels us, or motivates us. To what? To good works, because we have become new creatures in Christ, we should want to be in a position of service, bringing all the fruits of the spirit to bear on those we encounter. The good news of the Gospel is meant to be shared in not just a verbal, but in a very tangible way. Practically speaking we are the light on the hill, that the whole world that has been plunged into darkness, can see. Because of what we gain in Christ, our lives need to be an example to a dying world that Jesus paid the price for all so that none should perish. Can people see Jesus when they look at you? Can they tell that your life has changed? They should, because Christ's love compels us, and as a result we show that same love to compel others. We need to be an excellent witness by our words and deeds, it will affect many lives and bring the Kingdom that much closer…. So, what's your motivation?

Blessings, Rupert & Red.

APRIL 14

Exchanging The Perishable For The Imperishable

Meditation Verse: 2 Corinthians 5:2 NLT

We grow weary in our present bodies, and we long to put on our heavenly bodies like new clothing.

Scripture Reading: 2 Corinthians 5:1-10

The bible says in Ecclesiastes 3:11b (paraphrased), "He (God), has put eternity in our hearts." We all have a desire, all things being equal, to live long and prosperous lives. And long life is good, depending on the quality of that life. But as nature groans, we groan right along with it. Our bodies begin to perish from the day we are born because they were not built for eternity. This three-dimensional physical world was built with a time stamp. And until the new world and life eternal is ushered in, we are all on borrowed time. We are not long for this life, and anyone who has had the privilege to live for more than five decades can testify to the brevity of life. So, what are we to do in order to get the bodies that we are dying for? I say, make your calling and election sure. Don't you know that our lives are precious to God, and He has made a way for us to experience longevity? Is it not important to go beyond your dreams, and exchange the perishable for the imperishable? I know that I am looking forward to the day when illness and sleepless nights are a thing of the past, when my body and my mind are totally renewed to where I am in sync with Jesus!! I believe that Heaven is going to be so mind blowing and much more than we could ever think or imagine! Sick and tired of being sick and tired? Prepare yourself for your new suit, God has it waiting for you in just your size!!

Blessings, Rupert & Red

APRIL 15

Living For Christ Is Worth It

Meditation Verse: 1 Peter 5:10 HCSB

Now the God of all grace, who called you to His eternal glory in Christ Jesus, will personally restore, establish, strengthen and support you after you have suffered a little.

Scripture Reading: 1 Peter 5:8-11

We are not fans of pain! Personally, we don't know anyone who is. Sometimes though, pain is necessary to call attention to something potentially greater than the pain itself. Life itself is the result of labor pain. Pain may lead to the curing or the prevention of an ailment or disease. It is a sign that healing has begun. In many ways we can see that a positive end result can make the pain seem worth it. What is eternity worth to you? Is it worth the temporary inconvenience of being maligned, talked about, ridiculed, laughed at, mistreated, misunderstood, the loss of friendships, relationships, because no one understands your decision to live for God? Why does it seem that you have to give up so much and suffer for the cause of Christ? Can you stand on the promises of God alone when all else seems hopeless? Let me assure you that the pain is only a symptom of something "greater." God is working on your behalf even though the pain is present. He has promised to restore, establish, strengthen and support you, even though you have suffered. Be encouraged: "For our present troubles are small and won't last very long. Yet they produce in us a glory that vastly outweighs them and will last forever!" 2 Corinthians 4:17 (NLT). Forever is a long time and living for Christ is worth it!!

Blessings, Rupert & Red.

APRIL 16

Be The Light!

Meditation Verse: Matthew 5:16 HCSB

In the same way, let your light shine before men, that they may see your good works and give glory to your Father in heaven.

Scripture Reading: Matthew 5:13-16

It is easy to flip on a light switch whenever you enter a dark room. It is something that most of us take for granted, we never give it a second thought. Almost no one is thinking about the science of electricity and how the power connects to the bulb! The only time we give it any concern is if the light switch fails to work. It is hard to accomplish much without light. Our lives work the same way. The purpose of light is to dispel darkness, we are supposed to illuminate the atmosphere for change. It is the light that people see in us that will prevent stumbling, because of us becoming more and more like Christ. Jesus said that we are to let our light shine, Matthew 5:16a (NKJV paraphrased). He also said that: "I am the Light of the world." John 8:12, (HCSB). In other words, Jesus is saying is let the people see Me in you so that they will know who to praise! If we are conforming to His image, the switch should be permanently on. Give a dying world something beautiful and bright to see. Be the light that will prevent others from stumbling in the dark, and let God get the glory from your life!!

Blessings, Rupert & Red.

APRIL 17

Embrace The Joy Of The Lord!

Meditation Verse: Psalms 146:5 NLT

But joyful are those who have the God of Israel as their helper, whose hope is in the Lord their God.

Scripture Reading: Psalms 146

We don't know about you, but we need the joy of the Lord in our lives! Because joy is a catalyst for the fruits of the spirit. Because of His joy we have peace, because of His joy we have love, because of His joy we have self- control, because we have His joy, we have the strength to keep going!! God gives a joy that the world does not understand. Knowledge of our Lord and Savior, brings joy to the forefront. Because it is not dependent on circumstances, but on what you know. Joy also keeps hope alive, so many times it is easy to get discouraged and think that God does not care, but if we could just put our trust in God, the weeping may endure for a night, but Joy!! It is unspeakable and full of glory and comes at a price! Get to know God intimately, give Him your hopes and dreams, spend time, cultivate the relationship, read His Word, which by the way has a lot to say about joy. The more you know, the more you will grow and the greater your capacity for His joy! It will transcend every negative attitude, doubt or care, and lets you go on and see what the end will be. Receive the joy that Jesus gives to you, not as the world gives… It will become your strength.

Blessings, Rupert & Red.

APRIL 18

Who's Smarter Than The Creator?

Meditation Verse: Colossians 2:8 HCSB

Be careful that no one takes you captive through philosophy and empty deceit based on human tradition, based on elemental forces of the world, and not based on Christ.

Scripture Reading: Colossians 2:6-15

"God knows and sees all." That statement is used in most Christian circles. The problem is no one believes it. Either that, or we don't care that it's true. And believe me, it's true! Being in denial of this fact is made more obvious by our penchant for secret sins. Do we really think that we are smarter than God? Or is our guilt assuaged by the hope that where sin abounds, grace there much more abounds? Romans 5:20b (KJV paraphrased). The scripture says that we ought to be careful that no one takes us captive through philosophy or vain deceit, but I wonder, are we our own worst enemy? After all, the worse deception of all is self- deception. In order to avoid that horrible pitfall, every motive must be put through the integrity test. Only the truth will do and not the flawed traditions of man. Those traditions seldom operate in truth, but in what you deem to be right in your own eyes. We may not always understand what God is doing but based on the world's system and way of thinking, God is the wisest option! Actually, He is the only true option! Take your chances with the One who created the Universe, He will never leave you or forsake you. Just believe that through it all God knows what's best. Wisdom declares it, and that settles it, whether you believe it or not!

Blessings, Rupert & Red.

APRIL 19

Don't Come Down!!

Meditation Verse: Nehemiah 6:3 NIV

So, I sent messengers to them with this reply: I am carrying on a great project and cannot go down. Why should the work stop while I leave it and go down to you?

Scripture Reading: Nehemiah: 6:1-9

Focus is important! It is also difficult to maintain. There are so many things in this world that distract and most of the distractions mean you no good. Our lives are often busy and frazzled by everything that needs to be done. To multi-task is now a job requirement and an accomplishment. There is too much to do to get bogged down doing one thing, and one thing only. Time is of the essence, and we don't have any to waste! So often we take our eyes off the prize in an effort to win all the marbles. Stop trying to complete everyone's agenda! Take time to focus on the One who gave you purpose. People will try to pull you away from what is important to God to what is important to them. It is a snare of the enemy that will leave you drained, exhausted, and wanting! Nehemiah recognized that the enemy wanted him to lose focus on what God had assigned for him. God's plan and purpose for your life is too important for distractions. There is a prize for the high calling that is more precious than you know! Focus on Christ first and all the other things will fall in line. Therefore, my beloved brethren, be steadfast, immoveable, always abounding in the work of the Lord, knowing that your labor is not in vain in the Lord. 1Corinthians 15:58, (NKJV). Stay focused!! Don't Come Down!!

Blessings, Rupert & Red.

APRIL 20

Faith + Focus = Victory!!

> Meditation Verse: Nehemiah 6:16 NIV
>
> *When all our enemies heard about this, all the surrounding nations were afraid and lost their self-confidence, because they realized that this work had been done with the help of our God.*
>
> Scripture Reading: Nehemiah 6:15-19

Looking at Nehemiah again, his focus and faith in God gave him victory amidst enormous opposition and pressure. The enemy had been relentless in their quest to cause Nehemiah to fail. But Nehemiah and those with him refused to fall for the schemes and devices of his foes. All the rumors, lies, and pretense of protection, did nothing to sway or intimidate Nehemiah from his purpose. When the wall was built in record time, this caused not only his enemies, but the surrounding nations to be in fear. They recognized what could only be the power of God! When you are in the midst of opposition and your haters are trying to intimidate you and move you from your purpose, remember that God with you is much more than the whole world against you. He will cause you to see through the enemy's schemes, so you won't lose focus. When you put your trust in God, your victory will cause your enemies to scatter in fear, because they will realize in fact that they were fighting against not just you, but against God! God will cause you to triumph because you placed your faith in Him. When people see God working through you, the battle is as good as won!!

Blessings, Rupert & Red.

APRIL 21

Let God Re-Mold Your Mind

Meditation Verse: Romans 12: 2 NKJV

And do not be conformed to this world, but be transformed by the renewing of your mind, that you may prove what is that good, and acceptable and perfect will of God.

Scripture Reading: Romans 12:1-3

I like the JB Phillips translation of this passage as well: "Don't let the world around you squeeze you into its own mold, but let God re-mold your minds from within, so that you may prove in practice that the plan of God for you is good, meets all His demands and moves you towards the goal of true maturity." Romans 12:2. It is important to resist the mold and embrace transformation. The world's system and popular culture will try to conform you to their way of thinking. The way to thwart the enemy is by changing the way that you think. And the only way to do that is by renewing your mind, that is in opposition to being conformed to this world. You cannot feel your way through this. As commentator David Guzick puts it: "A life by feeling will never know the transforming power of God, because it ignores the renewing of the mind." (Source: Blue Letter Bible, blueletterbible.org) Transformation being the result, what happens on the inside then becomes evidence or proof on the outside. By focusing on God's Word, your growth will determine the will of God in your life. So, do not conform, renew and practice the presence of God daily, and watch the transformation!!

Blessings, Rupert & Red.

APRIL 22

What Are You Feeding Your Soul?

Meditation Verse: Mark 7:15 NLT

It's not what goes into your body that defiles you; you are defiled by what comes from your heart.

Scripture Reading: Mark 7:14-23

It seems that there is nothing you can eat that is good for you these days. Every food is likely to have some negative ingredient that will adversely affect your health. If they are not adding some preservative, they are spraying some pesticide, even the soil where the food is grown is contaminated. We must be so very careful what we allow in our mouths and eventually our digestive systems. Why was Jesus more concerned with what we allow into our hearts? Because the heart bears the consequences of eternity. And Jesus cares more about the spiritual than the physical. The wrong food may damage our bodies, but the wrong attitudes can defile our spirit man. You can usually tell by one's speech what resides in their heart. Jesus is saying that what man sees has no bearing on what defiles you, but God, who knows the thoughts and intent of the heart, has judged you accurately. Only He can reverse the cruel, selfish and self-centered attitude that is defiling you. Give Him your heart, He will regulate it and give you an upgrade. The food you eat may have nothing to do with your soul; but the character you build, has everything to do with your soul.

Blessings, Rupert & Red.

APRIL 23

Amazing Faithful God!

Meditation Verse: Lamentations 3:22-23 HCSB

Because of the Lord's faithful love we do not perish, for His mercies never end. They are new every morning; great is Your faithfulness!

Scripture Reading: Lamentations 3:16-24

God is Faithful!! We don't say that because it is "Christian Speak" or because we want to convince you. We say it because it is the simple truth! You may or may not be convinced but that does not change the truth. There are too many deposits of victory in our story to ever make us change our minds. God proves Himself to be just who He says over and over again. You see we believe in intelligent design. We are two of His precious creations and we know that it is because of him that we live. We are, because He is the Great I Am!! So everywhere we go we see His handiwork. The Sun, the Moon, the Stars, the Planets all align and rise, set, and move with clockwork precision. Day and night arrive when they are supposed to. We don't know what your definition of faithful is but what God promises He delivers. Never a question of if, but a solid when. He provides our needs even when we may not always seem grateful. He loves us still, covers us, comforts us, regardless of our moods or dispositions. His peace floods our souls! Know and believe that God cares for you in so many ways! Prove Him for yourself! We have, and you know what we've found? He's Faithful, that's just the simple truth! Relationship has its privileges!!

Blessings, Rupert & Red.

APRIL 24

We Should Care About The Less Fortunate!

> Meditation Verse: Isaiah 10:1-2 NLT
>
> *What sorrow awaits the unjust judges and those who issue unfair laws. They deprive the poor of justice and deny the rights of the needy among my people. They prey on widows and take advantage of orphans.*
>
> Scripture Reading: Isaiah 10:1-4

Some will say, "There he goes again!" Yeah, well God has laid it on our hearts to talk about social justice from His Word. All people deserve a decent quality of living. Unfair laws, practices, and policies are denying most of the population just that. I can find hundreds of verses that speak to the issue of compassion and love towards the less fortunate, and verses that speak of how ignoring them comes at a cost. I do not know where the term "Third World" came from, but labels for everything is a "thing" for society at large because of a need to believe that they are better than most and identifying inferior against superior is their sad but mistaken commentary on the human race. I know that God will vindicate those who have been denied unjustly by policies and practices, but He also has a church that He left explicit instructions to. There are those who claim to be Christians who feel that less fortunate means inferior, and there must be some reason why God is punishing them. They even twist the Word to try and prop up their prejudicial views. I say that those who have the ability to read and comprehend, cannot concur with their misguided interpretations. As people of God, we cannot condone these wicked acts as the norm. We must continue to fight against unjust laws, and not accept the status quo. God created one world and did not divide it into three. Man, in his greed for money and power did that. Heed the Word of God and do your part to expand the Kingdom by showing the same mercy that you were shown when you least deserved it… it really is that important to God.

Blessings, Rupert & Red.

APRIL 25

Do You Love Or Reject Wisdom?

Meditation Verse: Proverbs 1:7 HCSB
The fear of the Lord is the beginning of knowledge; fools despise wisdom and discipline.
Scripture Reading: Proverbs 1:1-7

As we read this verse on our bible phone app, it struck us both that you either desire wisdom or you are indifferent to it. Wisdom will either engage you or enrage you. We have said before that wisdom goes far deeper than knowledge, because it gives knowledge the advantage, in that you can correctly apply what you have learned. You see, Wisdom, comes from God, it is an attribute of The Almighty, and anything else is counterfeit. Oh, there are a lot of smart people, but there is a huge difference between being smart and being wise. Society uses terms far too loosely and meanings and definitions get watered down to where they would call a fool wise. If you want to learn the correct application for knowledge you must first realize that God, not you, not your teacher, or your Pastor is the beginning of all knowledge. It is from Him that all blessings flow. If God created the heavens and the earth and everything in between, then who knows more about anything than God? He is the Alpha and Omega of knowledge. Any pursuit of wisdom must first be confirmed with the truth that God already knows what you desire to learn and looking to Him is the best application of Wisdom you could ever have. So, with that being said, who is a fool? If you have no regard for God's wisdom or you reject wisdom as the truth you fall into that category. Because if you denounce God, you denounce wisdom, no matter what profound theories you may expound to try and solidify your position. It is the same as saying there is no God and we all know, what the Bible has to say in that regard! A fool is enraged by the preaching of the Gospel because he despises wisdom. He thinks he knows what he knows on his own merits and is adamant to any proof to the contrary. He may be considered smart in his own circles, but his disdain for wisdom makes him a fool. Don't be a fool!! All the education in the world won't make you wise if you don't know what to do with what you have learned. Truly know God, truly know wisdom, No God, no wisdom, it is as simple as that.

Blessings, Rupert & Red.

APRIL 26

An Expunged Record!

Meditation Scripture: Psalms 130:3 NLT
Lord, if You kept a record of our sins, who, O Lord, could ever survive?
Scripture Reading: Psalms 130

The mercy of the Lord is not only everlasting, but also ever present. The fact that we have been given life when it is death that we deserve is amazing enough, but God has not only made a way to eternity, but He has said that He will remember our sins no more. The price has been paid and we are forgiven. We surely would not survive if there were records kept. They shall never be laid to our charge, nor shall we be judged for them. But don't get it twisted. It is not a license to sin, but a chance to receive mercy, for who can stand before the King in his own righteousness? No one. The psalmist according to Matthew Henry, was so struck with the sense of the holiness of God, and the rectitude of the law that he is convinced that: "No mortal man can answer for himself before a Judge so perfect, concerning a law so divine." (Source: Blue letter Bible, blueletterbible.org) But praise God a way was made, and we stand covered in the precious blood of Jesus able to live a life of freedom! What a retirement plan!! To have goodness and mercy follow you all the days of your life, and then to dwell in the house of the Lord Forever!! Psalm 23:6 (NKJV paraphrased).

Blessings, Rupert & Red.

APRIL 27

Our Citizenship Is In Heaven

Meditation Verse: Psalms 137:4 KJV
How shall we sing the Lord's song in a strange land?
Scripture Reading Psalms 137:1-6

We love to travel!! We love to experience different cultures and customs, but we are not foodies by any means! We tend to stay in our lane, we are more of a meat and potatoes kind of couple! Through the grace and favor of God my gift has allowed me to travel around the world more than a few times and I consider myself to be blessed to be able to do what I love and to God belongs all the honor and glory! Nothing though, is like returning home. Back to my wife and family, familiar faces, and my own bed! But as much as I love my home and comfort zone, our spirits still yearn for that day when wars are over and peace reigns, when our mortal bodies will be changed, and pain and sorrow become a thing of the past. When corruption is vanquished, and integrity is the norm. Where jealousy and hatred are replaced with true relationship and love. We will sing a new song in a land that is truly our own. We believe it will feel as if we never left. This world, as beautiful and diverse as it is, is not our home. We have a home that is eternal in the heavens. Jesus said: "I go to prepare a place for you so where I am you will be also." (John 14:3 paraphrased). We are reminded every day that we are in a strange land, everywhere people have lost their moral center, no one wants to stand for righteousness, corruption is rampant, and we are ridiculed for putting our trust in a God we cannot see. So, while we must sojourn here on earth, we await the new Heaven and earth that God has promised us. We love our life, but there will be a time when God calls His own to take up residence in the place He has prepared for us. We want to be ready, make sure you are too.

Blessings, Rupert & Red.

APRIL 28

What Type Of Soil Are You?

Meditation Verse: Mark 4:14 KJV

The Sower soweth the word.

Scripture Reading: Mark 4:13-20

We are by no means farmers! We do not even come close to having a green thumb. We are probably among the least experienced at growing a garden of any kind. We do, however, know the power of a seed. We understand that if you place a seed in the ground, water it, cultivate it, let it get the right amount of sunlight, all things being equal, you should see some growth, and a potential harvest. The seed can be a game changer, the difference between eating or going hungry, even life or death. A seed is supposed to produce life. The Word of God is like a seed. It gets planted in our hearts and has the ability to bear fruit. But not every seed that is sown grows and bears fruit. The kind of soil in which it is planted makes all the difference. So, what type of soil are you? That is to say, how well will you hear? Because the Word must fall on good ground. You can read the Word, and even love it. But unless it is sown in your heart, you won't experience any growth or harvest. The enemy is quick to move in and steal your seed. That is because Satan does not want to see the Word taking root in a person's life. We need to make sure that our hearts are ready to receive, for some that may mean plowing up that fallow ground, knowing that we must be prepared when life throws its worst situations at you. Make sure your soil is in reception mode. Remember, Jesus said; "He who has ears to hear, let him hear!" Mark 4:9 (NKJV).

Blessings, Rupert & Red.

APRIL 29

God's Amazing Grace!

Meditation Verse: James 4:6 HCSB

But He gives greater grace. Therefore, He says: God resists the proud, but gives grace to the humble.

Scripture Reading: James 4: 1-10

When we think about the grace of God, our hearts fill with gratitude. His Grace!! Where would we be without it! We thank God that the more grace we need the more he gives and keeps on giving. Think about how many times you have felt discouraged, and you really don't know how to be about this life, just when you think of giving up, He gives more grace! When we are weak, He is strong, when we change, He is immutable, when we act sinful, He is forgiving, When we are bad, He is good, He gives us the grace we need to serve Him as we should. Do we deserve it? An emphatic NO! Yet God's undeserved favor is constant in our lives. It follows us, guides us, protects us, sustains us, and keeps us. But remember, grace comes to the humble and not to the proud. Grace and pride are eternal enemies, pride demands that God bless me in light of my merits, or lack thereof, but grace does not act on the basis of anything in me. It is simply the way the Father is, in spite of our imperfections. Aren't you glad that God gives grace instead of what we really deserve? Thank God for His amazing grace! Show Him how much you love him by making room for kindness to others. Walk in it, speak of it, and let it cause you to grow. So, when the trials and tests come, you can rely on it. And remember, His grace is sufficient…

Blessings, Rupert & Red.

APRIL 30

Wisdom: Available For The Asking...

Meditation Verse: James 1:5 HCSB

Now if any of you lacks wisdom, he should ask God, who gives to all generously and without criticizing, and it will be given to him.

Scripture Reading: James 1:2-8

A few days ago, we talked about wisdom, let's continue with that theme for another day! God wants you to have it! You just have to admit that you need it and accept that God will not be mad at you for asking. Trials are a good reason to ask for wisdom from God. We don't often know that we need wisdom until trials and tests come our way. When we find that we are faced with difficulties, we need wisdom more than we need mere knowledge. John A. Morrison said it like this; "Knowledge is the ability to take things apart, but wisdom is the ability to put things together." (Source: Blue Letter Bible, blueletterbible.org) I like that. So, to receive wisdom we simply ask of God, who will not despise us for asking. We are ready to go to books, men, ceremonies, anything but to God. God does not get tired of us. With Him there is no such thing as wearing out your welcome! His arms are open wide. When you desire wisdom, the place to begin and end is the Word. True wisdom will always be consistent with the Word of God. In fact, wisdom should be your motivating factor in your quest for relationship building, spiritual growth, love for your heavenly Father, and the family of God. Move in the direction of wisdom, your Father has an endless supply.

Blessings, Rupert & Red.

MAY 1

God's Breath: It's Why You Are Alive!

Meditation Verse: Genesis 2:7 KJV

And the Lord God formed man of the dust of the ground and breathed into his nostrils the breath of life; and man became a living soul.

Scripture Reading: Genesis 2:1-7

Some scientists say that all life began as a primordial ooze. Where is the breath that gave life to this ooze? An ooze cannot create intelligence. Ooze can only create more ooze! Everything reproduces after its own kind, so a pig cannot give birth to an elephant, and a turkey cannot give birth to a fox. God wanted to create man after His own image and likeness. A man with intellect, emotions and personality traits; because those are the qualities that God possesses. You were fearfully and wonderfully made according to the Word, Psalms 139:14 (NKJV), and the difference is God breathed His breath into you. We are alive because we are God inspired! Ooze cannot make anything fearfully or wonderfully, that has never been proven. Rejoice in the fact that God thought about you, and then created you with the ability to reason. We are thankful for the God of our salvation, our Creator, our Sustainer, Savior and soon coming King! We were never ooze because ooze cannot be intentional about us. How about you? Are you on the side of ooze, or Creator God? Are you happenstance or intentional? Are you temporary or eternal? If you are breathing, then the answer should be clear….

Blessings, Rupert & Red.

MAY 2

New Life; Free But Not Cheap

Meditation Verse: Galatians 2:21 NLT

I do not treat the grace of God as meaningless. For if the law could make us right with God, then there was no need for Christ to die.

Scripture Reading: Galatians 2:11-21

We have heard some religious folk and others who consider themselves "spiritual" say; "There are many paths that lead to heaven." The price of admission was paid by one man, Jesus Christ! Through grace are you saved. It is the unmerited favor of God. The gift is free, but not cheap. Because of the shed blood of Jesus are we made righteous. Simply put, if you are not in Christ, you won't make it in. So, what does it mean then, to be "in Christ?" It is an act of faith, an acceptance of who we are and what He did. The law of God was impossible for us to keep, and we kept messing up. When God saw us in our own strength, He saw failure, but through the shed blood of Christ, He saw victory. We like an analogy Pastor Rick Warren used: Think of an old note card as man, and the Bible as Jesus. The old note card represents all the shame and shortcomings in my life, things I have done and said that were not like Christ at all. Once I accept Jesus Christ as my Savior, I am forgiven, and I get to start over again. I am now in Christ and that old note card my life, is in the Bible. When you look at the Bible, you can't see that old notecard, you can only see the Bible. So instead of God seeing us in our sinful state, He sees Jesus covering us, the price has been paid and we are made righteous in Him! Thank God for His grace! God wants to see you live, not perish, share it with someone who needs to make that next step. We can all be living our best life!!

Blessings, Rupert & Red.

MAY 3

Possess The Land!!

Meditation Verse: Joshua 1:6 NLT

Be strong and courageous, for you are the one who will lead these people to possess all the land I swore to their ancestors I would give them.

Scripture Reading: Joshua 1:1-9

Joshua was exactly what God told him to be. He did not waver or doubt. He was willing to put himself in harm's way, in order to complete the mission that God had asked him to. His faith was as big as his courage. He knew and believed that they were well able to take the land that God had sworn to give them. Joshua believed God, and God gave him victory after victory. What sparked such confidence in this man that caused God's favor to shine so brightly his way? Joshua was obedient! His day never depended on how he felt, he did what God asked, when he asked! You don't have to have it all together, tough times can make you falter. It won't always be easy, in fact it probably will be hard more than it is easy, God is saying do not be afraid, be strong and courageous. He has already given you the victory! "Every place that the sole of your foot shall tread upon, I have given you!" Joshua 1:3 (NKJV). What an incredible promise! His condition was obedience and because Joshua was true to that instruction, he was successful in everything he did. God has given us great and precious promises, and our obedience is paramount to seeing those promises fulfilled. Can you walk? Walk over those circumstances and situations that have you on edge and anxious. God is greater, He will give you the land!!

Blessings, Rupert & Red.

MAY 4

Be Encouraged!

Meditation Verse: Psalms 71:14 NLT
But I will keep on hoping for Your help; I will praise you more and more.
Scripture Reading: Psalms 71

Listen, a word of encouragement today. Things may not always go the way you would like. There will be good times, and there will be hard times. There is no easy way out of tragedy and misfortune, but there is a way out. We need to remember that no matter how bad we think we have it, there is always some one who wishes that all they had were your problems. We live in a world where people care less and less about each other. There is a tendency to isolate ourselves, and then wonder why we are all alone. You are not. God cares and He loves you. It may sound crazy but praise Him in your circumstance! Let him know that your heart is broken. Tell Him that your hope is in Him. Don't give up!! Be persistent in your praise. Yes, we all will cry sometimes, and feel as if nothing will help. His love will lift you. Life is seldom fair, but God is always faithful. Place your hope in Him, He will come through for you.

Blessings, Rupert & Red.

MAY 5

The Battle Is Not Yours!

Meditation Verse: Ecclesiastes 7:9 HCSB
Don't let your spirit rush to be angry, for anger abides in the heart of fools.
Scripture Reading: Ecclesiastes 7:1-14

Anger is a dangerous emotion. Because it can linger and fester in your soul for a long time. When that happens the only one that loses is you. Most times people are either unaware that they have made you angry or they don't care. Either way, the best way to deal with anger is by not giving it room to grow. Because if you do, sin will be creeping at your door. Remember Cain, He allowed anger to get the best of him and murder was the result. God said, "Be angry but don't sin." Ephesians 4:26 (NKJV). In other words, don't let your anger move you to the point that you become out of control. Anger does not always have to be a negative force. You can channel that anger into a positive energy that motivates you to do and be better. We all make mistakes, but we don't have to be our mistakes. When someone makes you angry, remember that; "Vengeance belongs to Me, I will repay, says the Lord." Romans 12:19b (HCSB) Haters are going to hate that's a given. Choose your battles wisely and make sure you have on the correct armor! We know it is hard and you want to retaliate, but the God you serve is well able to fight for you…. the battle is not yours anyway. Relationship has its privileges!!

Blessings, Rupert & Red.

MAY 6

Your Priority Must Be God

Meditation Verse: Ecclesiastes 12:13 HCSB

When all has been heard, the conclusion of the matter is: Fear God and keep His commands, because this is for all humanity.

Scripture Reading: Ecclesiastes 12

Solomon tried all the things that life could offer, the pursuit of knowledge, the physical pursuit of pleasure, the material pursuit of wealth. Sounds pretty good right? Do you know what his bottom line was? Everything is meaningless! Wait! What?! The wisest human that ever lived summed up every one of his successes as meaningless?! Here is what his conclusion is to what gives life meaning: "Fear God and keep his commandments for this is the whole duty of man." Ecclesiastes 12:13b (KJV). That's it. All the rush and push for the other things won't satisfy. It is temporary at best. Does this mean that I must take a vow of poverty? No!! God wants you to prioritize, take care of what is important first. That needs to be God. Author John Mason wrote, "Seek not success, but truth, and you will find both. Measure wealth by the things you have which you would not exchange for money." (Source: Blue Letter Bible, blueletterbible.org) A wiser man than Solomon once said, "But seek first the Kingdom of God and His righteousness and all these things will be provided for you." Matthew 6:33 (HCSB).

Blessings, Rupert & Red.

MAY 7

Words Matter!!

Meditation Verse: Psalms 91:2 HCSB

I will say to the Lord, "My refuge and my fortress, my God, in whom I trust."

Scripture Reading: Psalms 91

If you live long enough you will discover the sad truth that you cannot put much faith in what people say. Whether it is what they are going to do for you, or advocate on your behalf. Unfortunately, not many people consider their word as their bond. It is just wisdom to think about what you are about to say before you say it. It is better to say what God says about you and put your trust in Him. In one of my favorite psalms, Psalm 91, the second verse says, "I will say," meaning that he is deliberate in this and confident in what he says. Some translations read: "I will say of the Lord," and some say, "I will say to the Lord," both imply confidence because he is declaring a truth that God is his protection, and he trusts and believes it. We, like David, need to speak the promises of God, because unlike man God keeps His promises. Even if you can't see it yet, we need to speak those things as though they were. Whether it is God's protection, favor, healing, or every blessing we seek, it is tied up in our words. Words matter, make sure that your words speak life, and add to the lives of those you come in contact with, and if you make a promise, Keep it!!

Blessings, Rupert & Red.

MAY 8

Spiritual Discernment Is Wisdom From God

Meditation Verse: 1 Corinthians 2:14 NKJV

But the natural man does not receive the things of the Spirit of God, for they are foolishness to him; nor can he know them, because they are spiritually discerned.

Scripture Reading: 1 Corinthians 2:6-16

Who is the natural man? The natural man is where we start life, the life inherited from Adam. Since we are born in sin we are at birth, unregenerate, unsaved man. Now natural life is not sinful, we all have to live, sleep, eat and work. But life on this level of the three dimensional, physical, material world, lacks spiritual insight. Therefore, it is not possible for the natural man to receive spiritual things. The things of the spirit seem foolish to the natural man. It would be wrong to expect the natural man to see the value in spiritual things, it would be like expecting a dead man to see the material world. Is it possible for a Christian to not spiritually discern things? Yes, if you refuse to spiritually discern, then you are thinking like a natural man, even though you may be saved. Once you have accepted Christ, your only concern cannot be "the bottom line," or "whatever works," you are mandated to walk by the spirit that has been regenerated in you. It is a new perspective, a better way of life, a glimpse into eternity, because that is the real life you are waiting for. Want to really understand the things of God? The connection is purely spiritual. That is how you come out of the darkness into His marvelous light.

Blessings, Rupert & Red.

MAY 9

Godly Behavior

Meditation Verse: 1 Peter 1:13 NLT

So, prepare your minds for action and exercise self-control. Put all your hope in the gracious salvation that will come to you when Jesus Christ is revealed to the world.

Scripture Reading: 1 Peter 1:13-21

Too often we gloss over the Word when we read, and don't fully grasp or comprehend what is being said. In order to apply the Word to our lives, we must rightly divide or interpret what the Spirit is telling us. Sometimes different translations can give a greater shade of meaning to what we read. Peter is saying in this verse that in order to prepare our minds, we must get rid of the old loose and sloppy way of thinking. We need to control what we think about or at least we can choose what to dwell on. To exercise self-control is to have an attitude of self-discipline that avoids extreme behaviors. We should have the mind of Christ, which brings us to the full hope of His salvation, past, present and future. To experience the riches of His grace and the unmerited favor of God. What does your life say? Do we emulate the love of God in our actions, so that the world may see and know without a doubt that we belong to Him? Live your life so that people will see Christ in you! Don't be a part of the silent majority. You may never know whose life you may have impacted for the Kingdom.

Blessings, Rupert & Red.

MAY 10

Keep The Faith!!

Meditation Verse: Luke 7:20 NLT

When the men reached Him, they said, "John the Baptist sent us to ask You, are You the One who is to come, or should we look for someone else?"

Scripture Reading: Luke 7:18-23

"Keep the Faith!!" Some people say this as they part ways, I guess to encourage one another. And that's fine, we can all stand to be encouraged from time to time, and even on a regular basis. When things are not going our way, it is easy to say but difficult to do! Sometimes an attempt to be positive outwardly, while inside you are falling apart, becomes an exercise in false bravado. I have heard Pastors talk about John the Baptist's lack of faith, as if he had lost his mind, I am sure every one of them would have had some questions for Jesus had they been in John's shoes! He was the forerunner, the heavenly mouthpiece, the voice crying out in the wilderness, preparing the way for the Messiah. I mean Jesus was his cousin, they were family! So, Herod threw him into prison, no big deal, surely cuz was going to get him out! But when that didn't happen doubt began to creep into John's mind and that faith began to fade. We all have felt that helpless at times. So, what do you do? You keep the faith!! Keep praying, keep believing, and never give up! God knows what He is doing so we have to trust the process. We can certainly relate to a dilemma like John's, but so many of Jesus' disciples paid the ultimate price. That may not be your reality, but in some countries, it is the cost for following Jesus. We may not be called upon to make the ultimate sacrifice, but we are called to "Keep the Faith!!"

Blessings, Rupert & Red.

MAY 11

Don't Be A Hypocrite!!

Meditation Verse: Luke 16:15 NLT

Then he said to them, "You like to appear righteous in public, but God knows your hearts. What this world honors is detestable in the sight of God.

Scripture Reading: Luke 16:10-17

What is your definition of hypocrisy? That is a strong word that most people take offense to but are quick to use. The truth is hypocrisy is a huge problem in our society and a serious character flaw. Those who practice it know that they do. My definition of a hypocrite is one who acts the opposite from their stated practices and beliefs, with no intention of changing. Their motive is to simply get away with everything that they can for their own advantage with no regard for who gets hurt in the process. They choose wrong, fully cognizant of what they are doing. And I would suspect that we all have been guilty of some form of hypocrisy. The Bible says, "for everyone has sinned; we all fall short of God's glorious standard." Romans 3:23 (NLT). The motives for our hypocrisy are wide and varied but none can make it acceptable. God knows the thoughts and intent of our hearts. He knows our every struggle and weakness. That is why He provided a way for those who desire to change. It is a heart transaction. Adrian Rogers once said: "At the heart of every problem is the problem of the human heart." (Source: Adrian Rogers, goodreads.com>quotes). God will fix that problem through faith in Christ Jesus, and that is true for everyone who believes no matter who they are. We can look and see hypocrisy at the highest levels. They try to justify it saying it is for the "greater good." We have no faith whatsoever in the "greater good," we believe in the "Greatest God!" I know that God detests hypocrisy, and we should too! God loves you enough to save you from it, love Him enough to be saved.

Blessings, Rupert & Red.

MAY 12

God's Goodness Is Ever Present

Meditation Verse: Psalms 27:13 HCSB
I am certain that I will see the Lord's goodness in the land of the living.
Scripture Reading: Psalms 27

To those who think that because you are a Christian you will never despair, you have not been a Christian very long, for to walk by faith and not by sight is not the easiest of journeys! That is just real talk! Jesus said that in this life you will have persecution, and trials and tribulations are the norm. Sometimes just watching the news can be a devastatingly negative experience. But we are Christians who desire to live a productive life while we are here and declare the goodness of the Lord! God's goodness is all around us even though sometimes it is hard to see the forest for the trees! There are days when we wake up and find it hard to put one foot in front of the other, but we find the reasons to go on rather than sit and complain. I want, I need to experience some goodness that makes me feel that no matter how bad it gets, it is always worth it. Despair is real y'all, but so is joy. David said he would have fainted, but he believed that he would see the goodness of the Lord in the land of the living. Psalm 27:13 (KJV paraphrased). The Word says, "And let us not be weary in well doing for in due season we shall reap, if we faint not." Galatians 6:9 (KJV). Be encouraged, God's goodness is all around us even if it is hard to see sometimes, and, we have said it before, due season always comes……

Blessings, Rupert & Red.

MAY 13

Watch Your Mouth!!

Meditation Verse: James 3:6 HCSB

And the tongue is a fire. The tongue a world of unrighteousness, is placed among the parts of our bodies. It pollutes the whole body, sets the course of life on fire, and is set on fire by hell.

Scripture Reading: James 3:1-12

"Be careful little tongue what you say," I remember the little Sunday School chorus that we sang as kids, a lesson many of us never really learned. Because we can't seem to control that little member of our body! A small bit controls a big horse, a small rudder can turn a large ship. If we can control our tongue, we can control our whole body. It is possible for our tongue to have tremendous power for good or evil. Some people just say what comes to their mind, others direct their tongue through their emotions or aspects of their carnal living. The tongue is likened to a fire, a world of iniquity, something spoken to us can and often does have a long-time effect. The sarcastic or critical remark can inflict lasting injury on another person. An encouraging compliment can inspire someone for the rest of their life. Commentator Donald Burdick put it this way, "It is as though all the wickedness in the whole world were wrapped up in that little piece of flesh." (Source: Blue Letter Bible blueletterbible.org) What I do know is, man has been able to master many things, but none have been able to master the tongue. So, why did God allow us such an uncontrollable member? Because we were never meant to live apart from the Spirit of God from the beginning. Our walk through this life was meant to be under the direction of The Holy Spirit and not our senses and emotions. They were meant to enhance your life, not control it. A life under the direction of the Spirit will speak words of life and correction with love. It will build up, not tear down. Let us be deliberate, with the Spirit's help, in the effort to speak in such a way, that our words don't harm, but cause joy, inspiration, kindness and even correction and rebuke with love. Of course, it is not easy to do, but nothing is impossible when you put your trust in God.

Blessings, Rupert & Red.

MAY 14

Every Joint Supplies!

Meditation Verse: Ephesians 4:16 NLT

He makes the whole body fit together perfectly. As each part does its own special work, it helps the other parts to grow, so that the whole body is healthy and growing and full of love.

Scripture Reading: Ephesians 4:1-16

Charles Spurgeon, one of the great preachers and commentators once said, "A church that is only united in itself, but not united to Christ, is no living church at all." (Source: Blue Letter Bible blueletterbible.org). Division is rampant in society today and unfortunately it has reached the church. There is a serious lack of maturity because we refuse to understand that "every joint supplies." Until we realize that we all need one another, and no gift is more important than the other, there will be no growth and the church will languish. God desires that we see the church as a body, so that at maximum potential it can run as a well-oiled machine. The eye cannot say to the foot I have no need of you, because the eye can only travel if the foot moves. God has designed us for relationship, first to Him and then to each other. We cannot operate in love and isolation at the same time. The evidence of maturity is when the leaders and the saints are all doing their jobs effectively. The coordinated and cooperative effort is what will foster growth and build itself up in love. Understanding that no one is perfect and that we are all striving for the unity of the faith regardless of the issues is the sign of a healthy body. Those of us that choose not to be a part of the body because of some past hurt or insult, must realize that there is no benefit in letting someone or something keep you out of the ark of safety. Your relationship is far too precious, and you are too valuable to God. Go, visit, join the church that God directs you to, and become a part of the body. God is waiting on you. Put your gift to work, let His favor rest on your life. Remember, every joint supplies, your contribution is never too small, if you just make yourself available, God has a way of working it all out for your good!

Blessings, Rupert & Red.

MAY 15

Psalms 19, God's Nature…

Meditation verse: Psalms 19:7-9 NKJV

The Law of the Lord is perfect, converting the soul; The testimony of the Lord is sure, making wise the simple; The statutes of the Lord are right, rejoicing the heart; the commandment of the Lord is pure, enlightening the eyes; the fear of the Lord is clean, enduring forever; the judgements of the Lord are true and righteous altogether.

Scripture Reading: Psalms 19

The character of the Lord is described in seven ways. The simple truth is that God reveals Himself in His Word. David in this psalm, praises creation as a way to see God, but depends on His Word for relationship. God's Word is an even greater revelation than creation, because it reveals His true nature as a covenant God, faithful and full of love for His creation. David here explains seven wonderful attributes, that are important for us to grasp as it gives; "all things that pertain to life and godliness." 2 Peter 1:3a (KJV). The Word of God is perfect, sure, right, pure, clean, true, and righteous. We should love these virtues and emulate them daily. We don't have the room to do a full dissertation on these seven characteristics of God's Word but remember in order for your relationship with God to grow, reading the 19th Psalm and studying it will certainly give you a perspective on how God desires your relationship to thrive, as you are obedient to His Word. David knew God's Word was alive and relevant to the times then as it is now. Be encouraged by this awesome psalm and realize that knowing God is possible, through His creation, but most of all through His Word.

Blessings, Rupert & Red.

MAY 16

Psalms 19 God's Nature Continued...

Meditation Verse: Psalms 19:7 NKJV

The law of the Lord is perfect, converting the soul; the testimony of the Lord is sure, making wise the simple.

Scripture Reading: Psalms 19

We are back with Psalm 19, it is the desire of the Spirit to go a little deeper into the seven attributes, today we will talk about the first two. "The law of the Lord is perfect, converting the soul." The Word is perfect, commentator David Guzick said, "while it does not give us all knowledge, all the knowledge that it gives is true and perfect."(Source: Blue Letter Bible blueletterbible.org) When you are able to discern God's Word in its proper context, it is never wrong, in science or history, no other book can explain the divine or human nature better. The perfection of God's Word does the work of converting the soul. The power in reading, hearing, and studying the Word is unmatched in actually changing one for the better, it revives, heals, assures forgiveness and cleanses. "The testimony of the Lord is sure, making wise the simple." Sure, means reliable and certain, also firm and confirmed. As a result, it can give the uneducated wisdom. Anyone with little education can have tremendous wisdom because they study and trust the sure Word of God. That is why we all need to develop a love for God's Word, it will give insight beyond your years and produce peace for the trying times. What an awesome God!

Blessings, Rupert & Red.

MAY 17

Psalms 19, God's Nature Continued…

> Meditation Verse: Psalms 19:8 NKJV
>
> *The statutes of the Lord are right, rejoicing the heart: The commandment of the Lord is pure, enlightening the eyes:*
>
> Scripture Reading: Psalms 19

Continuing today with verse 8 of Psalm 19, "The statutes of the Lord are right, rejoicing the heart." Right, meaning, to make straight, smooth, right, upright, as opposed to crookedness in mind or conduct; displaying how a person should behave. God's Word is right; morally, practically, physically, and spiritually. They are right because God is holy and true and always right. Knowing God's Word causes the heart to rejoice. We can find actual joy and pleasure in God's Word. "The commandment of the Lord is pure, enlightening the eyes." The Word of God is pure because it comes from a pure and holy God. The Word will never lead us into sin or impurity, unless you pervert its intent or motive. He will lead us into righteousness through pure communication. Therefore, it will enlighten the eyes. The light which will dispel or expose darkness, is what a pure Word will bring. Light that is clearly seen, will bring joy, comfort, peace, and confidence. God has declared that our eyes have yet to see what He has in store for those who love Him and follow His commands!! Allow your eyes to be enlightened by the right, joyful, and pure word of God, your life will never be the same!

Blessings, Rupert & Red.

MAY 18

Psalms 19, God's Nature Continued…

Meditation Verse: Psalms 19:9 NKJV

The fear of the Lord is clean, enduring forever; The judgements of the Lord are true and righteous altogether.

Scripture Reading: Psalms 19

Continuing with the 9th verse of Psalm 19, we read: "The fear of the Lord is clean, enduring forever," it is clean because it makes clean and therefore it endures. The Word of God will never fade, corrode or diminish because of impurity. God's Word is forever settled in heaven, it endures, because the grass withers, the flower fades, but the Word of God stands forever. Isaiah 40:8 (NKJV). It is deeply connected to God's majesty. The appropriate appreciation for God's Word is reverence and respect. That is the fear of the Lord. "The judgements of the Lord are righteous and true altogether." David summarized these beautiful attributes, declaring that the words of God are true and righteous altogether, there is nothing false or unrighteous in His Word. As one commentator, David Guzik puts it, "David wrote this psalm with just a fraction of what we have today as the Word of God. He probably had the first five books, Genesis to Deuteronomy, Joshua, Judges and perhaps Job and Ruth." (Source: Blue Letter Bible blueletterbible.org). He was truly a prophet of his day, his revelations coming straight from the heart of God. If David can glean so much from what little of the Bible was written in those days, then we have no excuse, we can say with confidence that God's Word is far more glorious than David knew!! Read it!

Blessings, Rupert & Red.

MAY 19

Psalms 19, God's Nature Continued…

> Meditation Verse: Psalms 19:10 NKJV
> *More to be desired are they than gold, Yea, than much fine gold,*
> *Sweeter also than the honey and the honeycomb.*
>
> Scripture Reading: Psalms 19

There is so much more that we can glean from this amazing 19th Psalm, but we will conclude today with a final thought. King David was an extremely wealthy man, but he is not famous or remembered for his riches. David was known for his heart that was established toward God. We know from the psalms, how David revered the Word of God, it's statutes and its precepts. The value that God placed on the Word was more desirable than gold, yes, he amplified more than much fine gold. Most men prefer gold to God and His judgements. What will you render to God? Will you value His Word over the riches that this world affords? The Word is to be esteemed not only over material wealth, but even more than the senses. It is sweeter than anything that you can see, taste, hear, touch or smell. If we were to place the value of God's Word above all, then love would be our walk and heaven would be our gain. Your relationship with God is more important than anything you can ever seek after or desire. It is the key to everything that you can want and need in this life. Matthew 6:33 NLT, says it this way: "Seek the Kingdom of God above all else, and live righteously, and He will give you everything you need." God loves you more than you will ever know… His Word proves it.

Blessings, Rupert & Red.

MAY 20

Justified By Grace!!

Meditation Verse: Romans 3:24 NKJV
Being justified freely by His grace through the redemption that is in Christ Jesus.
Scripture Reading: Romans 3:21-26

We love the fact that we are justified by His grace!! We just know that if we had to work to earn our salvation, that would be a job that we could never accomplish. None of us could. And it is not just the idea that we would mess it up every time, it is that we do and still He loves us!! It is hard to explain the grace of God in the midst of our frailties and shortcomings. Every day we realize that this race is not for the swift. There is always something that seems to be in our way, slowing us down, trying to get us to stop, or give in to the things that we know are temporary. There will always be an obstacle somewhere to overcome. Anybody who says there is not an enemy, cannot have a relationship with God. He, or she, or it, shows up in many ways, and not always in ways that are obvious. Don't let the hang ups in your life, and we all have them, make you think that you are beyond redemption. Christ loves you, and so much so that he extends you grace to make the crooked places in your life straight. God is not mad at you, and He does not get tired. He is calling you to Himself. His arm is not short, so as not to reach you, and His ear is not heavy as so not to hear you. Isaiah 59:1 (paraphrased). Being freely justified by the shed blood of Jesus is mind blowing. And it is all made possible by His grace which is free…That alone is priceless.

Blessings, Rupert & Red.

MAY 21

The Glass House Syndrome

Meditation Verse: John 8:7 ASV

So, when they continued asking Him, He raised up Himself and said to them: "He who is without sin among you, let him throw a stone at her first."

Scripture Reading: John 8:2-11

Self-righteousness is not a virtue; it is a problem. Because when we look at others and say or think that we are better than them, that is a form of selfish pride. These religious leaders in the passage did not bring this woman to Jesus out of a sense of duty, they sought her out to try and trap Jesus, why would they not punish her as per normal, they already thought themselves better than the woman, they wanted to prove to the people that they were better than Jesus also. For all of us who call the Name of Jesus and count ourselves among those who have accepted Christ, always remember and never forget that; "such were some of us," and if it were not for the undeserved, unmerited grace of God we would still be under the sentence of death. So, does that mean we condone sin? No, Jesus did not, but neither did He condemn the sinner. Our desire should be to speak the truth in love. Believe it or not the sin was not just in the woman's adultery, but in the way they sought to use her to trap Jesus, why did they just bring the woman, if she was caught in the very act, was there not a man there as well? How is justice served if they only seek to punish one of the offenders? Jesus of course saw through their scheme and exposed their motives as sin. In what was a true picture of grace, Jesus sought not to humiliate the woman, but to rehabilitate her, by telling her to go and sin no more. So should be our goal not to condemn and humiliate, but to love and rehabilitate and restore others to a place where they see the need for a Savior. Jesus saved that woman's life; we should look to emulate the Savior.

Blessings Rupert & Red.

MAY 22

Believe In His Name!

Meditation Verse: John 20:31 ESV

But these are written that you may believe that Jesus is the Christ, the Son of God. And that believing you may have life in His Name.

Scripture Reading: John 20:26-31

John was the disciple that Jesus loved. We think he gave himself that title, but we are not mad at him. He was in Jesus' inner circle, he was closest to Him, and we believe he understood Jesus' purpose spiritually, ahead of the others. He was the only one that did not run when Christ was crucified. Jesus gave John the honor of taking care of His mother, which he did, moving with her to Ephesus, and building a house for her where she lived out the rest of her days on earth. His description of himself was well earned. So, this last verse in the 20th chapter of John v.31, gives his whole reason for writing it. "That you may believe that Jesus is the Christ," have faith in Him, a faith that is not a blind leap based on the strong eye-witness account that John gives. He wants us to have the same relationship that he enjoyed, and in believing that you would have life, not just exist, but have life in His Name. Understand that the power of His Name goes beyond your recognition of the truth, but that truth transforms and translates into eternity, life everlasting. The book of John is a book about who Christ really is and the love He has for us. Embrace the Truth, and your life will take on new meaning and purpose.

Blessings, Rupert & Red.

MAY 23

Choose This Day Whom You Will Serve

Meditation Scripture: Joshua 24:15 NKJV

And if it seems evil to you to serve the Lord, choose for yourselves this day whom you will serve, whether the gods which your fathers served that were on the other side of the river, or the gods of the Amorites, in whose land you dwell. But as for me and my house, we will serve the Lord.

Scripture Reading: Joshua 24:1-28

It is a wise man who makes the decision to serve the Lord. Joshua was challenging the people to be faithful to the One who had brought them out of the Land of Egypt, through the wilderness, and finally to the land of Canaan, or the promised land. They had seen signs and wonders quite regularly and God had always provided for them. Yet, for us, this is the hard part, staying faithful to God even after He had so blessed us in ways we cannot imagine. Who wouldn't serve such an awesome God! Joshua sees this and as the head of his household declares; "As for me and my house, we will serve the Lord." Joshua 24:15 (NKJV). We always have a choice in everything we do. And it is clear when it comes to God, our choices have consequences. Because it will always come down to who you serve. Understand that you will end up serving something or someone. There is no one on the planet that does not. Like Joshua we need to be determined to serve God no matter what anyone thinks. Our relationship with God is not based on any man, but on the Lord and His love for you. Think back over your life and just remember how God has come through for you every time. It was not your friends, or relatives, or someone on your job, it was the Lord. Choose today but choose wisely. He is waiting on you.

Blessings, Rupert & Red.

MAY 24

Living Water In A Dry Place

Meditation Verse: Hosea 13:5 NKJV
I knew you in the wilderness, in the land of great drought.
Scripture Reading: Hosea 13:1-7

We don't know about you, but there have been times in our lives, that we have felt alone in a dry place, where it seemed as if nothing or nobody cared. Like we were in our own personal desert, our prayers seemed to be just reverberating and our strength sapped. We were in midbar (the Hebrew word for desert). There will be those times of wilderness experiences, a time when you realize that you were never in control. A time for you to understand your dependence on God. God will meet you in those dry places and minister to your spirit. You must however be willing to let go. Let go of the things you thought you could not live without. Let go of toxic relationships, bad habits, casting down imaginations that pervert your living. God wants to see us whole. We want to encourage you who find yourselves in midbar, don't be in a rush to leave until you have met God and communed with Him. He will give you what you need. He is the oasis in midbar. Get your refreshing, have your revival, take advantage of the heart of God ministering to yours. Midbar can be a good thing in the spiritual life of the believer. It is a reminder that God has promised never to leave you or forsake you. His mercy is everlasting, and His truth endures. Your relationship can still bloom even in midbar.

Blessings, Rupert & Red.

MAY 25

Walk This Way

Meditation Verse: Micah 6:8 NKJV

He has shown you, O man, what is good: And what does the Lord require of you but to do justly, to love mercy, and to walk humbly with your God?

Scripture Reading: Micah 6:1-8

Wow!! There is something to be said about the Wisdom of God! We love this verse because it is a recipe for how we should aspire to live! Even a skeptic at some point must see reason. If we were to take this verse to heart, and really practice what it says, the world would be the place that God intended for us to dwell. The number of problems and ills of this world that would just disappear would be incalculable! If only we would die to self and not make it about us but see how we can lift humanity through justice and mercy, to love others as we walk before God with a pure heart. If our leaders had the desire to treat everyone equally without regard to status, to lose the labels and bridge the divide between races, income equality, health care, elderly care, housing and mental illness. Our souls are expanding with the possibilities! To walk down any street without fear, to know that we are all neighbors, and that we care enough to see that people have what they need. Do you realize that all this would be possible if we were to adhere to the thirty-one words of this verse? This is what God requires. We may sound naïve, but we are tired of folk who call themselves Christian, and then promptly do the opposite of what Christ taught and commanded. They try to justify their agenda by twisting the Word. We are sick of slogans, mantras, promises that were never meant to be kept, people trying to keep their feet on the necks of others, offering a peace that they can't and never will deliver. All the politics and negotiating in the world will never produce what God's Word can. Sadly, we are too busy trying to be gods instead of walking with God. We have made such a mess of things on our own, we can't even get out of our own way! It is high time we listened to true Wisdom. We dare you to try it God's way. Micah 6:8, It is what He requires.

Blessings, Rupert & Red.

MAY 26

Can You Say Faithful?

Meditation Verse: Lamentations 3:22-23 NKJV

Through the Lord's mercies we are not consumed. Because His compassions fail not. They are new every morning. Great is Your faithfulness.

Scripture Reading: Lamentations 3:20-26

You do know that you are alive because God has shown you mercy? You do realize that it is the reason you are not consumed? If God did not show mercy toward us, we would all end up with what we deserve: death. If that sounds harsh it is meant to be! Our lives have been weighed in the balance and we have been found wanting. In other words, we have failed the life test miserably and our lives should be forfeit. We have been unfaithful, selfish, uncaring, without love or conscience. But God!! In His infinite mercy, He has given us another day to get it right! His faithfulness far exceeds our own, so we get another opportunity. God still wants to use us for His glory. He wants to see us succeed, and He has a plan for our lives. This passage says His mercies and compassion are new every morning. So, every day that you open your eyes, it means God is not through with you yet! It is a declaration of epic proportions! Great is His faithfulness! As long as we live, we want to be the recipient of His mercy and faithfulness! When you have experienced any type of victory in your life, you realize that it is only possible because of the Lord on your side. So, celebrate New Life!! It happens every morning!!

Blessings, Rupert & Red.

MAY 27

Pay It Forward!!

Meditation Scripture: Psalms 51:1 NKJV

Have mercy upon me, O God, According to Your loving kindness: According to the multitude of your tender mercies. Blot out my transgressions.

Scripture Reading: Psalms 51

This verse is about so much more than mercy, although it is a main point. What God has done in the life of a regenerated person is immeasurable. Words like thankful and grateful pale in comparison. To know that your sins are blotted out and thrown into the sea of forgetfulness brings a sense of peace beyond human understanding. So, what do you do with all the loving kindness, tender mercies, and forgiveness that we have and continue to enjoy? With all our heart, we extend the same to our fellow man. We say our heart because it takes the will of the spirit man to do this. You cannot do it in your own strength. God has set you apart because He has put His Spirit in you to show the love that He first showed you. This is not an option! Jesus said: "The way that you have freely received, is the way you must freely give." Matthew 10:8 (NKJV) (paraphrased). You cannot and should not want to keep this to yourself! What you have asked God to do for you, should motivate you to do, as much as you are able, for others. It is a part of His plan, and your participation is required. He has given you His grace, don't squander it.

Blessings, Rupert & Red.

MAY 28

Equal Opportunity Christians!

Meditation Verse: Romans 2:11 ASV
For there is no respect of persons with God.
Scripture Reading: Romans 2:1-16

My parents always told me, "We love you all the same, no one of you is loved more than the other." Now I thank God for my parents, because I know that they loved me, and I was shown that love every day of their lives, whether it was agape, or the tough love, the kind that came with the occasional backhand! But I know that they did not treat us all equally! As the 2nd eldest son, (my twin brother was older by six minutes), I saw preferential treatment given to the younger four, not in a big way, but in subtle ways that children see. While it never fostered any resentment in me, I have fond memories of my childhood that bear witness to this fact. Having children of my own, I now realize that although you love them unconditionally, you really can't treat them all the same. The lesson in this verse is that even though we are different, and God loves us the same, we are all given the same opportunity to accept Christ or reject Him, and the choice that we make will reap the corresponding consequences, regardless of who we are. You can't make enough money, or give enough money, you can't fool or deceive God into accepting the impure motives of your heart. There are no givebacks, takebacks, or I didn't know that can save you. If you choose to live for God, He will honor that, and if you choose to live for Satan, He will allow that too. And He will treat you accordingly, regardless of status, race, political affiliation, gender, or creed. God is no respecter of persons. If you surrender your heart, He will change it and give you the gift of eternal life with Him. See the value in the equal opportunity and choose God. We all are going to live eternally; it is just a matter of where.

Blessings, Rupert & Red.

MAY 29

He Paid It All

Meditation Verse: Hebrews 8:6 NKJV

But now He has obtained a more excellent ministry, inasmuch as He is also Mediator of a better covenant, which was established on better promises.

Scripture Reading: Hebrews 8:6

Why would you work if you didn't have to? I guess that would depend on your definition of work. My father always told us, "Do what you love to do, and you will never work a day in your life." Jesus did three things in the 6th verse of Hebrews 8, provided a more excellent ministry, mediated a better covenant and established it on better promises. Jesus' ministry was and is far superior to any other ministry or ministers. No other ministry could take away sins and provide forgiveness. The priests could only identify sin through the law and cover it, but not remove it. He mediated a better covenant, to mediate is to bring two parties together. The Abrahamic, Mosaic, and Davidic covenants were all steps in the redemptive covenant that reconciled man back to God. This was the new covenant that fulfilled and superseded the old. All this was established upon better promises, promises given through the Spirit of God, promises of favor and blessing and not cursing. This new covenant was obtained by receiving and believing, not by earning and deserving, meaning we don't have to work for it! Jesus paid it all for us. He said, "It is finished," on Calvary, by giving the ultimate once and for all sacrifice, courtesy of His Father's love. We can go on and on about why this covenant is so superior, but let's just say; Jesus did it all for you, offering a free gift of salvation, so again: Why would you work if you didn't have to?

Blessings, Rupert & Red.

MAY 30

He Kept You, When You Did Not Know

Meditation verse: Psalms 124:2-3 NKJV

"If it had not been the Lord who was on our side. When men rose up against us, then they would have swallowed us alive, when their wrath was kindled against us."

Scripture Reading: Psalms 124

I have no doubt that most of us if not all of us who put our trust in God, can remember a time, or two, when the Lord brought us out of some bad or rough situations. And while Satan is always busy, sometimes the crisis was of our own making. It is important to remember that the Lord is always on our side, but that it is us who try at times to lean on our own understanding. David led a dangerous life in the years before he became king; but David had a promise from God, and he would hold fast to his destiny, knowing that it would come to pass. We believe the challenge for us is to be steadfast like David. God has given us so much in the way of protection, that we have not even been aware of it. "He has given His angels charge to keep us in all our ways." Psalms 91:11 (NKJV paraphrased). There are situations that we have all gone through and seen, and when we just look back and wonder, how did we make it; well, it was God! He kept us, He sustained us, He prevented that car from killing you, those men from robbing you, and when your car broke down that night on that dark road, He kept you safe! We can personally testify that God has kept us safe all around the world! I personally have literally travelled millions of miles to all seven continents, and I have been kept safe from incidents of violence, accidents, and threats to my physical wellbeing. He has shown Himself to be faithful in our lives, because throughout our relationship He has kept His promises, even when we did not always keep ours!! And if He did it for us, He will do it for you!! We can truly say; "If it had not been for the Lord…. Thank You Jesus!!!

Blessings, Rupert & Red.

MAY 31

Raised With Christ

Meditation Verse: Colossians 3:1-2 HCSB

So, if you have been raised with the Messiah, seek what is above, where the Messiah is, seated at the right hand of God. Set your minds on what is above, not what is on the earth.

Scripture Reading: Colossians 3:1-11

There are certain behaviors that we should mirror, certain examples that should be followed, if we are indeed going to live the Christian life. If we know that Jesus has been raised from the dead, then our identification with Him becomes a reality. So, we were raised with Him, and because we were, then Jesus should be the One whom we emulate. Commentator David Guzick put it this way: "After His resurrection, Jesus left the tomb, so should we, we don't live there anymore. After His resurrection, Jesus spent time being with and ministering to His disciples, so should we, live our lives to be with and serve one another. After Jesus' resurrection, He looked forward to heaven, knowing He would soon ascend there, so should we, recognizing that our citizenship is in heaven." (Source: Blue Letter Bible blueletterbible.org). Jesus is now seated at the right hand of God, making intercession in heaven on our behalf. Setting our minds on what is above is to level up to the Christian living that comes from minds that are fixed on heaven, not as an obsession but as a goal. Seeking with desire and passion the Christ kind of life. We ought to love heavenly things and allow our minds to be influenced by them. Now that you belong to God, act toward those heavenly things with the priority that you treated those things in reference to the earth. The physical world can in no way take the place of the reality of heaven. The spiritual world is more real than the physical world in that it cannot die. Everything else will perish in the end. When the mortal puts on immortality, and death is not to be feared anymore, or as the old folk used to say: "When the wicked cease from troubling." Let's move toward that place in Christ that will keep our eyes heavenward, and not be distracted by things that neither last nor satisfy.

Blessings, Rupert & Red.

JUNE 1

His Grace Is Sufficient

Meditating Verse: Romans 3:20 NLT

For no one can ever be made right with God by doing what the law commands. The law simply shows us how sinful we are.

Scripture Reading: Romans 3:1-20

Under the law the whole world is guilty before God. It is so important to grasp the truth that the law cannot save us. The law shows us our sinful condition but has no power to rescue us from that condition. It is impotent and useless in that regard. It is not to say that we are all actively seeking to break the law, but because of our nature the propensity is to sin, and therefore we are unable to keep the law. This means the law now actively broken, can only condemn us and not save us. Even if you could perfectly keep the law, it would not make up for the past disobedience or present guilt. JB Phillips translation states it this way: "It is the straight edge of the law that shows us how crooked we are!" Romans 3:20b. Keeping the law is not God's way of salvation and blessing under the new covenant. To be made right with God is only through the acceptance of Jesus Christ and His finished work on the cross. We cannot be good enough on our own. We fail and fall short every day, and without the grace of God we are already condemned. You don't have to be perfect, just confess and believe. That's the qualifier. God's love is so much bigger than your sin and failures. He wants relationship with you and that is more than half the battle! It is a change of heart that will encourage you to live for God, and when you fall you have an advocate who will fight for you. Listen, there is no scenario that man can come up with that will improve your chances with the law. Our suggestion is to offer Jesus, He alone can take straight edge of the law and make your crooked straight! His grace is sufficient.

Blessings, Rupert & Red.

JUNE 2

God's Masterpiece

Meditation Verse: Ephesians 2:10 NLT

For we are God's masterpiece. He has created us anew in Christ Jesus, so we can do the good things He planned for us long ago.

Scripture Reading: Ephesians 2:1-10

God has given us every opportunity for relationship. It is almost impossible not to realize the love He has for us. We may find it hard to deserve it, but it is equally hard to dispute it. God call us His masterpiece, some translations say workmanship, but we kind of like the term Masterpiece. It has the connotation of something rare and beautiful, and something that was created with love and patience. God saved us to make us new, we do not evolve or develop into new creatures, the Bible says that the old has "passed away" and we are instantly new in Christ. We are given a new identity and a new name, God becomes "Abba Father," and we become sons and daughters. He created us for good works, not because works can result in salvation, (it does not), but works that validate the evidence that we are walking as God intended and that our purpose is real. The very purpose that God had in mind for us before the very foundation of the world. That's right, He thought about us beforehand and sacrificed His Son as a part of that plan giving us the spiritual transformation that we need to fulfill the things that God has ordained and to live life more abundantly. Do you know your identity? Has God given you a new name? Walk in the purpose that you have been given. Each step is a win for the Kingdom and glory of God.

Blessings, Rupert & Red.

JUNE 3

Mercy Triumphs Over Judgement

Meditation Verse: James 2:13 HCSB

For Judgement is without mercy to the one who has shown no mercy. Mercy triumphs over judgement.

Scripture Reading: James 2:1-13

I have always been offended by those who would show partiality to certain people just because of who they are. Don't get me wrong, there are those who are worthy of honor on a special occasion and some deserving of recognition for certain achievements or even heroic deeds. We are not talking about that. We are talking about those who feel entitled because they have a title or believe that they are better than others because they happen to be rich or famous. As a result, they believe the false narrative, lack humility and compassion for the regular guy. Jesus said, "For with what judgement you judge, you will be judged, and with the measure you use, it will be measured back to you. Matthew 7:2 (NKJV). People who say, "Only God can judge me," mostly use that as an excuse to sin, because people judge each other all the time. The question you should ask is this, is my judgement fair, honest, and trustworthy? Is it tempered with love and mercy? Yes, God is the final judge, and that, no man will escape. When you judge with partiality and not truth, you judge without mercy, so you should not expect mercy to be shown to you. Mercy triumphs over judgement, and thank God that it does, for the truth is we are all equal before God. At that time there will be no partiality, no plea bargain, no bail, suspended sentence, or parole. It will come down to two kinds of people, those who accept Christ and those who reject Him. We pray you are the former, and if you have not made a decision for Christ, we pray that you will before it is too late. Your money, position, status, or celebrity will not save you. Put your trust in the only One who can. Mercy triumphs over judgement.

Blessings, Rupert & Red.

JUNE 4

All In The Family

Meditation Verse: Ephesians 2:19 NKJV

Now, therefore, you are no longer strangers and foreigners, but fellow citizens with the saints and members of the household of God.

Scripture Reading: Ephesians 2:11-22

There is nothing in the world like family!! We say this without fear of contradiction, because we know that most can agree that this has been their own experience. Family makes the most sense in our lives, because we run the whole spectrum of emotions as we journey through this life. And if there is a group of people to whom we can relate, family tops the list. Whether we live in close proximity, or spread all over the globe, as is the case in my family, there is a bond that inextricably ties us together that we can neither adequately see nor explain. Whenever we get together there is a good time, and it is as if we were never apart. The love and memories that we share, serve to sever the passage of time, and even if just for a moment, it feels like a slice of eternity. The family was God's idea and concept, a plan to bind and build communities and nations around the world. Growing strong in love and peace, the idea that we would be the larger family of The Almighty. Somehow, we lost the true concept of family in the sense that we tended to build walls instead of bridges, and single-mindedness and isolation over community. We rejected God's intention and plan. It is not too late to fix that divide. God is waiting with open arms to welcome you back into the family. The original intent is one big family under God with all the rights and privileges that a Father bestows on His children. To be fellow citizens in a place called heaven where the love and memories will bless the tie that binds. The good times will be everlasting, and we will know the joy of not just a slice of eternity, but eternity in its fullness.

Blessings, Rupert & Red.

JUNE 5

Don't Live Without Praise!!

Meditation Verse: Psalms 145:3 NLT
Great is the Lord! He is most worthy of praise! No one can measure His greatness.
Scripture Reading: Psalms 145

If there is one thing that we know, it is that God is worthy of praise! It does not matter where you are, where you come from, or what your station in life may be. Whether you are black, white, brown, yellow or polka dot, God is worthy to be praised! If it is morning, noon, afternoon, or dead of night, Praise Him!! The best way to change your circumstances, navigate the complexities of life, or handle negative situations is to praise your way through! Most trials are too much for us to handle, some burdens too hard to bear, praise Him in the midst of it. Praising God will always yield peace of mind and calmness of spirit. Praise causes doors to open, hearts to change, causes compassion in those you least expect, heals the sick, and comforts the grief stricken. Praise is more powerful than you can imagine. Because it takes the focus off of you and what you cannot do and puts the focus on what only God can do! In truth you cannot live without praise, because you cannot truly live without God, and it is He, that inhabits your praise….

Blessings, Rupert & Red.

JUNE 6

Repentance Brings Blessing

Meditation Verse: Joel 2:12 KJV

Therefore, also now, saith the Lord, turn ye even to me with all your heart, and with fasting, and with weeping, and with mourning.

Scripture Reading: Joel 2:12-17

The call of this verse seems to have a sense of urgency. Sincere repentance is important to God, and the criteria is clear with which one ought to come. "Turn, God says, even to me with your whole heart." That word turn in Hebrew is "t'shuva," which means to repent. To make that 180 degree about face or, change direction. Because of God's warning the people decided to repent. True repentance can only be realized with your "whole heart," God demands nothing less. Giving all that you can in surrender to God. God is rich in mercy, no matter how egregious you believe your sin is, and feel that forgiveness can never be possible. With God nothing is impossible. Turning to go in a new direction requires a huge shift in your thinking. That is why God demands your whole heart. As you establish your heart towards Him, the change in your heart becomes evident, and now you get to exchange the old life with a new life and a new heart. It is a phenomenal change with eternal implications, so make up your mind to "T'shuva!!"

Blessings, Rupert & Red.

JUNE 7

We Are The Apple Of His Eye

Meditation Verse: Psalms 17:8 KJV
Keep me as the apple of the eye, hide me under the shadow of thy wings.
Scripture Reading: Psalms 17

This verse is precious to me for a number of reasons, first; the sheer poetry of the phrase is beautiful and second, my mother used to call me the apple of her eye; oh I know she said it to all her children, but it still made me feel special, even though at the time I did not really understand what that phrase meant. David was asking God to protect him as if he were the apple of His eye. The "pupil" is considered the "apple" of the eye and is protected by a complex series of bone and tissue, much like how a city is surrounded by mountains. The eyelid and lashes also create a protective covering, so we are to be protected as something fragile and unique. Then to be sheltered under His wings as a mother hen gathers her chicks under her wings to guard them from any hurt, harm, or danger. The combination of these two requests creates the most awesome picture of protection, a feeling of total safety and peace. But if we want to experience the peace of God then we must also accept the protection of God, because very seldom do the paths that we choose lead to peace. Knowing where to walk is just as important as knowing the destination. In order to walk in the peace and protection of God, make this verse a necessary part of your journey, it will illuminate the path you should take.

Blessings, Rupert & Red.

JUNE 8

Encourage The Law Of Love

Meditation Verse: Galatians 6:2 NLT
Share each other's burdens, and in this way obey the law of Christ.
Scripture Reading: Galatians 6:1-10

Man's inhumanity to man has always been. Unfortunately, it is accepted by a selfish and self-centered society. Even to those who have been raised with community and the values they espouse, showing love and compassion is seen as being weak. Humility is not seen as a virtue anymore. People use love and emotions as a way to gain an upper hand and control one another. We lie, cheat, and steal without remorse because we feel entitled, and we live in isolation because our own actions have trained us not to trust anyone. How is this any way to live? Who on God's earth has really said that this type of behavior is the new normal? What happened to empathy and caring, concern for each other, and taking the village to raise a child? God has wired us to have a vision that is greater than ourselves, the world view has perverted that idea to make us believe that it is all about ourselves. When we bear each other's burdens, when we mourn with those who mourn, rejoice with those who rejoice, give people a word of encouragement, a kind smile, involve ourselves in the community, sit with those who are ill, we become the change agents that we were intended to be, and the absolute truth is, it could mean the difference between life or death. Pain is real, my brothers and sisters, let's not dismiss or discount what another person may be going through. Fulfill the law of Christ, it was never about you, we are our brother and sister's keeper.

Blessings, Rupert & Red.

JUNE 9

Reverence The Lord

Meditation Verse: Proverbs 1:7a NKJV
The fear of the Lord is the beginning of knowledge.
Scripture Reading: Proverbs 1:1-7

Is it just us or did your parents use the "Fear of God" to make you behave? The possibility of hell was very real if we did not straighten up and fly right! Well while there is some truth to that statement, we believe that they used it as a phycological advantage as opposed to a theological truth. The Hebrew word for fear is "YIRAH" but it also means awe, reverence, respect, and worship. While I don't believe that it is foolish to have a healthy fear of God, we know it is more important to have a reverence, respect, and love for Him. God has blessed us with the ability to reason, discover, and yes to a great degree invent and create. But we lack wisdom if we think that we do these things on our own merit. Wisdom causes you to understand the purpose for which you are created. It allows you to rightfully apply knowledge. Anything that is created for good, can be perverted for evil. That is why we need to have "Yirah" for God and the abilities that He has blessed us with. If we misuse and pervert the purpose for which we were created, we will pay a price if there is no sincere repentance. "Do not be deceived, God is not mocked, for whatever a man sows, that he will also reap." Galatians 6:7, (NKJV). That is a spiritual as well as a physical truth. In order for us to put the right seed in the ground, our "Yirah" for God needs to be a daily acknowledgement.

Receive God's Wisdom today, He gives it without prejudice. Let the "Yirah of God be your daily goal. You will be blessed beyond measure for it!!

Blessings, Rupert & Red.

JUNE 10

Stillness Required, Patience Necessary

Meditation Verse: Psalms 37:7a NLT
Be still in the presence of the Lord and wait patiently for Him to act.
Scripture Reading: Psalms 37:1-17

Wow!! These words are so comforting, yet it is so hard to do! We all tend to micromanage certain situations and control is a huge issue for most of us, especially when things seem to be spiraling out of control. To surrender everything to God and be patient seems counterproductive at the very least. So how do we reconcile patience and trust and the obvious hemorrhaging of certain circumstances? We will offer what we think is the solution. To sit still in the presence of the Lord is to take a step back and listen for direction. God knows that your situation is urgent, but decisions should have the benefit of God's wisdom, because it is so easy to make a bad situation worse. Also having patience, does not mean inactivity, it is up to you to do the best that you can, and let God do the rest. The Word of God says having done all that you can, you must stand. Ephesians 6:13b (NKJV paraphrased). So, your patience comes with the belief that God is still in control, and He sees your efforts and will help you. The problem we have is God's timing, and God's will. Every situation and circumstance are not the same, but everyone wants an immediate solution. When you belong to God, He has already put a solution in place, we have to trust that He knows best. Everything will work out for our good even when we can't see it. So, listen for His voice, do all that you can, and stand with confidence that the outcome is in your best interest. Man will never do for you what God can, put your trust in His process, He, unlike man can do anything but fail.

Blessings, Rupert & Red.

JUNE 11

What's The Good Word?

Meditation Verse: Proverbs 12:25 NKJV
Anxiety in the heart of a man causes depression, but a good word makes it glad.
Scripture Reading: Proverbs 12

Words do matter! Nothing will lift your spirits like an encouraging word or an inspirational song. As music lovers we find comfort and calm in a favorite hymn or chorus. Being raised in church there are not many I don't know! I believe my mother had every hymnal known to man and she taught us every single one! But aside from the familiar tune, the words speak to you in ways that cannot adequately be described. Understanding the power of encouraging words can turn around almost any situation. It should be required learning for every human. We live in a society where stress and worry are now listed as a "condition" we all are faced with at times, some constantly. It can physically and emotionally take you down to the point where you could lose your very life. It is real and scary. Everyone is capable of being kind. Let us put that virtue to use and help uplift each other. Speak words that are affirming and life giving, you never know the effect it may have. It is like sowing seeds of love, and out of it grows a heart of compassion that spreads to others. Everyone has, or will go through something, sometime. Let's make our words count! Uplift, inspire and encourage someone today. You will be surprised at how good it makes you feel as well. Besides, it is important to God.

Blessings, Rupert & Red.

JUNE 12

Total Recall…

Meditation Verse: Psalms 77:11 NLT
But then I recall all You have done, O Lord; I remember your wonderful deeds of long ago.
Scripture Reading: Psalms 77

Every now and then we suffer with short term memory lapses. We hear that that happens as you get older. It is a baffling phenomenon. Forgetting something you just read or the inevitable walking into a room intent on doing or getting something and forgetting why you went in there in the first place! Those of us who are over forty can probably relate! What is even more strange is while the short- term memory fades, the long- term memory seems to grow stronger! We seem to have no problem remembering what happened long ago, good, bad, or unattractive! Memories linger and for those we would rather forget, we have 100% recall! We can all remember though, the situations and circumstances that we did not think we would get through, but we did. Problems we never thought would be solved, but they were. Trouble that we thought would surely ruin our lives, but we survived. Even situations where we deserved punishment, but fortunately we were spared. We want you to know whether you are saved or unsaved, you were the recipient of the grace and mercy of God. You never got out of any situation on your own, stop believing in luck, it does not exist! You were protected by the hand of Almighty God. Why? So, you would know and realize that it could only be God, and you would have a testimony, that would bring Him glory. His love for us goes deeper than you could ever think or imagine. As much as there are those who would rather have any other explanation, deep down inside you know it to be true. Because even you, when you were delivered suddenly, you breathed, "Thank God!" Just sit back and recall the events of long ago and you will find yourself counting your blessings. I encourage you to give the praise where it is due! Thank Him for all He has done, is doing and will do for you. Every day that you are alive is a gift. It is a sign that whatever you are going through, there is an end game. Trust Him, and if you have not yet put your trust in God, we encourage you to do so today! His grace and mercy are so much sweeter when the relationship is real. You will never have to wonder how you made it, you will recall that you never would have, if not for the grace and mercy of God.

Blessings, Rupert & Red.

JUNE 13

Done, Done, And Done!!

Meditation Verse: Romans 3:24 NLT

Yet God, in His grace, freely makes us right in His sight. He did this through Christ Jesus when He freed us from the penalty for our sins.

Scripture Reading: Romans 3:21-31

"What must I do to be saved?" This is a question that if you were to ask the average man or woman on the street, you would get a variety of answers. You need to do this, or that, be good, and don't be bad. It is all based on works. God says that salvation is absolutely free!! It is a gift that you can't earn or work for. It is the fundamental difference between Christianity and other religions. We like the way Rick Warren puts it. "All other religions are based on the word "do," this is what you need to do to get to heaven or paradise, you have to put in work. Christianity, however, is based on the word "done" you don't make it into heaven based on what you do, you get to heaven, based on what has already been done. Jesus has already paid the price for your salvation, through His work on the cross, that is why He said, "It is finished." The way has been made for you to receive His salvation. You make the decision to receive His grace, God gives it freely, but He won't force it on you. The choice as they say is yours. Free is good, but there is no other free gift in this world or life that will assure you of an eternal future with Christ. If you make Him your choice, you will not regret it! Do it today and begin to live your best life!! Remember, it is already done, done and Done!!

Blessings, Rupert & Red.

JUNE 14

Share Jesus Without Fear

Meditation Verse: Acts 18:9-10 NLT

"Don't be in this city afraid! Speak out! Don't be silent! For I am with you, and no one will attack and harm you, for many people belong to me."

Scripture Reading: Acts 18:1-17

Sharing Jesus without fear is a problem for many Christians. Most remain silent for many reasons. Depending on where you are in this world, it is estimated that between 2 and 17% of Christians actively share their faith. Two of the biggest reasons are, fear of rejection and ridicule, and a lack of knowledge. We all need to read the Word more, because faith comes by hearing and the more, we read and hear, the more our faith will grow. Think about your career, or what you do for a living, the more you learn, the more confident you become about your job, and the more competent you become at your job. Well did you know that it is also your job as a believer to share the gospel? If you are indeed grateful for the gift of salvation, you ought to tell somebody! I know not everyone is called to be a preacher, but we all have a sphere of influence, a circle of family and friends, who need the same opportunity that you were afforded. God said, "don't be afraid!" He has your back! Let the love of Jesus be evident in your life and people will ask you what it is about you that brings you so much joy! The body of Christ needs you more than ever, so be bold and unashamed of the gospel of Christ! Freely you have received now freely give!! Relationship Demands it!

Blessings, Rupert & Red.

JUNE 15

Got Your Ears On?

Meditation Verse: 2 Timothy 4:3 KJV

For the time will come when they will not endure sound doctrine; but after their own lusts shall they heap to themselves teachers; having itching ears.

Scripture Reading: 2 Timothy 4:1-5

What in the world are itching ears?!! Ears that will only hear theories and fables that they can agree with. Ears that can't and won't endure truth. As long as it does not convict, condemn, or contradict their lifestyles and beliefs. Revelation of God's Word becomes foolishness to them. And the truth is that the Bible says that these will and do exist, they always have, and always will. We are, most of us, comfortable with those things that challenge us the least. I don't want to be forced to think about, or deal with, anything that means I have to change. Because, if you do read the Word of God, it will change you, it will transform you, it will challenge your thinking, the way that you live, and the way that you treat people. The Word of God is powerful, and it is not for the faint of heart, unless you desire strength for your heart!! It takes courage to realize that we need to acknowledge a Being more powerful than ourselves, and we need Him to survive. We can do nothing in our own strength and every breath we take is because He allows it. It may not feel natural for you to surrender everything to God, but it is necessary for us to truly live and not merely exist. Open your ears and your heart to the inevitability of the Almighty. What is convenient is not necessarily truth.

Blessings, Rupert & Red.

JUNE 16

Change Your Ways!!

Meditation Verse: Jeremiah 26:13 KJV

Therefore, now amend your ways and your doings, and obey the voice of the Lord your God: and the Lord will repent him of the evil that He has pronounced against you.

Scripture Reading: Jeremiah 26:1-15

Here is the problem, we don't reverence God anymore. We don't do the right thing just because it's the right thing to do. Common courtesy is in short supply, we have failed to teach our children the true meaning of respect, and the people in positions of authority are mean spirited and self- centered. Corporations treat workers like slaves, no one wants relationships anymore, whether they be personal or business. Managers and owners confuse professionalism as arrogance, they try to force you to accept their low standards and then get revenge on you for pointing out their inadequacies. We fail to operate as a community because we are only interested in uplifting ourselves. So, nobody really benefits, and the only ones who lose are those who can least afford to. We could go on and on, but we refer you back to our initial statement: We don't reverence God anymore. When I was growing up even the unchurched had a respect for God. There was a moral center, a line not to be crossed, a sense of community, and the church was a place where you could get help. I am not saying that it does not exist, but far from the extent where we could see the difference in lives changed. We need to change our ways. Don't be the people that wake-up everyday intent on doing evil deeds. Respect and revere the One who made you, don't wait until you lose everything, and it is eternally too late. Be Wise!! Our very lives depend on it!

Blessings, Rupert & Red.

JUNE 17

Don't Be A Surface Christian

Meditation Verse: Titus 1:16a NLT
Such people claim they know God, but they deny Him by the way they live.
Scripture Reading: Titus 1:1-16

Who are such people? People who want you to see their "Surface Christianity," but don't really want to know you. No one is perfect, but it is impossible to be a witness for Christ if your words and life don't reflect your beliefs. Don't make your life a "show" for others, it will never go over well. Understand that if a child knew how to emulate what you do, and not what you say, then how do you really think that you are going to be effective for the Kingdom, with grown people seeing that your words don't match your actions? We need to grow up and get it together. Let people see the God in us by having our words line up with what we do. It is often said that we may be the only Bible that people see. That is an awesome responsibility, and we need them to see a good report. People are watching and paying attention to what we do and say. Operating in love is the first step to seeing lives changed. Plant the right seed and see God, the Lord of the harvest, raise up a beautiful garden.

Blessings, Rupert & Red.

JUNE 18

Do You Know Right From Wrong?

Meditation Verse: James 4:17 NLT
Remember, it is sin to know what you ought to do and then not do it.
Scripture Reading: James 4:13-17

How do we reconcile this scripture as an application to our daily lives? It seems simple enough as the difference between right and wrong. However, it goes much deeper than that; James knows that it is easier to talk about humility and dependence on God than to actually live it. But the more we learn, the more we are accountable to do it. The uncertainty of life alone should make us want to recognize what's good and then do it. Fear usually leads to inaction, or we fall back on the worldly areas that are familiar. As a result, even though we know what we should do, we cave to a carnal decision. God has written His laws on our hearts, and in order for us to change, our desires must change. What God has given us cannot be matched by anything human. So, there is an expectation of us. Jesus put it this way; "to whom much is given, from him much will be required." Luke 12:48b (NKJV). You can't live any old way and receive the blessing of God, that is idolatry. Don't let sin rule over you and take you away from what you know to be right. Greater light gives greater responsibility.

Blessings, Rupert & Red.

JUNE 19

Nothing But Love!

Meditation Verse: John 3:16 NKJV

For God so loved the world, that He gave His only begotten Son, that whosoever believeth in Him should not perish, but have everlasting life.

Scripture Reading: John 3:16-21

This world is a fickle place, everything changes, from relationships, jobs, financial status, one minute you are a hero, and the next a zero. Stability depends on other people's whims, values, and or bottom lines. Today you have a career or employment and tomorrow you could be on the street. When you depend on this world's system, disappointment is the only constant. There is only one thing that will never and can never change, God's Love. Knowing that God loves you no matter what; your failings, your brokenness, your sin, provides a rock-solid foundation for your life. God loves you with an everlasting, magnificent, beyond comprehension love. He just does not want us to mentally assent to His love, He wants us to make an intentional investment in it. God's very essence is love, and He created you, just to love you! God loves us so much it hurt. God sent His only Son to die. When Jesus died for us, He was saying that He loved us so much that He would rather die than live without us. That is the type of love that you can build your life upon. Real love that endures to the end and gives all. When you feel that your life is between a rock and a hard place, choose the "Rock," He is the solid foundation.

Blessings, Rupert & Red.

JUNE 20

God's Divine Order

Meditation Verse: Luke 13:30 HCSB

And note this: Some who seem least important now will be the greatest then, and some who are the greatest now will be the least important then.

Scripture Reading: Luke 13:22-30

We once read a meme that said: "You can't treat people like garbage and worship God at the same time." This resonated with us as we not only realized the premise of the statement, but understood that unfortunately, that is exactly what is happening. And we know that there are all types of people in the Body of Christ, and that no one is perfect, but there is a standard, a threshold, a line of decency and humanity that should be adhered to, no matter what your issue. God is not impressed with your status, your pedigree, your bank account, your race, color or creed. It will never be about you and what you possess, God is interested in your character, and how you treat Jesus and His creation. If you never thought about it before, think about this; your treatment of people, is directly related to your access to the Kingdom of heaven. If you believe that everything you were able to accomplish personally in this life will cause God to say, "Well Done," then your belief system is flawed. "Did you feed me when I was hungry? Did you clothe me when I was naked? Did you visit me when I was sick or in prison? Or did you treat people like garbage six days a week all the while claiming to love and serve Me on one day of the week? Jesus said that the way you treat people is the same way you treat Him. So, get over yourself and get proper perspective. God's love for His creation will always override your wealth, status or possessions. Remember the story of the rich man and Lazarus Luke 16:19-31 (HCSB), the rich man was just a rich man, but God knew Lazarus by name!! "The first shall be last and the last shall be first." You who have ears to hear….

Blessings, Rupert & Red.

JUNE 21

Are You In Opposition To God?

Meditation Verse: James 4:6b NLT
God opposes the proud but gives grace to the humble.
Scripture Reading: James 4:1-10

What does it say about a prideful spirit that it would cause opposition from God? What is so terrible about being proud of your accomplishments or reaching the goals you have set for yourself, or even in the education of your children? It is the idea that is what "I" have done and "I and I alone have accomplished this." That is the same spirit that got Satan thrown out of heaven. As created beings we can't take the credit alone for our accomplishments. Every breath you draw is a gift from God, and life, health, and strength, come from His gracious hand. It would not be possible to do anything without God's ability alongside you. When we think that we have done all on our own, that is the spirit of pride, working on the inside of us, pushing back against the glory that God deserves. Until you realize that every perfect gift comes from God, you will be blinded by a prideful spirit. Pride and grace work at cross purposes. Because a spirit of humility will always give credit where credit is due. It isn't that humility earns grace, it is that it puts us in a position to receive what God freely gives. We don't know about you, but we don't want God to be in opposition to us. Trade the spirit of pride for one of humility; not only will you experience an abundance of God's grace, but God will elevate you in response to your submission.

Blessings, Rupert & Red.

JUNE 22

Love Is Everything

Meditation Scripture: Colossians 3:14 NLT
Above all, clothe yourselves with love, which binds us all together in perfect harmony.
Scripture Reading: Colossians 3:1-17

The single most greatest, most excellent, most inspiring thing that you can do is Love!! In any walk of life, regardless of your status, if you name the name of Jesus as your Lord and Savior, it is the one command that transcends all others. EVERYTHING works by love, and if love is applied to every situation and circumstance, it will transform it! The greatest thing a Christian can do is operate in love. Can people see and feel your love, to the extent that they need to know what it is that you have that they are obviously lacking? When we operate in the principal of love, we change our lives for the better, our witness becomes credible, our character more trustworthy, and our words truth. Real love causes faith to grow, hope to rise, it is transformative and life affirming, and it begins and never ends with God. We don't love for love's sake we love because it is who God is. Our lives would be non-existent without it. Know that you were created by love, so that you can be loved, and so love in return. It is the currency by which we live. So, clothe yourself in it, bathe in it, rely on it, pray for it, speak it, breathe it, live it, do it!! Nothing else matters as much as love because it is all about love, and it matters to God, because after all; it is who He is!

Blessings, Rupert & Red.

JUNE 23

God Will Fight For You

Meditation Verse: Psalms 12:5 NLT

The Lord replies, "I have seen violence done to the helpless, and I have heard the groans of the poor. Now I will rise up to rescue them, as they have longed for me to do."

Scripture Reading: Psalms 12

Anyone who knows me knows how passionate I am about social justice. Now I believe in individual responsibility, and the infallible Word of God. But I also know that this world system is rigged against the worker and the working poor. So many people are under- employed, hardly employed and not working at all. There will always be those who don't want to work, but they are the exception and not the rule. Wages are so low that along with your work application, they also hand you a form to fill out for welfare, because the employers know that they are not paying you a wage you can live on. That is unjust, a sin, and an abuse of human rights. God has always spoken about the abuse of the poor since the exodus from Egypt. Why are we almost 5,000 years later, still talking about the poor in a land where there is plenty and some people who claim to be "Christian" are treating the less fortunate as if they deserve to be poor? Because nowadays, greed and self-centered behavior seem to be a pre-requisite for being wealthy. It is true that where your treasure is, your heart lies also. God is exposing the wickedness of the rich and powerful, their reign of greed and selfishness won't last forever. Just like the Israelites, left Egypt with all the wealth they could carry, a transfer of wealth is coming. He has heard the cries of the poor, abused and misused by a society that is only interested in selfish gain. They won't succeed, because justice is important to God.

Blessings, Rupert & Red.

JUNE 24

God Is Not Hiding From You

Meditation Verse: Deuteronomy 4:29 NLT

But from there you will search again for the Lord your God. And if you search for Him with all your heart and soul, you will find Him.

Scripture Reading: Deuteronomy 4:26-31

There is a secular song that has been playing in my head: "I've been searching, for so long, nobody like you, nowhere to be found. Makes me wonder, what I'd do, if I never had someone like you." It is about a guy who found true love but took her for granted and then lost her. Now he's searching but he can't find anyone like her. What does it mean to search for someone with your whole heart and soul? It is a search on a whole other level! It is a search for the true perfect love, and the pursuit of the relationship of a lifetime! Someone you can give your all to and feel secure. A love that is faithful and true and consistent. One who cannot only give you the desires of your heart, but will protect you from hurt, harm and danger. Someone who will be with you in sickness and health, good times and bad, and will comfort you when you have suffered loss. The best part is that they will never leave you or forsake you, no matter what happens. Not even death will separate you, because He holds the keys to death and the grave and He will walk you into eternity, where you will never part. That is the type of love you need above all others. There is no love that can compete with that love! Search first for the love that is like no other, and everything else that you need will fall into place. "I can search for all eternity Lord, and find, there is none like You."

Blessings, Rupert & Red.

Footnote: I've been Searching written by, Glenn Jones and Bernard Belle Published by Mom & Dad publishing and Davey Pooh songs.

JUNE 25

God Will Triumph Over Evil

Meditation Verse: Hosea 4:1b-2a NKJV

There is no truth, or mercy, or knowledge of God in the Land. By swearing and lying, killing and stealing, and committing adultery, they break all restraint, with bloodshed upon bloodshed.

Scripture Reading: Hosea 4:1-10

Where to begin? There is an evil that has taken over the land. True wisdom and understanding always begin with the knowledge of God. We have become like the people in Hosea; people don't want to hear about the knowledge of God, we are descending into chaos, and we are without restraint. Truth and mercy are becoming passe', we are too "enlightened" to follow God. We have a modern culture that is completely without boundaries. We embrace sayings like; "break all the rules," "living without boundaries," "peel off your inhibitions," "Find your own road." The message is the same, you answer to no one, the universe revolves around you. The ultimate result is bloodshed upon bloodshed.

We have no regard for our neighbor, we buy into the rhetoric that anyone who does not look like me is a problem or a threat, and the only answer is violence. Truth must be rooted in something other than personal opinion, and mercy has to go beyond self-interest. This is the tragic fruit of forsaking the knowledge of God. The enemy deceives us into believing that we are walking into the doorway of freedom, when actually it is a trap to the road of destruction. So, how did we get here and what is God's remedy to this horrific indictment? We will continue tomorrow with the why of it all and God's solution.

Blessings, Rupert & Red.

JUNE 26

God Will Triumph Over Evil, Part 2

Meditation Verse: Hosea 4:6 NKJV

My people are destroyed for lack of knowledge. Because you have rejected knowledge, I also will reject you from being priest for Me; because you have forgotten the law of your God, I will also forget your children.

Scripture Reading: Hosea 4:1-10

Yesterday we talked about knowledge, truth and mercy becoming deficient in people's lives, and why this is directly related to their destructive behavior. The Word says that "My people are destroyed for lack of knowledge," Hosea 4:6 (NKJV), think about it, in the natural, a lack of knowledge in any area could destroy you, how much more if you neglect the spiritual aspect of your life. This not only affects you but generations to come. From the time Adam rejected dependence on God, He began at once to die, and so it is with us from the moment we are born, we have inherited his very nature. When God's people are destroyed and waste away, it isn't because God lacks love and strength, it is because the people lack knowledge. Knowledge of God and His Word are inextricably mixed. Psalms 138:2 (NKJV), says, "You have magnified Your Word above all Your Name." When you begin to understand who God is, your conduct will change. Where there is no conviction of His omnipotence, omnipresence, and omniscience, there will be the gravest of sin, depravity, and moral decay. So, don't let a lack of knowledge cheat you out of your life. Seek the wisdom of God, exchange Adam's nature for His, and begin to operate in the will of God, that's your best life guaranteed!!

Blessings, Rupert & Red.

JUNE 27

Love One Another

Meditation Verse 1 John 3:11 NKJV

This is the message you have heard from the beginning: We should love one another.

Scripture reading: 1 John 3:1-15

A little encouragement and advice today. This message has never changed; Jesus commanded that we love one another. This is not a suggestion or a request. This is an expectation of everyone that claims to have a relationship with Christ. It is His command, and we are expected to obey. It is all well and good to talk about your personal relationship with Jesus, and how He is the center of your life, but if that does not translate into how you deal with your fellow man, your words are empty. I have said it before, and it bears repeating; how we treat others really matters to God. Psalms 15:3(NLT), in answer to the question of who can tabernacle or have relationship with God states: "Those who refuse to gossip, or harm their neighbors, or speak evil of their friends." This comes down to a faith decision, not an emotional one. Walking in love is not the easiest thing to do, but while practice won't make you perfect, it will yield much fruit. Make a concerted effort to walk in love; it will improve your treatment of people and increase your faith. Life is 20% of what happens to you, but 80% of how you respond, respond in love.

Blessings, Rupert & Red.

JUNE 28

That Name!! Jesus!!

Meditation Verse: Philippians 2:10-11 NLT

That at the name of Jesus every knee should bow, in heaven and on earth, and under the earth, and that every tongue declare that Jesus Christ is Lord, to the glory of God the Father.

Scripture Reading: Philippians 2:5-11

What's in a name? People are named for many different reasons, some for celebrities, some for famous places, some are combinations of parent's names, relatives, some even named for cars, or countries. I confess to never being very fond of my name, but I was not consulted, and there are I think, names that are, let's say less attractive than mine, so, yeah, I'm good! And while names in times past were given as a means of conveying a certain future or specific meaning, only one name was given to which the whole Universe would eventually be in submission to. The name of Yahweh (Jesus) is the Name that was given by God to be the Name above all names. It was given with manifest purpose and destiny. God has given His Son a name that has all power and authority, the living and the dead will answer to it, everything that has ever been created will be subject to it. No matter where you go you will not be able to escape its majestic reach! There is no other name given under heaven that can save you, cleanse you, and make you whole. It will transform everything it comes into contact with and bring dead things to life. The power of this Name is inexhaustible, relentless and unstoppable!! It can do for you what no other name on earth can, think about it: Nothing that you will ever do in this life will be more important. You can surrender now, or you can surrender later. Because you will eventually kneel, and confess, better to do it with rejoicing, than to do it in despair….

Blessings, Rupert & Red.

JUNE 29

Are You Breathing? PRAISE!!

Meditation Verse: Psalms 150:6 NLT

Let everything that breathes, sing praises to the Lord! Praise the Lord!

Scripture Reading: Psalms 150

Let all breath praise Him! That is everything that breathes!! No one is exempt. To withhold your praise is an offense! Why should the true reason you are actually breathing, not deserve your praise and adoration? If someone rescues you from certain death, the gratitude you would feel would be enormous, you will never forget them and would not be able to thank them enough! Hello!! If you belong to God your life has not only been spared from certain death, but you have been gifted with eternal life!! A thousand tongues would not be enough to sing to God His rightfully deserved praise!! So, go through this day and every day, thanking and praising Him not just for what He's done, but for who He is!! In fact, open your mouth right now and give Him praise!! Don't wait, later might be too late!! He deserves It!! Your Hallelujah! Belongs to God…. If you are breathing, you owe Him….

Blessings, Rupert & Red.

JUNE 30

In God We Do Trust

Meditation Verse: Job 13:15 NKJV
Though He slay me, yet will I trust Him. Even so, I will defend my own ways before Him.
Scripture Reading: Job 13:1-18

Job was a man who the Bible called "blameless and upright," so why would a man who seemed to be so faithful to God, suffer so much loss? There are so many angles to this story, we choose to follow the one about trust. Sometimes bad things happen to good people, tough consequences are not always about your mistakes. You can do everything right and yet still have your situation fall apart. It happens all the time, your job becomes redundant, a sudden death shakes your family, your hard work is minimized by your supervisor, a spouse walks away; The truth is sometimes you reap what other people sow. In a situation where you don't understand what is happening and you can't fathom why, you must trust that this too shall pass. Personally, it is hard to think about anyone enduring what Job had to endure, but the message is your dependence on God and God alone. "Yet will I trust Him," this is the attitude that got Job through this unbelievable trial. Trust in man is not an option, he will always fall short. Trust in the One who cannot fail. Life happens to all of us and living in this wicked and sin sick world is a challenge in itself. When you can't point to the reason for the trial take it up with God, He will vindicate you and cause you to come forth as pure gold. Don't let the enemy cause you to give up!! Trust God, He will make a way, no it is not fair, and maybe you did not deserve what happened to you. But with God's help you can bounce back. Trust Him!! He is trustworthy!!

Blessings, Rupert & Red.

JULY 1

Know Where Your Help Comes From

Meditation Verse: Psalms 121:1-2 NKJV

I will lift up my eyes to the hills – from whence comes my help? My help comes from the Lord, Who made heaven and earth.

Scripture Reading: Psalms 121

This is one of the first psalms that I memorized as a child, but I always thought that the second line was a statement and not a question. It was not until I was an adult and studied the psalm in earnest that I understood it as a question. "From where does my help come?" It comes from God of course, so looking towards the hills is an implication of looking towards the heavens or gazing heavenward. There is no help for us in the mountains, or hills or valleys, our confidence can only be in God, who created it all. We cannot rely on creatures, men, or any arm of flesh to give us the help that we need. Jeremiah 3:23 says: "Truly in vain is salvation hoped for from the hills and from the multitude of mountains, truly in the Lord our God is the salvation of Israel." (NKJV). We must see all our help laid up in God, in His power, goodness, mercy and grace. So, when we look up toward the hills, we must look beyond in order to see His splendid creation, inclusive of the heavens and universe. Understanding the awesomeness of God, the vast resources that are His, our faith tells us there is nothing our God cannot do. Now our problems don't seem insurmountable, because we have the Creator of heaven and earth on our side. He who spoke a word and formed this world from nothing, is more than able to provide whatever it is we need. This is a great devotional psalm, and one that can give you comfort and strength in any area. We pray you come to know Jesus as your help, it will make all the difference in your life.

Blessings, Rupert & Red.

JULY 2

True Peace Comes Only From God

Meditation Verse: Philippians 4:7 NKJV

And the peace of God, which surpasses all understanding, will guard your hearts and minds through Christ Jesus.

Scripture Reading: Philippians 4:1-7

How can one experience peace in a world that is so violent? It seems an impossibility because every day there are people without restraint and self-control committing atrocities against their fellow man. It is past epidemic, in fact it is pandemic, and it seems that no matter where you go, you don't feel safe. Where is peace in this horrific scenario? There is a peace that reigns supreme above what we can comprehend. God's peace is beyond understanding, which means you cannot grasp with your finite mind, why amid chaos, all is well. The Bible describes 3 aspects of peace that can be ours,

1. Peace from God, this is the peace that God gives as a gift to His people.
2. Peace with God, the peace that comes as a result of a relationship with Jesus Christ. Through His finished work on the cross.
3. The peace of God, the peace that is described in today's verse, which is beyond the very power of our thinking. This is not just peace that is beyond the thinking of the worldly man, this is beyond the comprehension of even the godly man, that is why it defies description and can only be experienced. But we can experience it daily, in the midst of every and any situation. "Father, today as I praise You, I surrender my day, my thoughts and actions to You, fill me with Your love and mercy so that I may impart it wherever I go. And grant me Your peace, that assures me that You are always in control, and I will forever praise You for Who You Are!! Thank You for Perfect Peace!!"

Blessings, Rupert & Red.

JULY 3

Religion Versus Relationship

Meditation Verse: Matthew 23:4 NLT
They crush people with unbearable religious demands, and never lift a finger to ease the burden.

Scripture Reading: Matthew 23:1-36

When you emphasize religion over relationship you force people into legalism. Legalism cancels the law of love. We must be careful that we don't bear heavy burdens that Christ never intended us to carry. Are there modern-day Pharisees among us? You had better believe it!! While there is merit to the Mosaic law, we have a better covenant, established on better promises. The accusations against those religious leaders apply to many today. While you should not let the law of God lose its authority with you, don't let the Pharisees of today bind you with heavy burdens that they themselves are not willing to carry. Peter said in Acts 15:10; (NKJV), "Why do you test God by putting a yoke around the necks of the disciples which neither our fathers nor we were able to bear?" Religion is meant to control you and put you in a position of bondage, there is no freedom in that. Relationship causes growth to become what God always intended for you to become. When you truly walk in love, you are walking in the grace of God and not in the attempt of your own self-righteousness. To walk in love is the best road you can travel. Don't be distracted by the restrictions and control of religion, the weight is too heavy to bear. Jesus said in Matthew 11:30, (NKJV), "For My yolk is easy and My burden is light." We are good with that!!

Blessings, Rupert & Red.

JULY 4

Religion Versus Relationship Part 2

Meditation Verse: Romans 7:6 NLT

But now we have been released from the law, for we died to it and are no longer captive to its power. Now we can serve God, not in the old way of obeying the letter of the law, but in the new way of living in the Spirit.

Scripture Reading: Romans 7:1-13

It is important to emphasize the difference between religion versus relationship again today. Because we identify with the death of Jesus on the cross, we are dead to the law, no longer bound by its control over us as a principle of justification or sanctification. Why? The law does not justify us, it cannot make us right with God, the law does not sanctify us, it cannot bring us into deeper relationship or makes us more holy before Him. Religion keeps you in bondage to a whole set of rules and regulations that were never meant to save you or give you new life. Galatians 3:24 (NLT), says that; "The law was our guardian until Christ came, it protected us until we could be made right with God through faith." Serving God in the newness of the spirit, gives us freedom to serve Him better, and not by trying in the natural to obey the letter of the law. We could not serve God in the flesh because as Paul said in Romans 7:18; (NKJV), "For I know that in me (that is in my flesh) nothing good dwells." The law could only serve to identify the sin in us. Our faith in Jesus justifies us and delivers us from rules and regulations. It is a shame when people feel forced to live a life of legalism with more devotion than walking in the Spirit. Religion operates in fear of doing wrong. Relationships operate in the spirit of love. Choose love over fear and free yourself from the bondage and letter of the law. Choose relationship over religion, and walk in the newness of life, in the Spirit of Christ Jesus. Remember, the letter kills, but the Spirit brings life….

Blessings, Rupert & Red.

JULY 5

God Has No Favorites

Meditation Scripture: Proverbs 22:2 & 7 NKJV

The rich and the poor have this in common, The Lord is the maker of them all.
The rich rules over the poor, and the borrower is servant to the lender.

Scripture Reading: Proverbs 22:1-9

These are statements of truth, however, the truth of the matter may not be entirely obvious to the reader. Both these scenarios become a snare to those who misinterpret the meaning. Both the rich and the poor have the same maker, God, and therefore in God's eyes they are equal. In the sense that they both must answer to a righteous God. So, even though both tend to view each other through their cultural stereotypes, they would be foolish not to understand what God is really saying here. We are all born into this world the same way, naked, helpless, sinful, and dependent on God from our birth. We will all be subject to the same illnesses, temptations, and sorrows. At the end of the day, we will all be subject to the same judgement. On that day, all pretenses and riches, rank and station, color and creed, will be left forever at the gates. It won't be about what you have, have accomplished, or even how much you gave, because the true motive of your heart will be exposed, your character revealed, and you will answer for the way you have treated people in this life. Having means will not give you a means to an end. Neither will having little to no means. Both rich and poor, borrower and lender, will have more in common than not. All would be wise to remember such....

Blessings, Rupert & Red.

JULY 6

God Sees You and Will Not Forget

Meditation Verse: 1 Corinthians 15:58 NLT

So, my dear brothers and sisters, be strong and immovable. Always work enthusiastically for the Lord, for you know that nothing you do for the Lord is ever useless.

Scripture Reading: 1 Corinthians 15:50-58

For believers, your faith should prompt you to good works as you now belong to Christ. Now that you have been given the victory over sin and death, your life should be a testament during this walk into eternity. Because we know that death is defeated, we should have a strong and unshakeable desire to work hard in everything because forever starts now!! Going to work would be a breeze if at the end of every week you received a million- dollar paycheck!! (If only!) Well, your labor for God will not be in vain, He sees you and will reward you; nothing, no matter how small, that you do for the Kingdom will go unnoticed. We are convinced that eternal life with no need for a health plan or any other type of insurance, and other benefits too numerous to mention, is a better package than you could ever receive from anyone in this world!! We don't need to waver, we don't need to fall, we don't need to quit! Hebrews 6:10, (NLT), says; "For God is not unjust. He will not forget how hard you have worked for Him, and how you have shown your love for Him, by caring for other believers as you still do." Be encouraged, believe God, His promises never fail.

Blessings, Rupert & Red.

JULY 7

Use Your Talents and Gifts For God

Meditation Verse: Psalms 84:10 NKJV

For a day in your courts is better than a thousand. I would rather be a doorkeeper in the house of my God than dwell in the tents of wickedness.

Scripture Reading: Psalms 84

There is no better privilege than to serve the Living God!! We all would do well to understand that salvation does not end with sitting in the pews. God expects you to use your gifts and talents to honor and praise Him. Think of all that he has done for you. It is not the magnitude of the service that is important, but the attitude of service no matter how small. To present yourself as a living sacrifice is the least you can do. God is not asking for martyrs, but people who will live for Him. Whether you are the preacher or the doorkeeper, your service to God is important. So, get up and be active in your place of worship! Give God your best and the glory He deserves from your life. As you work for the kingdom, your true purpose will unfold, your life will take on new meaning, and he will satisfy you with the desires of your heart. True worship is honoring God for who He is. Time, talent, and treasure, all have been given to you by God. So, use them for His glory, and let your legacy be one of service, and you will hear; "Well done my good and faithful servant; you have been faithful over a few things, I will make you ruler over many things. Enter into the joy of your Lord." Matthew 25:23 (NKJV).

Blessings, Rupert & Red.

JULY 8

Not Everyone Who Cries; Lord, Lord…

Meditation Verse: Matthew 23:27 NKJV
Woe unto you, scribes and Pharisees, hypocrites! For you are like unto whited sepulchers, which indeed appear beautiful outward, but are within full of dead man's bones, and of all uncleanness.

Scripture Reading: Matthew 23:23-36

Today is the anniversary of my birth. I want to say something that I feel needs to be said from my heart. We want this devotional to be uplifting and inspiring. We want it to encourage, and foster relationship with God. We also want it to reflect what is important to God and know what is in His heart. Because it is in that context, that will challenge your thinking, in that spirit, will you draw closer to Him. His Word is the key to all of that. With that in mind, hear me on this; "We want to say something about the Jesus that saved us and whom we serve. We want to say that the Jesus that we love may not be the same one you confess. Because as we read the rhetoric and hear and see with our own eyes and ears the comments and actions of some, and we said some "Christians," We are convinced that it is not possible that we are talking about the same Jesus!" Now if you are not a Pharisee, scribe, or hypocrite, then maybe we are not talking to you. We won't call any names because we don't want to make this a personal attack on anyone. We are, however, calling you out as a group, that you are working in total opposition to Jesus' mandate, and your desires and motives seem selfish and self-centered. You are a part of the reason that people want nothing to do with Christianity, you are a reason that people don't want to go to church anymore, you are a reason that people who try to show love are viewed with suspicion, you are the reason that people don't trust the true man of God. Simply because of what you are okay with; You are okay with people dying because they can't afford health insurance, you are okay with treating the immigrant and the foreigner like criminals, you are okay with people being treated less than because of the color of their skin, you are okay with the poor staying poor, and you are okay with lying to everyone about it all, and at the same time you confess to be followers of Jesus, the One who has spoken out against everything that you are okay with! Confused?? We are not, and we are perfectly clear and fully convinced that you are not confused either. The fact that you choose to take an anti-people stance, against the very people that Jesus bled and died for is not only sad, but an indictment on your soul. Mine is only an observation, but there is One who will judge, so if we are talking about the same Jesus, maybe you really are confused. Let us help you; the Jesus that we know said in Matthew 7:21, (NKJV) "Not everyone who says to Me, "Lord, Lord," shall enter the Kingdom of heaven, but he who does the will of my Father in Heaven." We pray you don't learn this too late… You need to know that it is important to God.

Blessings, Rupert & Red.

JULY 9

You Were Built For This!!

Meditation Verse: Psalms 18:33 NLT
He makes me as surefooted as a deer, enabling me to stand on mountain heights.
Scripture Reading: Psalms 18:30-39

One of the most amazing things that we have seen in our travels around the world, are the mountain deer and goats, running up and down the sheer side of a mountain. It is almost unbelievable how surefooted they are!! They run and jump from precipice to precipice never once stumbling, slipping, or falling! Anyone who has ever witnessed this will ask, how in the world do they do it?? They were created for it! They have mastered their environment. They have the skill set to live on the mountainous terrain. David says in this psalm that the Lord had given him the skill like a deer, to handle the rough terrain, to stand in mountainous places, his trust was in the Lord. What are the rough terrains in your life? What are you facing that you feel you won't be able to handle? Put your trust in the One who can give you the skill set to do more than just survive. Believe that you were built for this, and you can and will make it. Trust God to give you sure feet for the paths you must travel. See victory on the other side and march toward it! Despite the rough terrain, you have to navigate, be encouraged, God is in control, and if you let Him, He will help you master the environment. Then you will be able to stand on mountain heights. Remember, with God, all things are possible!!

Blessings, Rupert & Red.

JULY 10

But God!!

> **Meditation verse: Psalms 86:15 NKJV**
> *But You, O Lord, are a God full of compassion, and gracious, longsuffering in abundant mercy and truth.*
>
> **Scripture Reading: Psalms 86**

It seems that we can't stay away from the Psalms!! What can we say today about this magnificent verse of scripture that is basically self-explanatory? That God is a God of mercy is truly an understatement. In the face of all we are to the contrary, in our lives that are full of mistakes, selfishness, and sin, our treatment towards others, our lack of veracity, and all of the things that this miserable flesh contaminates, God. Still. Loves. Us. All the evils of men still cannot negate the goodness of God! He is intentional about His love for us, we would be otherwise condemned, but Christ suffered the cross to redeem us from our sin. He is long suffering, despite our stubbornness to repent. He knows us intimately and yet patiently waits until our desire is to know him that same way. Once you understand the magnitude and sheer power of God's love you will never be the same. Amid everything you are going through, or ever will face, the only constant you have is God's love and presence. Conform to His image of grace and truth, the peace you will have will be incalculable, and you will wonder how you lived so long without it!! But God!

Blessings, Rupert & Red.

JULY 11

Difficult Trials

Habakkuk 3:17-18 NLT

Even though the fig trees have no blossoms, and there are no grapes on the vines; even though the olive crop fails, and the fields lie empty and barren; even though the flocks die in the fields, and the cattle barns are empty, Yet I will rejoice in the Lord! I will be joyful in the God of my salvation.

Scripture Reading: Habakkuk 3

It is always hard when you are going through difficult trials, and they seem to strike at inopportune times. It is challenging to understand how these trials can work out for our good. If we are honest, we sometimes doubt, and feel that God has abandoned us, and we feel let down and angry. If, however, we want to get through a disappointing situation, the answer is in our "Yet Praise." Because storms come to all our lives, it is a part of this fallen world, no one escapes it. The answer is not to be blind to it, but to yet praise through it. Why? Because "Yet Praise" shifts your focus to the One who is bigger than any problem you may face. It centers your spirit, strengthens your faith, and increases your endurance. Habakkuk saw desolation in the Judean countryside, but during it all, his thought was to Yet Praise the Lord! You see, being joyful and praising God, has nothing to do with the way you feel. Feelings are never a good barometer in deciding what to do, it is based on what you know to be true. Yet praise will move you to that position. It is so important to keep emphasizing this point! Your condition now will not determine your outcome. Let your praise bring you to your conclusion. Be determined that your "Yet Praise" will be heard. God inhabits the praises of His people; He will hear you and will bring you out.

Blessings, Rupert & Red.

JULY 12

He Alone Is Worthy!!

Meditation Verse: Psalms 63:3 HCSB

My Lips will glorify You because Your faithful love is better than life.

Scripture Reading: Psalms 63

The faithfulness of God is truly amazing! Most take for granted their rising in the morning, able to stretch and move and think for yourself. We forget that it is because of a loving God, whose tender mercy and favor, sustains us from one breath to the next. The Word says that: "In Him we live, move, and have our being." Acts 17:28a (NKJV). Truer words were never spoken. His faithful love is better than life, not even a thousand lifetimes can compare to the eternal love of our God, no matter what we may be going through, we ought to give Him the fruit of our lips, because despite the trials and hardships, life with Christ is worth it. Here is the absolute truth; Your life is meaningless without God in it. Your accomplishments and success come to naught unless you know and acknowledge where your help comes from. If God withdrew himself from you, you would be looking at the shadow of death, what will the success and money mean then? This life is temporal, but God's love and mercy are faithful and everlasting! Let the Lord's glory be known, tell of His excellent greatness, He alone is worthy of your praise!! We all long for the day when sorrow is no more, but until then, don't let the enemy steal your praise! Remember; God's faithful love is better than life.

Blessings, Rupert & Red.

JULY 13

In The Beginning: God!

Meditation Verse: Genesis 1:1 HCSB
In the beginning God created the heavens and the earth.
Scripture Reading: Genesis 1

As I was meditating on this verse, the Holy Spirit showed me several revelations. You can start to read at any point in the Bible and get a glimpse of God, even an understanding of His mercy, grace, and yes, judgement. But you will never fully grasp the awesome power of God until you read the first verse of Genesis. God has always existed, so with Him there is no beginning and no end. Eternity is an immeasurable, infinite continuum, a concept that is hard to wrap around a finite mind, even with the attempt of an explanation. So, in the beginning has nothing to do with eternity, it only exists as a measure of time. God decided to create something out of nothing, so He started with time. In the beginning is our reference point. That declaration is your starting point, not of belief, but of understanding who God is to the extent that you can. As you continue to read, faith comes, and God's plan is revealed for your life. But you must get a revelation of the beginning to settle in your spirit that you were created for forever. Time is only temporary, to give us an opportunity to prepare for eternity. Seize that time, foster relationship, only God can turn time into forever, He created the beginning, He will see you to that glorious day when time will be no more….

Blessings, Rupert & Red.

JULY 14

Persistence Has Its Rewards

Meditation Verse: Luke 11:9 HCSB

"And so I tell you, keep on asking, and you will receive what you ask for. Keep on seeking, and you will find. Keep on knocking, and the door will be opened to you."

Scripture Reading: Luke 11:5-13

For a good part of my life I had thought, that when you petition God for anything, you just ask once and then leave it alone. To do anything more would show a lack of faith. I had heard that taught by many popular preachers and I accepted it as true. But that was when I did not really search the scriptures as I do now. I will research anything that does not agree with my spirit, not because I want to prove anyone wrong, but because I have developed a Berean mentality. I must search for myself to see if it is so. Acts 17:11 (NKJV). So, in studying the 11th chapter of Luke, I discovered that God respects and honors persistence. There is reward in persistence of prayer, because it is not a measure of unbelief or doubt, but a measure of faithfulness. Like the man in bed with his family, finally got up to give his neighbor bread, and the woman who showed up in court every day until the judge heard her case, and like the woman with the issue of blood, who fought through the crowd because she knew Jesus could heal her, persistence has its place in the believer's life. Can you think of anything that you were praying for, and you just gave up because you felt the answer was, no? Sometimes we talk ourselves out of a blessing because we don't really believe that God is for us. And so, we give up, often at the moment of breakthrough, never realizing how close we were to the goal. Jesus is saying no, keep on asking, keep on seeking, keep on knocking, it is not a futile exercise, those verbs are continuous. Jesus is looking for persistence, not just people throwing up wishes, that is not productive prayer. Our willingness to be persistent is what will get us through the hard times. Consistency in prayer is the key to watching God move in your life. It is not just the prayer that will produce results, but faith will grow because of what you say, and that faith pleases God. So, stay persistent in your asking, seeking, and knocking, God will give you victory!

Blessings, Rupert & Red.

JULY 15

You Can Trust God

Meditation Verse: Nahum 1:7 NLT

The Lord is good, a strong refuge when trouble comes. He is close to those that trust Him.

Scripture Reading: Nahum 1:7-8

Trust: An assured reliance on character, ability, and strength or truth of someone or something. Are you trustworthy? Are you someone who can be depended upon? I like this definition of trust, it implies relationship, and you must be able to be trustworthy in that relationship, but you also must trust the one who is in relationship with you. God knows those who have put their trust in Him. Spurgeon, the great commentator put it like this "God knows us, He knows our prayers, tears, he knows our wishes, He knows that we are not what we want to be, but He knows what we desire to be." (Source: Blue Letter Bible blueletterbible.org). Someone who knows us that intimately, who sees our groans, and our ups and downs. Who understands and forgives us when we fail, even when we are constantly beating ourselves up because of our weaknesses. Even when we don't trust ourselves, we can put our trust in Him! When we stand amid chaos, we need to be able to rely on that strength of character that God provides. Know that God is the One in whom you can put your trust completely. Others, including yourself will fail you, but God will never fail you. I need to be close to God, so that when trouble comes, and it will, He knows I am trusting in Him. God already knows all the plans and purposes for our lives. You just need to trust that He will guide you to, through and out of whatever we face in this life. He is close to those that trust Him...

Blessings, Rupert & Red.

JULY 16

Rejoice, Pray, Give Thanks, Repeat...

Meditation Scripture: 1 Thessalonians 5:16-18 NKJV

Rejoice always, pray without ceasing, in everything give thanks; for this is the will of God in Christ Jesus for you.

Scripture Reading: 1 Thessalonians 5:12-22

Rejoice, pray, and give thanks, the trifecta for a relationship of gratitude! We say that God is good as easily as we say good morning, but do we really believe it? Or is it just something that we say? To be grateful is not to be unaware of adversity. It is the ability to give thanks regardless of the adversity we face. For us to be thankful in everything we must receive thankfulness in our hearts. Because it is through your heart that you will discern God's goodness. It is not possible to be thankful "for" everything, but it is possible to be thankful "in" everything. It is one of the many reasons why prayer is necessary continuously. Believe me, your prayer life will establish your level of gratitude, because you cannot praise without it! It is like water without the wet, it won't happen! The more you put these things into practice the more you will understand the goodness of God. The more you understand the goodness of God, the more you will praise, the more you praise, the more you will be able to say in earnest, from your heart, God is good! Rejoice, pray, and be thankful unto Him, and watch gratefulness flow from your heart.... It is His will for you.

Blessings, Rupert & Red.

JULY 17

Recall God's Goodness

Meditation Verse: Psalms 77:11-12 HCSB

I will remember the Lord's works; yes, I will remember Your ancient wonders. I will reflect on all You have done and meditate on Your actions.

Scripture Reading: Psalms 77

Your memory should be precious to you, it is the keeper of your life's hopes, dreams, and accomplishments. What is sometimes problematic, it is not selective. It will remember the things you treasure, but also the things you would rather forget. So, at times it is a blessing and at times it may seem to be a curse. But notwithstanding that, you pray against losing it altogether. It is worth it to remember the bad in order to keep the good. What do you do, however, when the bad seems to outweigh the good? When the enemy fills your mind with all the things that challenge your resolve, and paralyzes you from moving forward? Despite the enemy's attempt to immobilize you, just remember all the times that God has brought you through. Remember the good things he has brought to your life, the way he has kept you and shown you, His favor. The fact that you are standing today is proof that He has brought you through some situations. You can move forward because you remember the goals you've achieved both large and small, that could only have occurred by God's grace, mercy, and favor. So, when the enemy comes in like a flood, allow the standard of the Lord to come against it! You remember how He came through before; He will do it again! His mighty acts are not limited, His strength and power are everlasting!! God can do anything but fail!! Now that is worth remembering!!

Blessings, Rupert & Red.

JULY 18

Only God!

Meditation Verse: Titus 3:4-5 NLT

But - When God our Savior revealed His kindness and love, He saved us, not because of the righteous things we had done, but because of His mercy. He washed away our sins giving us a new birth and new life through the Holy Spirit.

Scripture Reading: Titus 3:1-11

Just a gentle reminder, we did not save ourselves, we were saved by God's grace and God's mercy. There was never anything that we could have done to rescue our lives from eternal separation from God. On our own we could not have been good enough, benevolent enough, caring enough, or even loving enough. Going to church does not save you, giving does not save you, being on various boards and offices of the church does not save you, reading the Bible does not save you, reciting the ten commandments does not save you, in and of themselves none of these wonderful works, will save you. "He saved us," this is the essence and benchmark of the gospel. God is the initiator; we receive from Him before we can give anything back. Our very lives belong to Him whether we believe it or not. Nothing happens without Him, and we cannot do anything without the breath of life that was breathed into our very soul. So, the only thing we can render is our hearts to receive His love and pardon so that our useless works become acts of love and obedience, because of the new life that we have been given because of the Holy Spirit. It was never about you or what you can do, it is about what God has done for you…

Blessings, Rupert & Red.

JULY 19

Are You Speaking Life or Death?

Meditation Verse: Proverbs 18:21 NKJV

Life and death are in the power of the tongue, and those who love it will eat its fruit.

Scripture Reading: Proverbs 18

Until we realize that words matter, we will either be speaking to our growth or to our demise. A thought unspoken is a thought that dies unheard, but once said can never be taken back. Once words enter the ear gate it becomes record. James said that the tongue is the one thing that cannot be tamed, but our self-control must improve if we are going to walk in love. Too many apologies whether heartfelt or duplicitous will begin to land on deaf ears. How someone feels will always negate or confirm what was said. Don't be that person that causes bad feelings to surface whenever they are around. To live in a world where everyone "speaks their mind" has very little to do with truth. It is, recurrently, a lack of self-control, and a desire to inflict pain. Gossip and innuendo are only tools of assumption, which is the lowest form of knowledge. It does no one any good to engage in it and it can murder the reputation of one who is the target. God has a higher elevation of living that He wants us to aspire to. Yes, people will come and go and leave their mark or lack thereof, but the legacy we should desire to leave should be one of love, not dissention and treachery. Let brotherly love continue… take the high road, uproot and grow away from that negativity, even poisonous trees have roots.

Blessings, Rupert & Red.

JULY 20

Confession Is Good For The Soul

Meditation Verse: 1 John 1:10 NLT

If we claim we have not sinned, we are calling God a liar and showing that His word has no place in our hearts.

Scripture Reading: 1 John 1:5-10

But I am a good person!! We believe it was Jesus who said, "There is no one good but One, that is, God." Luke 18:19b (NKJV). When it comes to sin there are no good people. The Bible records in Romans 3:10 (NKJV), "There is none righteous, no, not one." We must first recognize that the problem is in us before we can do anything about it. Just as the law revealed that we have inherited a sin problem, the remedy is revealed in the Word. We need the courage to confess, "I am a sinner and I need the shed blood of Jesus to cleanse me." When we deny our sin, we are self-deceived, and we are denying God's Word. You want to be good? You can only be good when you have the only one who is good living inside you. We are not talking about perfection here; we are simply talking about relationship. "Confess," translates a verb in the present tense that means that we should keep on confessing. 1John 1:9b (NLT), says: "He is faithful and just to forgive us and cleanse us from all unrighteousness." What an incredible promise! So, even though sin is always present, so is the remedy, not the license to sin, but to lead us out of sin, so that we can have fellowship with God. Let the truth of God transform you, so that you come to realize the importance of confession, it's not just good for the soul, it is good for eternity.

Blessings, Rupert & Red.

JULY 21

Obedience Pleases God

Meditation Verse: Proverbs 21:3 NLT

The Lord is more pleased when we do what is right and just than when we offer Him sacrifices.

Scripture Reading: Proverbs 21

How many times have we, as either a child or an adult, regretted the choices we made, when the consequence was far worse than the decision all because we chose not to listen and obey? At this point everybody should have one hand if not both hands up! Here is the moral of all your stories: "Obedience is better than sacrifice!" 1Samuel 15:22b (NLT). Animal sacrifices was a way to keep in right standing with God. It was a way to pay for sins that had been committed throughout the year. It was also a way to make petitions known, and a way for praise and worship to be offered. There were so many sacrificial rituals, that the religious spent most of their time at some type of altar or another! There had to be an easier way, and there was in the Person of Jesus Christ. He was the one and only perfect sacrifice, that once and for all paid the price and sealed our futures with the glorious gift of eternal life. God knew that His grace was sufficient, He only asked one thing, Obedience. Throughout the Old and New Testaments, the idea of obedience was instilled so that consequences to the contrary could be avoided. If we obey the law of Love, everything else would be covered. The way we treat others is far more important to God than we imagine. Why? Because God takes the way we treat others personally. Here are a few reasons why that is true: "Love your neighbor as you love yourself." Galatians 5:14b (NLT), "Assuredly, I say to you, inasmuch as you did to one of the least of these my brethren, you did it to me." Matthew 25:40 (NKJV). And just for good measure, "And just as you want men to do to you, you also do to them likewise." Luke 6:31 (NKJV). We encourage you, obey God's Law of Love and you will save yourself a life full of regret. This is what pleases the Lord.

Blessings, Rupert & Red.

JULY 22

Live Holy, See God

Meditation Verse: Isaiah 6:3 NKJV

And one cried to another and said: "Holy, holy, holy is the Lord of hosts; The whole earth is full of His glory!"

Scripture Reading: Isaiah 6

Holy, holy, holy, is the Lord God Almighty! Holiness is not just a personality trait of God; it is characteristic of His entire being. It is also a requirement of God. There should be a noticeable difference in the way we conduct ourselves. To be holy is to be set apart. What does that mean exactly? Does it mean we don't interact with our fellow man? Does it mean that we esteem ourselves above others? Does it mean we don't enjoy life or have fun? None of these examples are true. A life of holiness is the emulation and the aspiration to conform to the image of Christ. It is being set apart for His purposes. It is growing in grace and in the fruit of the Spirit. It is avoiding evil and a life of excess. It is not cultivating arrogance and pride. Being holy is recognizing that God is first, and then putting Him first. Giving Him the praise, worship and honor that He deserves. Loving God above the things of this world. If all the things of this world were to dissolve and fade away, God would remain. He is not creature, He is Creator. So, why live your life for something that is temporary? Live your life holy, that is the eternal expectation, for then you get to see God.

Blessings, Rupert & Red.

JULY 23

Eternity; Our Destiny, One Way Or Another…

Meditation verse: Psalms 90:12 NKJV
So, teach us to number our days, that we may gain a heart of wisdom.
Scripture Reading: Psalms 90

It is not our wish to appear morbid, but truth transcends all emotion, and a dose of reality is always needed to put things in proper perspective. This verse is from a Psalm written by Moses, around the time that God told the people of Israel that they were going to lose a generation in the wilderness because of their sin. If you are twenty years old and you were told that you would live only thirty-eight more years, how would you spend it? In relation to eternity that works out to less than a minute!! That is a sobering thought. From the moment we are born we are marching toward the grave. Time is never really on our side. When we understand the brevity of life, then it should be a priority to redeem the time, a desire that counts as wisdom. We don't know about you, but we want to spend the rest of our days in the joy of the Lord. Do not forfeit your life, living it outside of Christ. It matters not what you accomplish in this life if it is not tied to eternity that relationship with the Almighty brings. It does not mean that you stop living, it means you change the reason for which you are living. This life is tough enough, but even more so when you try to live it on your own. Make God your chief joy and heaven your goal. Develop a heart of wisdom. Eternity is not an alternative lifestyle, it exists as our destiny, one way or another.…

Blessings, Rupert & Red.

JULY 24

Got Prayer?

Meditation Verse: Luke 11:1 NKJV

Now it came to pass, as He was praying in a certain place, that one of His disciples said to Him, "Lord teach us to pray, as John also taught his disciples."

Scripture Reading: Luke 11:1-4

Prayer!! The most powerful weapon in the arsenal of the Christian. Communication is everything! The best relationships are anchored in honest communication. It establishes boundaries, increases trust, brings understanding, and ensures longevity. It is a necessary two-way street. Without it, any relationship is doomed to failure. A failure to communicate is usually rooted in three things, fear, stubbornness, and selfishness. Why would you want to be in a relationship where you don't or won't communicate? Your relationships should mirror the one with your Heavenly Father. Communicating with God, through prayer, will bring you to the seat of wisdom, that if applied will cause some relationships to flourish and some to cease. God knows what is best for you and when you keep the lines of prayer open, it will bring peace to your life. Make it a priority to pray to God in season or out of season, good times, or bad. It is possible to have great resolve and make better decisions because of prayer. Talk to God throughout the day, every day! Prayer works! God's ear is always open, He will hear and answer; it will be for you the beginning of a beautiful relationship.

Blessings, Rupert & Red.

JULY 25

Are You Redeemed? Say So!!

Meditation Verse: Psalms 107:2 NKJV
Let the redeemed of the Lord say so, Whom He has redeemed from the hand of the enemy.
Scripture Reading: Psalms 107

If you name the name of Jesus, you have an obligation and a duty to say why. We were all given the mandate of the great commission. A wise pastor once said that we should learn to share Jesus without fear. Fear is the one thing that paralyzes progress. It has more side effects than most medicines. Fear can take over your whole way of life but think about this; most people don't fear talking down someone or making fun of them or exposing their personal issues. Why is it that we have a hard time telling people how good God is and all the things that He has done in our lives? We should be shouting from the rooftops, going from pillar to post and everywhere in between. Whatever others might think or say, the redeemed have overwhelming reasons for declaring the goodness of the Lord. Spurgeon says: "Ours is a particular redemption, so we must offer a particular praise. The Redeemer is so glorious, the ransom price so immense, the redemption so complete, that we are under sevenfold obligations to give thanks unto the Lord and exhort others to do so." (Source: Blue Letter Bible blueletterbible.org) So, let go of your fear and let God be exalted! Boast in the Lord and the joy of your salvation! He has redeemed you from the enemy! Victory is not only yours, but also guaranteed!! So, what more do you need?! Let the redeemed of the Lord say so!!

Blessings, Rupert & Red.

JULY 26

First Things First

Meditation Verse: Matthew 6:33 NKJV

But seek first the kingdom of God and His righteousness, and all these things shall be added unto you.

Scripture Reading: Matthew 6:25-34

To first seek the kingdom of God should be the choice of all who are saved, because truthfully, how you live everyday will either reinforce that decision or deny it. We should also remember that statement in its immediate context. Jesus talked about worry in this chapter, we ought to exchange the habit of worry with the passion of concern for the kingdom. What is being demanded in this verse, is a commitment to find and do the will of God. This must be given priority so that God's divine order will take place in our lives. "All these things," include a supply of what is needed by the God of all provision, the portion of indescribable peace, and joy indescribable that only God can give, and life everlasting. Our greatest desire should be to aspire to true relationship with God and be a part of the fellowship of the kingdom. This can only be accomplished when we put God first, live righteously to the best of our ability, and watch God do the rest...

Blessings, Rupert & Red.

JULY 27

Because Of Christ, We Can!

Meditation Verse: Ephesians 2:18 NLT

Now all of us can come to the Father through the same Holy Spirit because of what Christ has done for us.

Scripture Reading: Ephesians 2:11-18

It is one thing to acknowledge something, it is another to act as if it is so and put it into practice. Jesus said: "I am the Truth." John 14:6a (NLT). You believe it, or you don't. if you do then no other truth will do, if you don't then you believe like the world that everyone has their version of "truth." The body of Christ is not made up of sects, and so-called religions. It is made up of those who have claimed Jesus Christ as "The Truth." We come to Christ because of what He has done for us, not because of anything you did or can do for anyone else. To all of us he gave equal access. There is no distinction between Jew and Gentile. Equal. Access. Ephesians 2:18 says "Now all of us can." That word can in this context means ability, we all have the ability to come to the Father. It is a choice, you can't make it for me, and I can't make it for you, but there is no exclusion, we all can. The only one who can reject this choice is you. When one group tries to influence another of anything other than what this verse means, they are not walking in truth. They are not acting as if it is so and living it. It should be impossible to take this verse out of context. The whole chapter brings it to this conclusion. Don't let anyone tell you that one person is more worthy of salvation than another. You have equal access because of "The Truth." Jesus said it! And that settles it, and we are so grateful because of it....

Blessings, Rupert & Red.

JULY 28

It Is Who You Know That Counts

Meditation verse: Psalms 9:10 NKJV

And those who know Your name will put their trust in You; For You, Lord, have not forsaken those who seek You.

Scripture Reading: Psalms 9

Until you know God's name, you won't be able to grow your trust. Knowing means having an intimate understanding of someone or something. It implies relationship. And without relationship, things can't grow. Knowledge is important for growth to occur. In knowing someone you also must be willing to be vulnerable and transparent. What we sometimes fail to realize is that God already knows us intimately, He is simply waiting on us to do our part. You want the blessings of God? Get to know Him, to know Him is to trust Him, and He will never leave you alone or forsake you. The wonderful thing about God is, with Him you will always get the better and best part of the relationship. So, let go and let God! He can be trusted to see you through! Knowledge can be a beautiful thing!!

Blessings, Rupert & Red.

JULY 29

The Godless Lack Wisdom..

Meditation Verse: Psalms 14:1 NLT

Only fools say in their hearts, "There is no God." They are corrupt, and their actions are evil; not one of them does good!

Scripture Reading: Psalms 14

What is the definition of a fool? Both the Biblical record and Webster's dictionary describe the fool as lacking in judgement and prudence. The Bible in fact has a lot to say about fools, reason enough to pay close attention! If the truth is to be told, we have all acted foolishly at one point or another in our lives. Usually the result of a selfish and self-centered mindset. The result of foolishness is sin and vice versa. The Bible calls the man or woman a fool that says there is no God. To deny the one who created you and gave you life, seems foolish to us, but we suppose that there are those who think that we are the foolish ones! You may call us unreasonable but, we cannot wrap our heads around the fact that our bodies, that are so wonderfully complex and intricate, with it's cellular, and nerve structure, developed organs and brain function, was the result of some random explosion. What has corrupted the thinking of man that he would try to negate the beauty of creation and deny the existence of a Creator? To not see God in all creation is to walk around as if you have no sight! We have always said, and it bears repeating: Without God in your life, life will never truly make sense. No matter how much knowledge you attain, you will never be able to create something out of nothing. It is only the wisdom of God that gives you the power to create in the first place. You can't create love, peace, hope, joy, faith, emotion, these things exist only because of the will of God. There are many things that man may improve on, but that ability only comes from God. Don't allow your intellect to supersede your reason for being. Don't believe that your creativity is a sign of complete independence. Don't determine that you don't need God. In other words, don't be a fool!!

Blessings, Rupert & Red.

JULY 30

Are You Hungry Yet?

Meditation Verse: Matthew 5:6 HCSB
"Those who hunger and thirst after righteousness are blessed, for they will be filled."
Scripture Reading: Matthew 5:1-12

Ever get those hunger pangs that cause you to put everything on hold until you get something to eat? We mean real food, just a snack won't do! In this modern western hemisphere, most people do not know what it is like to be truly hungry. When Jesus was teaching, he was talking in a time and culture, where hunger was a stark reality. We hunger and thirst after many things; power, authority, success, happiness, wealth, but do we really hunger and thirst after righteousness? The desire to live in a way that is pleasing to God. Spurgeon the great commentator said, "It is not enough to know that my sin is forgiven, oh that my nature could be changed, so that I, a lover of sin, could be a lover of that which is good!" (Source: Blue Letter Bible blueletterbible.org). Not so that we could just live holy, but to also have a hunger to see more righteousness exist in our families, communities, cities, and throughout the land. It is a passion and zeal that needs to be just as intense as true hunger and thirst can be. Jesus promised that this kind of hunger and thirst will be filled; but unlike a good meal that can leave you feeling stuffed, this is a profound filling, that will leave you completely and totally satisfied, yet still wanting more....

Blessings, Rupert & Red.

JULY 31

Walk This Way!!

Meditation Verse: Psalms 23:6 NKJV

Surely goodness and mercy shall follow me all the days of my life; and I will dwell in the house of the Lord forever.

Scripture Reading: Psalms 23

This is the final verse of what may well be the world's most popular and famous psalm. Millions of people have memorized this psalm in its entirety. It is to us a psalm of unbelievable comfort and courage. We both learned this psalm in Sunday School as children. We have recited it countless times; and sat down to read it hundreds of times over the years. It has never failed to give us comfort and strength when we needed it. The saint and sinner alike have either read it or recited it in times of trouble or need. It is like a balm of healing power to the soul. It is simply titled, The 23rd Psalm, a psalm of David. David's poetic yet powerful declaration at the end of this psalm, fills us with hope, as he says, "surely goodness and mercy shall follow me." A truth that has manifested itself over the years, that David experienced first-hand. One that we can attest to as well because God's goodness and mercy has brought us to this point in our lives. Anyone who can look back over their lives and not believe that the mercy of God has been instrumental to their actual survival is just dishonest. We are alive because of His mercy. Why? Because God is good!! We need His love and mercy in our lives every day, it is both the reasons why we live, and the result of relationships. God never leaves us, so His benevolence follows us even through the valley of the shadow of death. Life and people may disappoint, but He never disappoints. And even when this life is ready for physical transition, our dwelling place with God is secure forever. Don't take God's goodness and mercy for granted. Let it be an intentional plan for your life, present and future. That is the path that will lead you into the house of the Lord forever.

Blessings, Rupert & Red.

AUGUST 1

Forward! Ever Forward!!

Meditation Verse: Philippians 3:13 NLT

No, dear brothers and sisters, I have not achieved it, but I focus on this one thing: Forgetting the past and looking to what lies ahead.

Scripture Reading: Philippians 3:12-16

FOCUS!! There are enough distractions on this journey that will throw us off the proper path. There is always much to do, and as many reasons why you ought not to! There are constant plans afoot to cause you to waver. You must realize that the enemy will try to make you look backward to the point of immobilization. There will be times when you will be required to put the blinders on and concentrate on the task in sight. Then there will be times to take them off and enjoy the view. God has an expectation of maturity from His children. Develop that childlike faith and use it to move forward. Like a child that can't wait to grow up to take on more mature responsibilities, such should be our attitude. But with growth, should come understanding, because you can grow without maturing, but you cannot mature without growth. Sometimes it is good to reminisce, but don't let it cause you to live in memory lane and forget what lies ahead. Like Paul, we are not perfect, but we must look forward if we want to progress. Faith will increase for the journey if we focus on what is important. Here is the best advice; Keep your eyes on Jesus who is the author and finisher of your faith, Hebrews 12:2a (NKJV paraphrased), in that way you will not only know your destination, but you will finish strong!!

Blessings, Rupert & Red.

AUGUST 2

Your Word Establishes Your Character

Meditation Verse: Psalms 138:2 NKJV

I will worship toward Your holy temple and praise Your name for Your loving kindness and Your truth; For You have magnified Your word above all Your name.

Scripture Reading: Psalms 138

How important is your word to you? Do you say what you mean and mean what you say? Are you trustworthy? Can you be counted on when needed? Or do you say one thing and do another? God expects us to live with integrity. Our worship is or should be in obedience to God, no, not perfect but authentic. The manifestation of His character in us is what we should be seeking. Because God is faithful and full of mercy, our lives should reflect truth. If it is important enough to God to esteem his Word above His name, our word should be our bond! God has proven Himself trustworthy time and time again, and the veracity of His word is irrefutable. Integrity is not an emotion; it is a practiced principle which means it can be learned. It builds character and brings freedom. Practice integrity, let truth speak for you, allow it to become more important than your name, and then your name will become important to others, not for your sake, but for the sake of the Kingdom. God will elevate those He can trust.

Blessings, Rupert & Red.

AUGUST 3

The Difference Between Now and Then

Meditation Verse: Mark 10:31 NLT

But many who are the greatest now will be least important then, and those who seem least important now will be the greatest then.

Scripture Reading: Mark 10:17-31

We don't get celebrity worship!! Why would you idolize someone who has no intention of doing anything for you? Who does not know or even care that you exist, not to mention that you do not fit into their immediate or long-term plans! We are not talking about admiration; to admire someone for their skill, talent, passion, contribution, or dedication is warranted or even encouraged; but to be unreasonably obsessed with people on a superficial level is just foolishness. It is also a violation of the first commandment. God has painted a clear picture of people who are impressed with themselves, and those who see value in that; "They have their reward." Matthew 6:16b (NKJV). There is a big difference between now and then, and a lack of humility will follow you into a useless then! When you become wise enough to discover that only God can save, satisfy, promote, touch, heal, and deliver you, then you will realize just who is worthy of your worship. Man's validation of you cannot give you a seat in the Kingdom. Only relationship with God can give you that. Bottom line? You will eventually stand before God, and there is not a celebrity in this world that will be able to speak for you! Make sure that the One who speaks for you will say, "Well done, my good and faithful servant, you were faithful over a few things, now I will make you ruler over many things." Matthew 25:21 (NKJV). That is the difference between now and then....

Blessings, Rupert & Red.

AUGUST 4

There Is No Life Without Christ

Meditation Verse: Psalms 18:2 NKJV

The Lord is my rock and my fortress and my deliverer; My God, my strength, in whom I will trust; My shield and the horn of my salvation, my stronghold.

Scripture Reading: Psalms 18

Do you ever stop to wonder how trivial we are with our words? We tend to over-exaggerate situations or even their importance by our choice of description. "I would give my right arm for those shoes!" "This chocolate cake is to die for!" "That suit is everything!" "I would kill for some food right now!" These types of expressions have become part of our everyday vernacular. This is by no means a criticism, merely an observation. This is just another aspect of human nature that intrigues us. It causes us to think, how do we describe something or someone who is indeed indescribable? Words like awesome, amazing, and phenomenal come to mind. When we think of how God saved us, delivered us, and set us free, we are at a loss for words. It is beyond description. We could not over-emphasize it if we tried. Man's description falls short, God's does not, he declared; "I AM!!" "I Am your rock, your deliverer, your fortress!! I Am all that you could ever need or want, because I AM!!" There are a lot of things that you could live without, no matter how much you believe you need it. Truth is, without Christ, you cannot truly live.

Blessings, Rupert & Red.

AUGUST 5

Stay The Course!

Meditation Verse: Hebrews 2:1 HCSB

We must, therefore, pay even more attention to what we have heard, so that we will not drift away.

Scripture Reading: Hebrews 2:1-4

Growing up in Mom and Dad's house was no joke! Discipline and whippings were given generously when needed. There were six of us, so they stayed busy. Oh, I had the best childhood ever, I had no remembrance of hard times. We had enough food, clothing, a roof over our heads and parents that loved us and demonstrated it daily. When you feel that secure, you feel that you have all you need, and you don't realize so much the things you did without. As you get older though, you want more and more independence, and precipitously, what mom and dad had to say became irrelevant. Advice was received with an "eye roll" and you start to distance yourself from their principles. We then make decisions based on our own desires and often shortsighted thinking. Frequently, regret sets in and you wish that you had listened and heeded their advice. Principles remain principles, truth remains truth, right remains right. These things are immutable. God wants to save you from regret. His Word is good advice. While we may have a desire to drift away and do our own thing, the consequences are too costly. Get back to the place where you can feel secure. God loves you and demonstrates it daily. Heed His Word, learn His principles, walk in His truth. Remember, the only way to prevent drift is to make sure your anchor holds and grips the Solid Rock!

Blessings, Rupert & Red.

AUGUST 6

Intelligent Design; It's A Thing!!

Meditation Scripture: Romans 1:20 NLT

For ever since the world was created, people have seen the earth and sky. Through everything God made, they can clearly see His invisible qualities, His eternal power, His divine nature. So, they have no excuse for not knowing God.

Scripture Reading: Romans 1:18-25

We know that we have talked about this a few times, but it is hard for us to fully understand how people can walk around day after day, month after month, year after year, oblivious to the truth that there is a God. How is it possible to live among such beauty that exists in this world, the way our senses come alive when we gaze upon its natural wonders. Even if you have not been privileged to travel, the images portrayed on television, photographs taken by friends, the beauty in the country or island right where you are should bring you to the conclusion of intelligent design. Just an upward glance at the day or night sky should be enough to bring praise to your lips! We understand that the world can be an ugly place because of the greed and evil of man. That is in total opposition to what God desires, and reflects the attitude that they (man), don't believe that they have anyone to answer to. The truth is that none of their conceited, self-absorbed thinking will count as an excuse. In the face of all that is around them, the irrefutable evidence, they still believe that their own intellect is too important to worship the Creator. Stop! Look! Listen! What you are experiencing and seeing is created by the One that you can't see, yet the proof that He exists is everywhere! Don't be too smart for your own good! Acknowledge your Creator while there is still time. Worship the One true God who is your reason for being. You are already out of excuses. Don't wait till you are out of time…

Blessings, Rupert & Red.

AUGUST 7

Always Faithful, Never Forsaken

Meditation Verse: Psalms 37:25 NKJV

I have been young, and now am old; Yet I have not seen the righteous forsaken, nor his descendants begging bread.

Scripture Reading: Psalms 37

We are not yet ready to say that we are old, although some mornings will contradict that statement! I guess you could say we have moved beyond the young stage! We have spent a considerable amount of time on this earth. My wife and I have travelled extensively and have seen more of this world than some will see in ten lifetimes. We say that not in a conceited way, but to make a point. Our God is faithful!! We certainly have not been perfect by any stretch of the imagination, but God has blessed us beyond measure. Notwithstanding the struggles, turmoil, and pain we have endured, we have also experienced the favor and grace of God, joy, peace, contentment, laughter, and the unconditional love of family! To say that our life so far has been amazing would be an understatement! I need and want you to know that God is still in the blessing business. Trusting God may not be easy sometimes, but it is to your advantage! Does that mean that you get everything that you want? No, but you will have everything that you need, and that may be all you want. God expects us to do our part however, just because you are here does not entitle you to favor, but when you honor God in everything, He will honor you. Give your life to Him and He will never forsake you. Your best life is only one decision away. It will be more than you could ever ask, think or even imagine!!

Blessings, Rupert & Red.

AUGUST 8

Correct Hearing Gains Wisdom

Meditation Verse: Matthew 11:15 NLT
Anyone who has ears should listen and understand!
Scripture Reading: Matthew 11:1-19

As I was reading this morning, I came across this verse and it had me thinking, my mom would always say to us growing up, "Why won't you listen? You were born with ears!" It is easy to tune out what we don't want to hear, we develop convenient filters to keep out what we consider noise. To hear with understanding requires a sensitivity that comes from God. It is called wisdom. It is necessary for you to hear with clarity. Believe it or not we train our ears to hear only what we deem important to our flesh. There are times when we need to take into our ear gates the words that God is speaking to us. There is a level of hearing that we all need that goes beyond the physical. It is perfected through an open heart and brings you to the place of understanding that God is telling you something that is relevant and important for your life. Don't tune out when you know that God is speaking! Sometimes we just don't want to listen, and we just don't want to know. That attitude is always to our detriment. God has placed the desire for His voice in our hearts, but the choice is ours, hearing is the first step, doing is the next. There is a reason why we were born with ears, so, listen!!

Blessings, Rupert & Red.

AUGUST 9

Whom or What Do You Love?

Meditation Verse: 1 Timothy 6:10 NKJV

For the love of money is a root of all kinds of evil, for which some have strayed from the faith in their greediness, and pierced themselves through with many sorrows.

Scripture Reading: 1 Timothy 6:2-10

One of most misquoted scriptures in the Bible, most people lose the truth of this very important verse. There is nothing evil about money in and of itself. This is more about the condition of your heart than the need for currency. When you love something to the exclusion of everything else, it causes chaos in your life. When you get to a point where you would do any and everything to acquire it, evil is lurking at your door. The nursing and enabling of a bad habit will cause that evil to surface in your life. The love of money can motivate any sin on the face of this earth! There is nothing wrong with having nice things, it becomes problematic when those things have you! When your heart is set only upon what you can gain in this life, you lose all perspective on eternity. Don't let the love of money rob you of your relationship with God, and the expectation of heaven. The desire to be rich can only be truly balanced with the desire for spiritual gain, everything else will fall short. You will never see a trailer following a hearse!! The gold you have may be a precious and desirable commodity in this life, but in eternity, God paves the streets with it! Love God, not money!!

Blessings, Rupert & Red.

AUGUST 10

Worship Is A Beautiful Thing

Meditation Scripture: Psalms 29:2 NKJV

Give unto the Lord the glory due to His name; Worship the Lord in the beauty of holiness.

Scripture Reading Psalms 29

Praise Break!!

This verse says it all! God is worthy of our praise! He is Sovereign! He is the Creator of everything! Did you know that we were created for His praise, His worship, and His glory? If God is Alpha and Omega, the beginning and the end, then He is also our beginning and our end. Our lives are in His hands! God is your present, your future and your eternal destination! Live your life to give Him glory! "We laud and magnify your Holy Name, we praise You O God, heaven and earth are full of your glory! There is none like You, past, present and future, forever You are God and God alone! You only are worthy of all praise, honor, and glory! Bless the Lord, O my soul; And all that is within me, bless His Holy Name! Psalm 103:1 (NKJV)." Everything that is created praises God. You who have speech and the ability to articulate have no excuse! Praise Him now!! Do not ever let a rock cry out in your place...

Blessings, Rupert & Red.

AUGUST 11

Forgiveness: Doing The Hard Thing

Meditation Verse: Matthew 5:7 NKJV
Blessed are the merciful for they shall obtain mercy.
Scripture Reading: Matthew 5:1-12

"I forgive you." Those words are among the most powerful that a person can utter. They are also among the hardest. We are all told that forgiveness is more for you than the offender, and while that is true, it can be very difficult to reconcile the pain of being hurt. Depending on the offense, the memory of it can keep you up at night. That is why forgiveness cannot depend on your mood. If you give in to how you really feel, forgiveness will never take place. To forgive means that sometimes we deny ourselves justice, and that just does not seem fair. That is why forgiveness is not just a matter of the will, it must also be a matter of the heart. God expects us to develop a heart of mercy, because He has shown us mercy. The realization of God's forgiveness concerning our own lives, puts us in a place where we have a debt that we can never repay. Our penalty was death, but God denied Himself justice so that we could receive His mercy. So, who are we to deny forgiveness to another when we have received the benefit of so much more? This is a hard lesson to learn because we want so badly to see others pay for what they did to us. Don't take all that on! Cultivate a heart of mercy, God will honor your efforts and bring you to a place of peace. The benefits will eventually outweigh the pain.

Blessings, Rupert & Red.

AUGUST 12

Earthly Minded Or Heavenly Bound?

Meditation Verse: Matthew 16:26 NKJV

For what profit is it to a man if he gains the whole world, and loses his own soul? Or what will a man give in exchange for his soul?

Scripture Reading: Matthew 16:24-28

How do you see and understand your value? Are you interested in only what you can acquire, or does it mean more to you to develop your character? Do you prefer quantity over quality, or the preservation of morals? Do you live for a life of excess, or do you prescribe to the ideal that less is more? Does the more the merrier excite you, or would you rather live your life in isolation? We ask all these questions with a focus to determine priorities. At different times in our lives, certain things take precedent over others, and that is fine, it helps to give our lives balance. Look, the struggle is very real in this world and for most people, their only priority is survival. However, unless we make Christ the focal point in our lives, we will lose perspective on our purpose and forget that there is more to life than the acquisition of "things." Unless we keep eternity in our view, we will pursue that which is only temporal. We must realize that we were meant for an eternal relationship, and that must take precedence over anything and everything else. It makes little sense to chase after things which will produce no life to the detriment of your soul. Success by the world's standards may be gratifying, but it won't truly satisfy. Why? Because it won't last. True success is measured by what you do with Jesus and how you treat people. The way to be truly wealthy is to seek first the Kingdom of God, settle that priority daily, and take nothing else in exchange. It will bring the transformation that will seal your future. Walk in that. Wouldn't you rather gain heaven than this world?

Blessings Rupert & Red.

AUGUST 13

Seek To Be A Blessing

Meditation Scripture: James 1:27 CEB
True devotion, the kind that is pure and faultless before God the Father, is this: to care for orphans and widows in their difficulties and to keep the world from contaminating us.

Scripture Reading: James 1:19-27

We are God's most prized creation! He loves us with an everlasting love. It is pure and unconditional. While he desires relationship with us it is entirely our choice. God knows that for us to love correctly, that love must first flow from Him. When you mishandle, mistreat, or abuse one another, you are rejecting His love and choosing the influence of the world. God desires that His relationship with you, mirrors that with your fellow man. You decide to love what God loves and hate what He hates. That constitutes true devotion. Relationships cannot work at cross purposes. You cannot claim to serve God and mistreat His people. We have an obligation to the less fortunate. There will be those who struggle no matter how hard they work. Living for them is slowly becoming unsustainable. There is a big difference between working and paying bills and working to pay bills. This evil world system has been perverted to operate that way. Those of us that have the ability should do what they can to help no matter how small it may seem. God sees it as pure and undefiled devotion. Want to live a life that is pure and pleasing to God? This is how you do it. Show care and compassion, operate in opposition to the world's system. Share the devotion that God has shown you, be a blessing to others, it is important to God.

Blessings, Rupert & Red.

AUGUST 14

You Better Recognize!

Meditation Verse: Ephesians 6:12 NLT

For we are not fighting against flesh and blood enemies, but against evil rulers and authorities of the unseen world, against mighty powers in this dark world, and against evil spirits in heavenly places.

Scripture Reading: Ephesians 6:10-18

The dynamic of good versus evil exists in parallel worlds. It is always hard to fight against something that you cannot see. So, it makes sense in the natural to fight what you can see. But if you can't recognize your true enemy, your fight will frustrate you and you will never have the sense of true victory. The reason for the dysfunction of this physical world is the spiritual forces of evil bent on its demise. What you see is being controlled by what you can't see. You are either walking with God or the evil one. 1 John 5:19, (HCSB), says it like this: "We know that we are of God, and the whole world is under the sway of the evil one." Satan has temporal influence over this world system, it is his oppressive methods that he employs that cause destruction, and he is using man to do it. When you are blinded by the things of the world and to the deception of the "god of this world," then you will see man as your problem and hence you engage in the fight against flesh and blood. People of God, recognize your true enemy and pray for those under the sway of the evil one. Let God fight your battles, and do not stand against the enemy without your armor, Ephesians 6:13-18, (HCSB). The sway of the wicked one is temporary, don't invest in that, put your trust in the One who holds eternity and has never lost a battle!

Blessings, Rupert & Red.

AUGUST 15

We Can Have It All!!

Meditation Verse: Psalms 24:1 NLT
The earth is the Lord's and everything in it. The world and all its people belong to Him.
Scripture Reading: Psalms 24

Ownership! People talk and sometimes brag about the things that they own. Their possessions. They worked hard and maybe sacrificed in order to buy their favorite things. And it is fine to have a nice house, a nice car, and nice things. Now the deed, the chattel mortgage, and your receipts may say that these things are yours, but at the end of the day, we own nothing! We have talked about this before; we are merely stewards of everything. All that we have is on loan from God. Earth, Sun, Sea, and Sky all on loan. Beautiful views, vistas, belong to God. Stars and moon at night, on loan. All creation was put here for man to enjoy, but even we belong to God. Be very clear about what this verse says: Everything and all, two words that leave no misunderstanding as to who has ownership. So how do you want to belong? Do you want to be just His creation or His heir? We become heirs of salvation and joint heirs with Christ when we give up who we are for who He is. Relationships bring true ownership! Are you in the will? Take advantage of something that can never be taken away, eternal and joint ownership with God....

Blessings, Rupert & Red.

AUGUST 16

What Makes You Righteous?

Meditation Verse: Mark 2:17 NLT

When Jesus heard this, He told them, "Healthy people don't need a doctor, sick people do. I have come to call not those who think they are righteous, but those who know they are sinners.

Scripture Reading: Mark 2:13-17

When you are willing to admit that you are wrong, that is a sign of maturity. Growth only occurs when you apply the wisdom that suggests the need to do and be better. When you think you are sick you monitor your symptoms, when you know you are sick you seek medical treatment. Jesus said He did not come for those who think they are righteous, but those who know they are sinners. There are those who believe that their lives are fine as long as they manage to stay out of trouble, mind their own business, and do their best not to lie and steal. And those are good principles in practice, and good for you if you can live within the boundaries of society's laws and fly under the radar as it were. Those are worthy goals, but they don't make you righteous. If you think that you are not a sinner, you have made a serious error in judgement. People think that their lives without Christ are just fine. God is calling but they don't believe He is talking to them. The Word says, "for all have sinned and fall short of the glory of God."

Romans 3:23 (NKJV). You think you are righteous, only God can make you righteous, and for that to happen you have to admit that you are a sinner. Admit that you are wrong and that you need Jesus to be made right. That is the wisdom that grows you to do and be better, you really can't afford not to.

Blessings, Rupert & Red.

AUGUST 17

Change Your Seed

Meditation Verse: Matthew 7:20 NLT
Yes, just as you can identify a tree by its fruit, so you can identify people by their actions.
Scripture Reading: Matthew 7:15-20

One of the hardest lessons to learn is that "you reap what you sow." This is not only a physical truth but a spiritual principal. When we think that we have gotten away with something, the consequence always shows up, and in ways that we least expect it. God commanded everything to produce after its own kind. Think about that for a minute, you can't expect a harvest of wheat if you have planted corn. Similarly, you cannot sow evil and reap good. You cannot circumvent that law any more than you can ignore gravity. There is no deception in the truth. Your deeds display your character. Your harvest will always expose your intention, and your actions will speak louder than your words. God has identified His Son; He is the source of life. His desire is to allow you to tap into His harvest, so that you can reap eternal life. You want to be identified as good fruit? The answer is simple, change your seed…that seed is Christ…

Blessings, Rupert & Red.

AUGUST 18

Religion Or Worship?

Meditation Verse: Mark 2:27 NLT

Then Jesus said to them, "The Sabbath was made to meet the needs of the people, and not people to meet the requirements of the Sabbath."

Scripture Reading: Mark 2:23-28

The words of Jesus are profound yet not complicated in its interpretation. While there are deep spiritual truths implied, there is a practical application which is not burdensome. In this verse Jesus is saying, human need is more important than religious ritual. Sometimes we forget amid man-made traditions that we were made for dominion. We were created to be in charge, but we traded dominion for a lie. Jesus came to restore our relationship, to bring us back to our true purpose, to give us back the life we lost. God's priority has always been His people and when we mirror that example, we begin to understand, that loving our fellow man is consistent with the image of God, that same image in which we were made. In the context of this verse Jesus was saying to the religious leaders of the day that they had missed the whole point of true worship. It is through true worship that the needs of the people were met, not an attempt to put them back in bondage. You can't tell somebody they are free and then make it impossible for them to live. The whole keeping of these man-made laws was out of harmony with God's true purpose. Our good intentions do not necessarily amount to truth. Meet the needs of the people and you will be fulfilling the law of Christ. They will know it by your love.

Blessings, Rupert & Red.

AUGUST 19

It's Time!

Meditation Verse: 2 Corinthians 6:2b NIV
I tell you, now is the time of God's favor, now is the day of salvation.
Scripture Reading: 2 Corinthians 6:1-13

Everything in this three-dimensional physical world is marked by time. There is past, present, and future. None of us can exist in all three at once, because we are all bound by the earth realm. Time evolves either positively or negatively, mostly as a direct result of our decisions. Past decisions can dictate present circumstances, and those circumstances can reveal how a future may play out. For a simple example, Let's say you were caught committing a crime, that prior bad act has you presently in court, with the possibility of prison being in your future. Time has a way of immobilizing you yet can still run past you. You can't catch it, can't beat it, can't hold it, yet you can waste it. Whether you want to or not, you use it. And depending on how you manage it, it can create memories, build relationships, foster growth or breed regret. But with all that time can do and be, it cannot exist outside itself. The best measure of it is now. Now is the best use of the dictate of time, you can't use yesterdays or tomorrows. God designed it that way. He knew that because of the rigid structure of time we can only live in the now of it. That is why there is "No time like the present." It is the only time that matters. That is why God has said in His Word, "Now is the time of salvation." You can't afford to wait. You don't have the time for it. You only ever have this moment. Nothing beyond it is promised. So, give your life over to God, only He can turn time into eternity… do it now!

Blessings, Rupert & Red.

AUGUST 20

A Unified Body

Meditation Verse: Philippians 2:2 HCSB

Fulfill my joy by thinking the same way, having the same love, sharing the same feelings, focusing on one goal.

Scripture Reading: Philippians 2:1-4

If the body of Christ is going to thrive and grow, then there is one thing that must take place. We must have unity. Jesus knew and understood that a house divided against itself would not stand. Our focus should be on the same goal, knowing that the best way to achieve it is by unity in our purpose. We must have the same mind and feeling about how the goal is reached. We ought to recognize the importance of being on one accord. Even though we may have different levels of understanding we can still agree on a common goal. The goal is unity in the faith. It is possible to have union without unity. Just being together does not guarantee unity. To think and love the same, having the same feelings will move the kingdom in the right direction. If we determine to have purpose above self, we will be on our way to a good start. Unifying the body of Christ, conforming to His image, allowing ourselves to decrease while giving Him increase is how we will achieve unity of the faith.

Blessings, Rupert & Red.

AUGUST 21

An Honorable Life

Meditation Verse: James 3:13 NLT

If you are wise and understand God's ways, prove it by living an honorable life, doing good works with the humility that comes from wisdom.

Scripture Reading: James 3:13-18

If you desire to understand God's ways you must first ascribe to Godly wisdom. Mere human wisdom will not measure up to an honorable life. Human wisdom may have good intentions but will lack a heart filled with motives that are pure. Good works with humility are the hallmark of an honorable life. Humility is strength with grace under pressure, and good works can only come from the One who is good living inside you. It is the good that does not look for a return. It is the life that does not seek praise but gives God the glory. It is why we were created, for works that will reflect to whom we belong. Letting our lives bring glory to God is more important than any earthly legacy you can leave. Only what you do for Christ that will last.

Blessings, Rupert & Red.

AUGUST 22

The Wonder Of It All!!

Meditation Verse: Psalms 8:3 NLT

When I look at the night sky and see the work of Your fingers, the moon and the stars you set in place...

Scripture Reading: Psalms 8

We love verses that talk about creation! When we look around at the things that are not man-made, things that are beyond description, things that you would not believe except your eyes are a witness to, our hearts move to a whole new level of worship! To say that God is awesome is really an understatement! It is a blessing to sit amid creation and realize that all this is for us to enjoy! It gives us such a deep appreciation for life, health, and strength. God is truly an awesome God! It makes our troubles seem small because we look at what God can do in the expanse of the universe, and we know that He's got us!! Out of every created thing, He decided to make us in His image and likeness. It is us He is after, us He wants to commune with, us He desires for relationship, us He loves, and us He wants to forgive! God is so good on so many levels, we can't tell it all! You must praise Him for who He is! If you ever need to feel loved, wanted, safe, valued, and forgiven, step one is get up, go outside, and as always look up and call on His great name!!

Blessings, Rupert & Red.

AUGUST 23

Lost And Found

Meditation Verse: Hebrews 3:7-8 HCSB

Therefore, as the Holy Spirit says: Today, if you hear His voice, do not harden your hearts as in the rebellion, on the day of testing in the wilderness.

Scripture Reading: Hebrews 3:7-19

The lesson of the children of Israel's disobedience that caused them to wander in the desert for forty years, is a sobering reminder to heed the word of the Lord. It is one thing to be lost and not know it, it is quite another to be lost and know exactly where you went wrong. God has provided a blueprint or map to show us the way to salvation. He speaks to us through His Word, and by His Spirit. The longer you hear his voice and ignore it, the harder it will eventually be to hear it at all. The wilderness is not where you want to be. Why keep going around that same mountain? Get it right with God, you have too much work to do. You know you were out of the will of God, make that detour while the road is still open, and you can make it home. There are too many who are lost and don't know it. They need you to show them the way.

Blessings, Rupert & Red.

AUGUST 24

The Power Of The Word

Meditation Verse: Hebrews 4:12 NKJV

For the word of God is living and powerful, and sharper than any two-edged sword, piercing even to the division of soul and spirit, and of joints and marrow, and is a discerner of the thoughts and intents of the heart.

Scripture Reading: Hebrews 4:11-13

Your health is important! You do everything you can, or at least you should, to ensure good health. That means making the right choices in food and exercise and recreational activities. Your spiritual health, however, is even more important. So, your choices should be even more prioritized in this realm. God's word diagnoses the condition of man with skillful precision. He can expose our spiritual health, our weakness, our unbelief, our lack of obedience. The benefits to reading God's word is inestimable. It goes far beyond the value of just reading and memorizing, the power of the Spirit through the word is transformational. It does what mere intellect can never do. God's word brings health, fruitfulness, healing, cleansing, provides counseling, prosperity, and keeps us from sin. The Word has authority and power, and nothing can stand against it. It brings life to all, and to those who would receive, eternal life. Most importantly the Word is Jesus Christ. The Eternal Ever Living Word! He is really the reason the word is alive! The reason why you read it and feel convicted is because God knows how to pierce your heart. You might as well surrender because you are in a fight, and if you go it on your own, you will lose. Win with the Living Word, anything else just won't cut it!

Blessings, Rupert & Red.

AUGUST 25

Kindness, A Simple Price To Pay

Meditation Verse: Proverbs 16:24 NLT
Kind words are like honey, sweet to the soul and healthy for the body.
Scripture Reading: Proverbs 16

It costs nothing to be nice! When you connect with people with a conscious effort to be kind, it will not only improve their day, but it can also cause a domino effect. It will also make your day brighter and you will feel a difference in your overall attitude. There have always been self-absorbed and mean people in this world, but it seems to have increased enormously in our lifetime and it is troubling. We have often wondered why we can't see the importance of treating one another with dignity and respect. Our lives are stressful enough with the business of just living, think how much of that stress we could eliminate if we tried to be kind. God said that we should have love one for another, kindness is a by-product of love, it demonstrates compassion for others and eases the pain of whatever they may be going through. We all have troubles in this world, Jesus said that we would. It is the nature of this world system. Be intentional about being a part of the solution, rather than part of the problem. Determine to be kind! It may add years to your life, besides, it is also important to God…

Blessings, Rupert & Red.

AUGUST 26

A Recipe For Life

Meditation Verse: Proverbs 3:5-6 HCSB

Trust in the Lord with all your heart, and do not rely on your own understanding; think about Him in all your ways, and He will guide you on the right paths.

Scripture Reading: Proverbs 3:1-12

These verses have been a solid lesson and blessing in my life. The two men that I have looked up to for most of my life, have counseled me constantly with this passage of scripture. My father, and my father-in-law. My Dad called it "the recipe for an effective, successful life." My father-in-law would always quote this passage, and since I have known him, he signs every card; Proverbs 3:5-6. You have to be all in with your whole heart. When your trust is in God, He takes that seriously, His commitment is to be by your side, and to guide your every step. But you must not allow your intellect to interfere with your heart (spirit man). When you start thinking that you know better, the recipe is incomplete, and your G.P.S. (God Provided Signal) becomes weak. For God to guide you, you must admit that He is Sovereign and not let pride trip you up. Then and only then will your life truly make sense. Trust Him, that is the beginning of the recipe for an effective, successful life.

Love and Blessings, Rupert & Red, Proverbs 3:5-6.

AUGUST 27

Humility, The Gentle Giant

Meditation Verse: Philippians 2:3 NKJV
Let nothing be done through selfish ambition or conceit, but in lowliness of mind let each esteem others better than himself.
Scripture Reading: Philippians 2:1-4

This verse alone is a lesson in humility. There is so much to be unpacked here that time and space will not allow. But this is oh so necessary for us in the journey to achieve unity in the faith. Four things we would like to touch on.

1. Selfish ambition: there is nothing wrong with ambition, if it is not self-absorbed. When all you want to promote is self, there is a problem. When the desire is to bring God glory, then there is nothing more to fight about because the goal is unified.
2. Conceit: When you live with the feeling that you are, more important, more able, and more talented, than anyone else, you are out of God's will. You are operating in "empty glory" and fighting against the unity that God requires of us.
3. Lowliness of mind (Humility). This is in complete contradiction to the world's mindset. Lowliness of mind in the natural is not considered an attractive trait. Again, though if the goal is to bring God glory, it is not going to happen by imposing your will on someone else. Humility seeks the good in everyone. A good dose is required to carry out the will of God.
4. Esteeming others better than yourself. The attitude of confident superiority over everything or everyone is not the foundation for healthy human relationships. When you esteem others as better than yourself, you will naturally have a heart for other's needs and concerns. This type of mentality brings unity into the body of Christ. Finally, the

key purpose here is to operate in humility. These ideas are restricted because a secular mind lacks the spiritual ground for ideas like this to grow. The truth is that God's purposes will ultimately prevail. That is what we should strive to achieve.

Blessings, Rupert & Red.

AUGUST 28

Supreme Love

Meditation Verse: 1 Corinthians 13:7 NLT

Love never gives up, never loses faith, is always hopeful, and endures through every circumstance.

Scripture Reading: 1 Corinthians 13

Love is Supreme! It is the only virtue that should be elevated above all! Nothing and no one can claim supremacy save love! It is not only necessary to our existence it is the reason we exist at all! We have chosen verse seven of this most endearing chapter, in which the virtues of love are extolled so eloquently. It speaks of the highest form of love "agape." Paul was emphasizing how love never gives up and bears up under all circumstances. This type of love has little to do with emotion but must function on a higher level. Most of us can bear all things, hope all things, and believe all things, but only for a while! To have the tenacity that this love requires, can only be achieved with the help and grace of God. We don't know about you, but it is hard work to let the irritants of this world roll off your back, especially as you grow older. But love keeps on believing, hoping and bearing and never gives up! To love as God loves should truly be our primary goal. Want to measure your spiritual maturity? Read the entire chapter of 1 Corinthians 13 and replace the word love with Jesus, (it works best with the NKJV), then read it with your name. We got a long way to go right? It may sound a little far-fetched, but one thing we have realized, your gifts and giftedness have little to do with spiritual maturity, your demonstration of love does…

Blessings, Rupert & Red.

AUGUST 29

The Best Partnership!

Meditation Verse: Proverbs 16:3 NIV
Commit to the Lord whatever you do, and He will establish your plans.
Scripture Reading: Proverbs 16:1-9

Here is a little encouragement in what we believe to be true. God wants to see you succeed. Everyone needs to commit their works to the Lord. Because we are to do everything as unto the Lord, He should be included in your plans. Not that our salvation is based on our works, but if God has laid something on your heart, it is probably wisdom to acknowledge that and partner with Him. A surrendered life is already a commitment, why would you want to make any plans without putting the Lord in the center of it? Solomon had the right idea; God can establish your plans and make your dreams come true! So, place your dreams in the Master's hands, work your plan and give Him the glory! He deserves it anyway!!

Blessings, Rupert & Red.

AUGUST 30

Chill, God's Got You!

Meditation Verse: Psalms 46:10 NKJV

Be still and know that I am God; I will be exalted among the nations, I will be exalted in the earth!

Scripture Reading: Psalms 46

This familiar verse of scripture is like a double-edged sword. These are words of both comfort and warning. For the enemies of God, it is a warning and a promise that nothing that you do will thwart the ultimate purpose and will of Almighty God. It will always be his Omnipotence against your impotence. No matter where you sit or stand you will eventually kneel. God will be exalted not only in the nations but in the entire earth! You might as well be still and recognize that you cannot prevail against the One who created heaven and earth! On the other hand, to those that love Him, find rest and peace in those same words. God is saying be calm and relax, for He will fight our battles, He will show us His strength and His great Name. We need not fear for our enemies are already defeated and our victory is already assured. We will see this played out by God's Name being exalted through all the earth. We must understand though that our timing is not God's timing, He will not fail. So, be still and know that God is in control. He is the great comforter. So, chill, God's got you!

Blessings, Rupert & Red.

AUGUST 31

The World's Way Or The Word's Way?

Meditation Verse: Proverbs 22:6 AMP/paraphrased.
Train up your children in the way that they should go [teaching them to seek God's wisdom and will for their abilities and talents], even when they are old they will not depart from it.

Scripture Reading: Proverbs 22:6

Okay! This will not take long, and it may step on a few toes, but there is too much at stake to have people all caught up in their feelings!! We have taken the liberty of paraphrasing the scripture verse, in order to make it a little more inclusive.

Most parents believe that they have a handle on how best to raise their children, and the general school of thought is: "You can't tell me what to do with my child!" And from the classroom to the playground, we have seen the result of that same attitude in the children! In some cases, the parent's behavior is just as bad or worse than the child's! For all the experts out there, there are only two ways to do anything and that includes raising children; the right way or the wrong way. Kids are going to do what they see and not so much of what they are told. So, training is just as much modelling a lifestyle that they can emulate as well as instructing them in how they should behave. That ought to be a given. There is the world's way, and then there is the Word's way. Here is the difference, the world's way promises nothing that will last or fulfill, the Word of God declares that even if a child loses their way, they will find their way back. I don't have the time or space to go through all of the variables, but this we do know and believe, no one knows more about raising children than God. So, whether you believe it or not, He is the best chance of true success for our children, and the only chance for them to experience eternity when the world's success will mean absolutely nothing.

Blessings, Rupert & Red.

SEPTEMBER 1

Never Give Up!!

Meditation Verse: Galatians 6:9 NKJV

And let us not grow weary while doing good, for in due season we shall reap if we do not lose heart.

Scripture Reading: Galatians 6:1-10

My mother would always say, "you need to develop patience, patience is a virtue!" Do you remember as a child how everything that you looked forward to would take forever to arrive? Whether it was a trip, a party, a birthday, or Christmas the expectation to be good during that endless wait seemed hardly worth the effort! But the wait was forgotten the moment the reward was received. Likewise, the pain and weariness of childbirth becomes a memory when you hear that baby's first cry. Or the long hours of study and hundreds of exams before the final walk across the stage to receive that diploma or degree. This world can and will be a drain on your patience and resources, and you will come to the point where you want to just give up, cease from your labor, and throw in the towel. But don't lose heart, God sees your struggle and He can and will strengthen you. We cannot see the end from the beginning, but God can! In time God will reward your efforts. Like the farmer plants a seed and expects a harvest, we must move from planting to expectation. Just stay focused on the purpose, there will never be a wrong time to do the right thing, and with God as your resource; the harvest will come in!! Believe that!!

Blessings, Rupert & Red.

SEPTEMBER 2

Unconditional Praise!!

Meditation Verse: Psalms 63:3 NKJV
Because your loving kindness is better than life, my lips shall praise You!
Scripture Reading: Psalms 63

Our praise of God should be unconditional!! Regardless of how they wronged you, how they made you feel, whether loss or gain, rich or poor, sad or happy, your circumstance should not negate your praise. If you can read this, you should praise. It is important to praise God for what He has done, it is more important to praise Him for who He is. We don't only praise when we feel like it. Because if that were the case, our mouths would seldom open! We will admit there are times when it is the last thing, we feel like doing, however, feelings are the last things we should put our trust in! It is God's loving kindness that warrants our praise! His mercy and grace sustain us, our lives are irrelevant without it! It is not," we live therefore we are," it is "We live because He is I AM" it is as simple as "this and that," God's loving kindness is better than life, because "this" life is short, but His love is everlasting, the love which will make "that" life eternal, Got it?

Blessings, Rupert & Red.

SEPTEMBER 3

In God We Trust?

Meditation Verse: Mark 10:24b NKJV

But Jesus answered again and said unto them, "Children how hard is it for those who trust in riches to enter the kingdom of God!"

Scripture Reading: Mark 10:23-31

In what or whom do you put your trust? The world has played a magnificent part in deceiving masses of people with a false picture of success. Why are we so driven and programmed in the selfish pursuit of temporary riches, lifestyles of excess, by any means necessary? Losing in many cases our sense of humanity believing ourselves to belong to some elite class of people who are better than those who have less. Even to the point of abusing those who struggle even on their behalf. Jesus is not against anyone being rich, but when you don't understand that your money cannot save you, give you true peace and comfort, cause you to love your neighbor or buy you true love, then you unfortunately have missed the point. If your trust is in anything or anyone but Almighty God, then it is misplaced. "For what will it profit a man if he gains the whole world and loses his own soul?" Mark 8:36 (NKJV). The acquisition of wealth is not in and of itself a bad thing, but with all your getting, get understanding and "lay-up for yourselves treasures in heaven, where neither moth nor rust destroys and where thieves do not break in and steal." Matthew 6:20 (NKJV) Trust God to protect your investment in eternity.

Blessings, Rupert & Red.

SEPTEMBER 4

World Peace Or His Peace?

Meditation Verse: John 14:27 NKJV

Peace, I leave with you, my peace I give to you; not as the world gives do I give to you. Let not your heart be troubled, neither let it be afraid.

Scripture Reading: John 14:25-31

"Peace," a state of tranquility or quiet, freedom from civil disturbance, a state of security or order within a community, provided by law, a state or period of mutual concord between governments. These are a few of the many definitions of peace as defined by Webster's dictionary. Notice something similar in all these definitions? They are all for a state or a period of time. This is the peace that the world offers, fragile, lacking stability, and temporary. In some parts of the world, they have managed to achieve this type of peace, and in others they have promised peace but so far have been unable or failed to deliver. Jesus promised peace that is everlasting and sure. The ability to receive peace and maintain it regardless of the trials and tribulations we face. This is a peace that the world does not understand. True peace is not the absence of problems, it is its presence in the midst of them. Peace that is meant for our highest good, peace that comes from a heart untroubled and not fearful. Jesus describes it as His peace, freely given to those who trust in Him. This peace can only come from relationship, so establish yourself, and walk in His peace, once you experience it, you will never want to be without it. His peace be unto you.

Blessings, Rupert & Red.

SEPTEMBER 5

Fear Is Not An Option

Meditation Verse: Psalms 56:4 NLT

I praise God for what He has promised. I trust in God, so why should I be afraid? What can mere mortals do to me?

Scripture Reading: Psalms 56

Trust in the promises of God is preeminent if you don't want to live a life that is consumed by fear. It is not that the faith walk will not feel intimidating at times, but we don't have to give in to the spirit of fear. God has promised us a sound mind full of love and power in its place. It will give you the ability to stand against the enemy and his devices. When you praise Him for the promises in your life, you will feel the strength to mount up with wings like the eagle. You will know that man cannot do anything to you. Because your trust is not in a mere mortal. God will always fight your battles. In fact, He is fighting for you right now! You don't even realize what He has already saved you from! That is reason enough to praise Him right now! His Word is full of His promises, the more you read and hear, the more your faith will grow. The more your faith grows, the less you will be afraid. It is the formula that yields the best results. God will honor your faith, because that is what pleases Him.

Blessings, Rupert & Red.

SEPTEMBER 6

We Are What We Think

Meditation Verse: 2 Corinthians 10:4 NLT
We use God's mighty weapons, to knock down the strongholds of human reasoning and to destroy false arguments.
Scripture Reading: 2 Corinthians 10:1-8

The term "carnal Christian" should be an oxymoron, but the truth is, part of the Christian's greatest struggle is his/her thought life. It is not so much the thoughts that come to you, but the thoughts that you dwell on that matters. Casting down imaginations is preventing certain thoughts from taking root that you know are not pleasing to God. They are really arguments against the mind and methods of God. They want to debate God, thinking that they have a better way. It is their way of exalting themselves against the knowledge of God. If it sounds strange that I am speaking of thoughts as if they have life, it is because when we dwell on certain thoughts to the point where we speak them into existence and they become reality, we actually give them life! That is why it is important to renew our minds. Focusing on God and His Word is the first step to renewing our minds. In order to effect change you must change the way you think. Carnal or worldly thinking will not win any battles. Remember, "The weapons of our warfare are not carnal." 2Corinthians 10:4a (NKJV). Your thought life is reflective of the decisions you will make. "For as he thinks in his heart so is he." Proverbs 23:7a (NKJ). Carnal thoughts will come, that is a given, "you can't prevent a bird from flying over your head, but you can stop it from making a nest in your hair!"

Desire the mind of Christ.

Blessings, Rupert & Red.

SEPTEMBER 7

God Is In Control

Meditation Verse: Proverbs 21:1 AMP

The king's heart is like channels of water in the hand of the Lord; He turns it whichever way He wishes.

Scripture Reading: Proverbs 21

This verse, as in many others in this chapter, is more about the realization of truth than manipulation. Here it is, God is Sovereign! He can do what he wants, when He wants, in whatever way He chooses. The king held the power of life and death in his hands, that is power! But God, is still in control. God holds and guides the human heart. It is ultimately His plan that will prevail. If God can channel the king's heart in any way He chooses, then our hearts are indeed subject to his command. While some things seem to go in our favor, and some it seems to our detriment, trust that God is working it out for our good. We have to willingly place our lives in His hands, for His purpose and glory, because whether we accept Him or reject Him, God has the final say. Whatever the king does, sooner or later he will have to bow his knee to the King of kings!! Like water flows in the direction of a chartered course, so are we subject to the purpose and plan of His sovereign will. So, you might as well get in the flow!!

Blessings, Rupert & Red.

SEPTEMBER 8

You're All I Need

Meditational Verse: Psalms 23:1 NLT
The Lord is my Shepherd; I have all that I need.
Scripture Reading: Psalms 23

Millions of people have memorized this entire psalm, it is recited as much as, if not more than, the Lord's Prayer. The first verse, however, has almost inexhaustible implications. From Genesis to Revelation God is depicted as a Shepherd, to, for and by His people. Jesus himself said in John 10:11, (NLT), "I am the good shepherd. The good shepherd sacrifices His life for the sheep." David said "The Lord is MY Shepherd, right now he belongs to me, and I am His, it is personal and present tense. Secondly, "I have all that I need," my temporal needs are met because the Shepherd sees to it. Regardless of what may come I have what I need, not because I have an endless supply of money in the bank, but because my God has an inexhaustible supply of everything! In this world system some people never can get enough, satisfaction is an elusive commodity, but the righteous have a gracious spirit of gratitude that comes from a heart of contentment. It is all about knowing "the source." Think about this, if you can truly say that the Lord is my Shepherd, in the biblical relational sense, then every promise and blessing that you need belongs to you.

Blessings, Rupert & Red.

SEPTEMBER 9

There Is Pride We Use, And Pride We Need To Lose.

Meditation Verse: Proverbs 21:2 AMP

Every man's way is right in his own eyes, But the Lord weighs and examines the hearts (of people and their motives).

Scripture Reading: Proverbs 21

Staying in Proverbs for verse 2 of this very engaging chapter, is another teachable truth. There is justifiable pride and then there is pride that we justify. And just like you believe I said the same thing, we don't always understand the difference. When your child struggles in school, yet still makes the honor roll, or your spouse graduates from a tough course and gets that promotion, or your friend exercises discipline, loses weight and keeps it off, you have good reason to be proud of them. But pride gets in the way when you make it about self; it comes naturally to justify ourselves, we do it with sincerity, believing we are entitled, or we talk ourselves into certain situations knowing that it is wrong, but stubborn pride causes us to deceive ourselves. Because everyman is right in his own eyes. We may be confident in ourselves, but God knows, He has already discerned our motives, we say, "but in my heart I know, or "I must follow my heart, (actually feelings)." Duane Garrett, commentator said it this way, "Yahweh's discernment goes beyond those who fool others, He even finds out those that have fooled themselves." (Source: Blue Letter Bible blueletterbible.org). Your self-confidence is misplaced. Your pride cannot be justified by the heart. Place your confidence in God, He will lead you the right way, so that your pride won't result in a fall. Walk with Him, keep your eyes on Him, then your way will be right in His eyes.

Blessings, Rupert & Red.

SEPTEMBER 10

Religion Or Right Living?

Meditation Verse: Proverbs 21:3 MSG

Clean Living before God and justice with our neighbors mean far more to God than religious performance.

Scripture Reading: Proverbs 21

Day three diving into the third verse of Proverbs 21.

Just because you go to church, pray, and sing in the choir, it does not exempt you from doing justice, or give you a pass from unrighteousness. It is plainly stated in God's Word that His requirements for a godly life (doing justly and showing mercy) are far more important to Him than the most pious and extensive showings of devotion. God deserves your devotion and adoration, and your service, but He also wants you to show love to your fellow man. As the saying goes, "Don't be so heavenly minded that you are no earthly good!" Your sacrifices offered to God, if given in faith and with repentance are well received, but if you fail in your moral duty to your fellow man before God, He is not pleased. If you abdicate the law of love in your interaction with people, you lose the best part of why you had a relationship in the first place, because without love everything you do becomes form and fashion. Lips that praise God but a heart that is far from His. Matthew 15:8b (NKJV paraphrased). God is not willing that any should perish, but you ignore the Word of God at your own peril. Yes, render unto God the praise and devotion that He deserves, but remember He is watching to see how you treat His most precious creation. Obedience is always better than sacrifice!!

Blessings, Rupert & Red.

SEPTEMBER 11

The Lamp Of The Wicked

Meditation Verse: Proverbs 21:4 AMP

Haughty and arrogant eyes and a proud heart, the lamp of the wicked (their self-centered pride), is sin (in the eyes of God).

Scripture Reading: Proverbs 21

We cannot seem to get away from the 21st chapter of Proverbs! This chapter is so full of wisdom, read it again and again and get it into your spirit.

This verse is talking about the actions of wicked men. Sin exists in this world, and all have fallen prey to it at one time or another. Some though, make sin their practice and their business. Those that carry themselves in insolence and defiance before God. They rail at God's very existence because He exposes their evil motives. They worship at the altar of greed and self-centeredness. They do all they can to satisfy their lusts with no regard for anyone else. All this is sin in the eyes of God. It does not matter what we think, or think we know. It is what God says that matters. There is a price to be paid for this way of life, and the end of it is not pleasant. There is a solution: Love God and live for Him. It is not wisdom to exchange eternity for the temporal. The relationship and blessings of God are far too precious to be squandered in your own greed and lust. That is a broad road that has no eternal value. The lamp of the wicked will be extinguished. Chose to be right in God's eyes, that is where the true light is, what say you?

Blessings, Rupert & Red.

SEPTEMBER 12

Tend Your Garden!

Meditation Verse: Genesis 2:15 NLT

The Lord God placed the man in the Garden of Eden to tend and watch over it.

Scripture Reading: Genesis 2:4-17

Adam was charged originally with taking care of Eden. A place that was made especially for him. He was given the freedom to live his life with one restriction, do not eat from the tree of the knowledge of good and evil. One job, one restriction. With freedom comes responsibility and restraint. Without it, you will descend into chaos. God had purpose and position for Adam, but his dependence was to be totally on his connection to God. Once Adam perverted his purpose, his connection was forever broken. He was no longer free, but a slave to his senses, and tied to only what the ground would yield. Because of Adam's disobedience we too, were born with our connection broken, dependent on our senses, and tied to the expectations of the world. But praise God, we don't have to stay that way! God has a plan that will allow you to tend your garden and fulfill His purpose for you. He sent His Son for your redemption and to reconnect you to His plan for your life. You see, we were never meant to live apart from dependence on God. His plan and purpose for your life is far more important and exceeds the world's expectation of you. When you realize that, then you will walk in freedom. You will be able to tend your garden, connected to the One who originated life for you to enjoy now and through eternity. He did it just for you. Live your life the way it was meant to be, connected to the source of all that is good, the giver of life, the One who created you for His glory. He has a garden waiting for you.

Blessings, Rupert & Red.

SEPTEMBER 13

Don't Throw Away God's Covering.

Meditation Verse: Genesis 3: 6b-7a NLT

So, she took some of the fruit and ate it. Then she gave some to her husband, who was with her, and he ate it too. At that moment their eyes were opened, and they suddenly felt shame at their nakedness.

Scripture Reading: Genesis 3:1-7

It would be easy to blame Eve for the fall of man, but that would be inaccurate. Though she did play a role and was certainly deceived, the serpent tricked her, but it was Adam who had received divine instruction who was in full out rebellion in taking part in this sin. And that is what sin is, rebellion against God. The "I" factor. I am going to do this anyway, I know what is good for me, I deserve this, I make my own decisions, I will not be told what I can and cannot do." Let me say this; "Men, our instructions from God are not to be ignored. The consequences are not worth it." Notice that nothing happened until Adam ate the fruit. The Bible says in the NLT version that it was "at that moment," that the eyes of both Adam and Eve were opened, and the light of God left them, the spiritual communication was severed, and they were left naked and ashamed. They threw off God's covering, for a covering of itchy leaves. Men, when you throw off God's protection, you lose the ability to protect your own family in the way that God intended. Every attempt to cover your nakedness before God is foolish, and appealing to any man-made remedy is bound to fail. Let the blood of Jesus Christ cover you, sustain you and keep you, it will never lose its power and your family will forever thank you for it.

Blessings, Rupert & Red.

SEPTEMBER 14

Speak Up!!

Meditation Verse: 1 Peter 3:15-16a HCSB

But honor the Messiah as Lord in your hearts. Always be ready to give a defense to anyone who asks you for a reason for the hope that is in you. However, do this with gentleness and respect.

Scripture Reading: 1 Peter 3:13-17

Three of my favorite books in the New Testament are 1st and 2nd Peter, and James. They both give practical and valuable insight into the Christian life. Now let me state that all of God's Word is profitable, just that these books speak to me in a personal way. God wants to be first in your life, anything else that is necessary for your living should be secondary. Your heart should first be established toward Him, so that life in general will be easier to bear. Your knowledge of God's Word is also a command, you cannot speak to others about your faith if you have not developed it to some degree. It does not mean that you should be the fount of all knowledge, but your desire to have relationship should cause you to seek God, and the best way is through His Word. And as a Christian you have a mandate from the Great Commission to go and tell others. Your heart and passion will speak through the Holy Spirit, who resides in you. However, you can't talk about what you don't know. And a silent Christian is not always the most effective witness! You have been empowered; you must activate that power. The greatest thing you can do in this life is sow seeds for the Kingdom!! Move past the fear and speak up for the One who saved your life! God is looking for those who would speak on His behalf, it will reward you with a blessed life.

Blessings, Rupert & Red.

SEPTEMBER 15

Declare That He Is Faithful!!

Meditation Verse: Psalms 92:2 HCSB
To declare your faithful love in the morning and your faithfulness at night.
Scripture Reading: Psalms 92

Webster's dictionary defines the word "Declare" in one instance as, 'to state emphatically." Emphatically is defined as "tending to express oneself with forceful speech." I believe this was David's intent when he wrote this psalm. He declared God's faithfulness, day in and day out! Did you lie down to sleep last night? He has been faithful; did you rise this morning? He has been faithful. The first verse of this psalm says, "it is a good thing to give thanks!!" So, not only is it good to praise God, but His faithfulness toward us is also worthy of constant praise! It is so easy to take for granted that our days belong to us and that it is in our own strength that we accomplish the day's tasks. We assume the sun's rising in the morning, it's setting at night, the air we breathe, the food we consume, the roof over our heads. We need to stop and declare emphatically that God is faithful! Life I know is unfair at times, we endure many things that we do not understand, but this is a fallen world system, and a lot of times the price we pay is that the innocent suffers for the guilty. But we cannot allow it to negate our praise, because regardless of the unimaginable, God is still faithful!! We declare that God is faithful with our heads bowed and tears falling from our eyes, we declare His faithfulness when we don't understand, we declare that God is faithful, because we are inhaling and exhaling, we won't know everything or understand much of anything, even question most things, but it won't change the fact that God is faithful. When it feels like it will never be okay again, God loves you and has put people in your life that love you, so, when you are loved back to love, and you will be, you will arise and declare emphatically; God is Faithful!!

Blessings, Rupert & Red.

SEPTEMBER 16

Follow For The Fullness

Meditation Verse: 2 Thessalonians 3:5 NLT

May the Lord lead your hearts into a full understanding and expression of the love of God and the patient endurance that comes from Christ.

Scripture Reading: 2 Thessalonians 3:1-5

This beautiful prayer was directed to the Christians in Thessalonica; however, it is relevant to us today. For us to live at any level of spiritual maturity we must be willing to recognize spiritual authority. You cannot be led in anything or lead anything if you are not willing to follow. The full expression of God's love is understood by your desire to die to self, and to be dependent on the life that Christ gives. Simply put; you become a recreated creature in Christ, the old you has passed away, and you pass from a sentence of death to one of life in the regenerated spirit that connects you back to the spirit of God. If this is not your experience, you cannot grow in your present state. God does not just pour spiritual maturity and stability into us; it has to be done by us cooperating in accordance with His will. It is a process that will cost you, but when you come to full understanding of God's love and Christ's sacrifice, the joy outweighs the pain. He will give you strength to endure, to move past the pain and into His presence and peace. Let this be our prayer, to walk in the fullness of everything God has for us, so that others may see and be willing to follow into the newness of life.

Blessings, Rupert & Red.

SEPTEMBER 17

Let God Fight For You!

Meditation Verse: Psalms 20:7 NLT

Some nations boast in their chariots and horses, but we boast in the Name of the Lord our God.

Scripture Reading: Psalms 20

In the ancient world, most people put their trust in what they could see, and in their ability to overwhelm their enemy, with the vastness of their armies and weapons. The sight of thousands of chariots and horses no doubt struck fear in the hearts of those whose job it was to engage in battle with their impressive foes. But David could boast about a name that was above every name! A power that was unequalled and unmatched! An ally that was without peers! Strong enough to turn back any army or force on the face of the earth! The name of God that assures victory! What's in a name you say? Everything that you need to conquer any trial, battle, situation and circumstance you could ever face. David's trust and belief were well placed. Time after time, battle after battle, war after war, God proved Himself as the Ultimate Warrior! David knew what we must learn that God with you is more than the whole world against you! Where do you place your trust? Are you losing heart because you feel you are in a battle that you cannot win? Turn it over to God and let Him fight your battles! It was never really yours anyway. Trust in the name of the Lord, it is a strong tower the righteous run into it, and they are safe. Proverbs 18:10 (NKJV paraphrased).

Blessings, Rupert & Red.

SEPTEMBER 18

And He Shall Reign Forever!

Meditation Verse: Psalms 93:2 HCSB

Your throne has been established from the beginning; You are from eternity.

Scripture Reading: Psalms 93

If you have ever read or studied history, you will know of men who boasted of ancient dynasties, cities and cultures that existed long ago. Kings and kingdoms that reigned for centuries. Man has always sought to establish vast empires of power and enduring legacies. Throughout all the rich history of long ago, one thread of evidence runs through all of it. They were all here one day and gone the next. Born an instant ago and dead the next. Only the Lord reigns eternally!! The believer can boast of the fact that he dwells under an immortal ruler that will still flourish after everything else has passed away. The Kingdom of God is unmovable, unshakeable, and forever established. It is the fool who is in rebellion against it. He can't change it, overpower it, or outlive it! God is from everlasting; His rule is the only sovereign one and no one else will ever sit on His throne. And the good news is whosoever will, may come into relationship with the Eternal God!! Your ethnicity, creed, nationality or station in life will be neither a requirement nor a deterrent. Only that you enter under the shed blood of Jesus Christ, believing that through His death and resurrection you have now received eternal life. Kings and kingdoms will all pass away, God has secured eternity on our behalf. He is truly the King who will reign forever. Amen!!

Blessings, Rupert & Red.

SEPTEMBER 19

The Sign Of The Times…

Meditation Verse: Psalms 55:10 NLT

Its walls are patrolled day and night against invaders, but the real danger is wickedness within the city.

Scripture Reading: Psalms 55

The Word of God is instructional and prophetic at the same time. The truth is as Solomon said, "There is nothing new under the sun." Ecclesiastes 1:9 (NKJV). There is no situation that the Word does not cover. As it was then it is now over 2000 years later. We live in a society where there are people that ignore the obvious. The governments are corrupt, and there are leaders that have no compassion or empathy towards its citizenry. We send troops all over the world to defend freedom, yet we fail to protect our own. We build walls of many types, to "guard" our cities and keep "certain" people out, but evil is already in our midst. We attempt to isolate ourselves, but we are no safer. The real danger is the wickedness inside the city. Our best defense is the Word of God. It will give you the truth and not lie. It is our responsibility to discern the times that we live in. The treacherous pretend to be your friend while all the time plotting your demise. Your so-called leaders will lie to you and betray you to fulfill their own evil agenda. David realized this when his own son betrayed him and tried to usurp the throne. We need to check ourselves. Who is sitting on the altar of your heart? Do you have the walls up when it is really you that you are running from? Realize that your life will never be safe until you allow the True Life inside you. We have got to tear down the walls that keep us afraid and prevent us from living our best life. God will be your fence and place a hedge of protection around you. He won't turn you away, He won't build a wall to keep you out, He won't lie to you and betray you with evil intentions, He loves you too much….

Blessings, Rupert & Red.

SEPTEMBER 20

God Had You In Mind

Meditation Verse: Jeremiah 1:5 NLT

"I knew you before I formed you in your mother's womb. Before you were born I set you apart and appointed you as my prophet to the nations."

Scripture Reading: Jeremiah 1

Just a little encouragement for you today; did you know that you existed in the mind of God and that He planned your purpose before you were born? That God loved you and created you for Himself? The call of Jeremiah was not so much a singular call as it was a call to the nations. Yes, His call to Jeremiah was specific in nature, it was not given to entertain Jeremiah, but so he could know the will and plan of God for his life. And God wants the same for us. We have not all been called to prophesy, but God has a specific plan and purpose for each of our lives. Just knowing that God desires to give our lives purpose before we even existed is humbling. That we were set apart in His mind says that God was thinking about you! You are not a mistake, however you got here, God allowed it to work out His purpose. Understand that you were born for greater!! Rise up and don't miss this blessed opportunity, you were called by God on purpose for purpose!! Shout hallelujah and thank You Lord! We were born for Destiny!!

Blessings, Rupert & Red.

SEPTEMBER 21

God And God Alone

Meditation Verse: Exodus 20:3 NLT

"You must not have any other god but Me."

Scripture Reading: Exodus 20:1-18

This won't take long; There should be a fundamental understanding of who God is, what He brings to our lives, and how we should live as a result. After all it is because of Him that we are even alive! This first commandment implies explicitly that God will not tolerate anyone or anything before Him or replacing Him. He is to be the only God that we worship and serve. In ancient Israel there was a tendency to worship gods like Baal, the god of weather and financial success, (materialism), Ashtoreth, the god of sex, romance and reproduction (hedonism). We are tempted to worship those same gods today just without the old-fashioned names and images. Nowadays just about anything is priority to giving God first place or preeminence over our lives. The implication is not that it is okay to have other gods as second and third place, it means literally no god before His face. It is not enough to add God to our lives, He requires that we give our lives over to Him. Anything short of this command is idolatry. Sounds serious? That's because it is. We owe everything to the One who gives life, sustains it and keeps it. So, if God is not number one in your life, remove what is and give your life to God, He is worthy and deserves it!!

Blessings, Rupert & Red.

SEPTEMBER 22

I Pray for You, You Pray For Me.

Meditation Verse: Luke 22:32 NLT

"But I have pleaded in prayer for you Simon, that your faith should not fail. So, when you have repented and turned to me again, strengthen your brothers."

Scripture Reading: Luke 22:32-38

Jesus is aware of the spiritual battles going on behind the scenes. That is why He is the best advocate to have, our personal High Priest who is always interceding on our behalf. Jesus knew that Satan wanted to crush and defeat Simon and devastate his faith. Simon would falter but his faith would not fail. That, however, had nothing to do with Peter, it was because Jesus had prayed for him. Peter was restored, but his obligation now was to do the same for others. That same obligation rests with us. We are called to pray for one another, to build up, lift and restore and strengthen when we are weak, and our faith is faltering. You may say, but I can't pray like Jesus! Never underestimate the power of an earnest prayer! God knows, and understands and hears you when you pray, and your backup is Jesus himself! He takes our prayers before the Father, that is your seal of approval. So, pray for one another, let's love and strengthen our brothers and sisters, that they may develop a faith that will not shrink. That is how the kingdom on earth becomes like the Kingdom of Heaven!!

Blessings, Rupert & Red.

SEPTEMBER 23

Desire Relationship

Meditation Verse: Luke 12: 34 NLT
Wherever your treasure is, there the desires of your heart will be also.
Scripture Reading: Luke 12:22-34

In the human heart, there is built a desire to worship. This is not appointed to a select few, but every man to whom is given the breath of life. However, the choice of to whom or to what you give your worship is entirely up to you. The correlation between your heart and what is most important to you is not suggestive but a fact. Your commitment will determine what your primary interests are. Now I am not saying that you should not pursue an education, a career, or a desire to provide and care for yourself and family, but if your pursuit of material things becomes the singular focus in your life to the exclusion of all else, then your desires are earthbound, and you have fallen into idolatry. When you fail to put first the Kingdom of God and its righteousness, your heart will never be established toward God ordained priorities. Jesus warned about the dangers of the location of the heart concerning materialism. Placing God first is wisdom, for it is God who gives the power to get wealth. Here is the caveat; it is so you can establish his covenant in the earth. When you understand that everything you have belongs to God and that you are merely a steward, your perspective on material things will shift, and your heart will set its sights on what is truly important, the benefits of relationship, and the only One deserving of your worship.

Blessings, Rupert & Red.

SEPTEMBER 24

No King, No Kingdom

Meditational Verse: Luke 17:20 NKJV

Now when He was asked by the Pharisees when the kingdom of God would come, He answered them and said, "The kingdom of God does not come with observation;"

Scripture Reading: Luke 17:20-26

Whenever the Pharisees questioned Jesus, it was never in the attempt or purpose to gain insight or knowledge, they were only seeking to entrap Jesus. They had a superior attitude and thought they were smarter than most. And Jesus was no exception. So, when they asked Jesus about the coming of the kingdom, Jesus perceived their sarcastic attitude and answered, "You won't ever see the kingdom by hostile examination" (I am paraphrasing), the translated Greek word observation is better translated "hostile examination". Demanding that Jesus put up and produce the kingdom or shut up and stop claiming He was the Messiah, was the whole intent of the conversation. Their hostility blinded them to what was in front of them. If their motives had been pure, they would have realized that the kingdom along with the King was in their midst. Don't get so caught up in life that you miss the reality of what is in front of you. When you harden your heart to the things of God, you have put your soul in jeopardy. If you don't see the need for the Savior and relationship, then you won't know when the kingdom comes. And like many today, we long for the kingdom to come, we pray for it. The whole of creation groans for it. But here's the catch; you can't want the kingdom and reject the King.

Blessings, Rupert & Red.

SEPTEMBER 25

Anchor To The Solid Rock!

Meditation Verse: Hebrews 2:1 NKJV

Therefore, we must give the more earnest heed to the things we have heard, lest we drift away.

Scripture Reading: Hebrews 2:1-4

Do you listen to understand, or do you listen to reply? Many of us do the latter. To give "earnest heed" is to listen for understanding and to follow through with an intentional action. We must give earnest heed to the words of Jesus, for if we do nothing, we leave ourselves open to drift away. The story is told about an ungodly farmer who died, and it was discovered that in his will he left his farm to the devil. In court they did not know how to deal with such a request; how do you leave your farm to the devil? In the end the judge decided that the best way to carry out the wishes of the deceased was to allow the farm to grow weeds, the soil to erode, and the house and barns be left to rot. In other words, do nothing. We can leave our lives to the devil in the same way, by doing nothing and allowing our lives to drift wherever the winds and tides may take us. Drifting naturally happens when you are not anchored to a rock or something solid. Let that solid rock be Jesus, He is the Original Rock! The storm and the winds will come, you need to be intentional about Who your life is adhered to, be very sure, that your anchor holds.

Blessings, Rupert & Red.

SEPTEMBER 26

When You Have Done All: Stand!

Meditation Verse: 2 Corinthians 4:8-9 HCSB

We are pressured in every way but not crushed, we are perplexed but not in despair; we are persecuted but not abandoned; we are struck down but not destroyed.

Scripture Reading: 2 Corinthians 4:7-15

It may be hard to believe that the suffering this verse talks about is still going on today. Yet there are those in parts of the world near and far where the physical ramifications of this verse are an everyday stark reality in their lives. Paul was a hunted man, everywhere he went there were those who wished to do him harm. But there are other ways that people suffer, it is not just a physical thing. Though most of us live comfortable lives, the pain and suffering we sometimes experience can take a serious toll on our well-being and peace of mind. The question is can you put your trust in God and depend on him to see you through? How do you maintain, when you are feeling pressured, perplexed, persecuted, struck down, and not feel crushed, in despair, abandoned, or destroyed? The enemy may not attack us in the same way physically, but he will attack our minds with a vengeance. Our decision and desire to live for God needs to be without limits. We must find every solution in Him. Our joy in the middle of sorrow, our peace in the midst of conflict, our strength in the midst of weakness, our hope in the midst of our sickness, our relief in the midst of hurt and pain. Like Paul, we must know the power and victory of Jesus in our lives, because we will constantly find ourselves in situations where only the power and victory of Jesus will meet our needs. Life can deal us some crippling blows, and pain and sorrow will be real, but we can't let the enemy take our minds. The promise is the weapons may be formed, but they won't prosper. Allow God to guide you, it may be dark to you now, but this too shall pass, you will see the light, because in Him, there is no darkness at all.

Blessings, Rupert & Red.

SEPTEMBER 27

Become A Vessel For Him.

Meditation Verse: 2 Corinthians 4:7 NKJV

But we have this treasure in earthen vessels, that the excellence of the power may be of God and not of us.

Scripture Reading: 2 Corinthians 4:1-7

"This treasure is the greatness of the gospel of Jesus Christ, and the glory of God made evident through that gospel". David Guzick. (Source: Blue letter Bible, blueletterbible.org). So, this treasure in earthen vessels is a confirmation of the life that God wants to endow us with. He considers us capable of carrying His Word within us, and the light of His Word shines forth throughout time and all generations. Who is worthy to be a "container" for God's light and glory? The smartest person is not smart enough, the purest person is not pure enough, the most talented person is not talented enough!! Yet here we are by God's grace and mercy, clay pots filled with His story. But only so God can receive the glory. The excellence of His Word can stand by itself, it is a privilege to be allowed to carry it. So, what are you doing with your privilege? Are you a light and example for excellence, or are you a bulb that has been extinguished by fear or lack of motivation? Get up and shine! It is not about us! God has placed His excellence in you for a purpose! The kingdom is depending on you!

Blessings, Rupert & Red.

SEPTEMBER 28

Know Where You Are Walking

Meditation Verse: Psalms 119:105 NKJV
Your word is a lamp to my feet and a light to my path.
Scripture Reading: Psalms 119: 105-112

It is possible to walk the path of life without knowing where your steps are leading you. The psalmist is saying here that the Word of God made his steps clear. There are many ways to walk, and God has instructed us in His Word that we should walk worthy, uprightly, humbly, integrally, and in the light. All of these are not possible without God's Word lighting your way. It not only shows you how to walk but where you should walk. Light brings clarity and understanding, so you are shown the path you should take, Psalms 119:30a (NKJV) says, the entrance of Your word gives light, because even though we may know right from wrong, our conscience is at most times weak and influenced by the flesh. The light of God's Word will teach our conscience the truth about moral choices. Where and how you walk will produce choices in your life. It determines whether you set your feet on good ground or dangerous ground. Your walk is also influential and an example to others, you may literally have people walking in your footsteps! So, make sure your steps are ordered by God, then whoever follows you will be confident of their destination.

Blessings, Rupert & Red.

SEPTEMBER 29

It Is On The Inside!

Meditation Verse: Psalms 119:11 NKJV
Your Word I have hidden in my heart, that I might not sin against You.
Scripture Reading: Psalms 119:9-16

Real Quick: We too like the psalmist need to understand the importance of hiding God's Word in our hearts. It is wisdom to receive it in our minds, but it is the act of hiding it in our hearts so that it becomes more than just mental assent, that will become our defense against sin. It is a simple equation actually, the more knowledge you gain in any area, the more prepared you will be to execute the application of that knowledge to your advantage. God's Word will give you the best advantage over sin, so when temptation comes (and it will) you will not yield. The truth is that the temptation to sin is an ever-present reality in this world. It always seems to be knocking at our hearts, so when that happens; just let the Word answer the door....

Blessings, Rupert & Red.

SEPTEMBER 30

Justice Not Revenge

Meditation Verse: 1 Thessalonians 5:15 NKJV

See to it that no one repays evil for evil to anyone, but always pursue what is good for one another and for all.

Scripture Reading: 1 Thessalonians 5:12-22

This passage of scripture is not at all hard to understand. The believer should never seek revenge or vengeance against anyone. The pursuit of justice through the proper channels, or the defense of oneself and family in case of a sudden attack is another matter but taking matters into our own hands for revenge is something that God commands we do not do. "Vengeance is Mine I will repay" says the Lord. Romans 12:19, (NKJV). Evil for evil will never yield a satisfying solution. While I admit that this can sometimes be difficult to do, we are required to do those things that will produce a good result, to bring about a peaceful end. People can and have done unimaginable things to others, but "Do not be deceived, God is not mocked, and whatever a person sows, that he will also reap." Galatians 6:7, (NKJV). For many of us this will be a true test to trust God. The desire for revenge can be a consuming and destructive emotion. Just leave it to the One who always gets the victory. God is well able to fight for you, in fact He said He would. Power will always belong to and remain with God.

Blessings, Rupert & Red.

OCTOBER 1

Be Mindful Of Your Words

Meditation Verse: Psalms 19:14 NKJV

Let the words of my mouth, and the meditation of my heart, be acceptable in Your sight, O Lord, my strength and my Redeemer.

Scripture Reading: Psalms 19

We have talked about the challenges of our "thought life," and how it is important to think on things that are true, honest, lovely, and of good report. We have also said that the mind is where most of our battles are fought, and reality in the flesh means sometimes the battles are brutal. Our three-dimensional body seems to be constantly at war with itself. It is why we need to guard our hearts with all diligence and cast down imaginations that defy Godly behavior. What we dwell on is what we will produce. Sowing and reaping are both spiritual and physical laws, and they are a part of what governs the universe. Our words do matter and what we say is evidence of what we have sown into our hearts. Jesus said it this way; "Out of the abundance of the heart, the mouth speaks." Matthew 12:34b(NKJV). Whatever you meditate on will be evidenced by the words that you speak. We pray that you allow this verse to penetrate your spirit man and be a blessing to others by the words of your mouth, it really is that important to God, relationship matters.

Blessings, Rupert & Red.

OCTOBER 2

GOD Is Greater!!

Meditational Verse: 1 John 4:4 HCSB

You are from God, little children, and you have conquered them, because the One who is in you is greater than the one who is in the world.

Scripture Reading: 1 John 4:1-6

It is up to us to trust and believe in the resources that we have on the inside of us, because even if we don't it will not make it any less true! That resource is God living inside of you, which will guarantee victory if we rely on Him instead of relying on the flesh. Once we understand it, we will increase our confidence and decrease our fears. We may have spiritual and physical enemies but none greater than the One who dwells on the inside of us. Getting past or going through the inevitable trial and or test can sometimes be overwhelming, and no one can claim that pain or disappointment are not real. The confident hope that God is in control, should give us strength in an otherwise weakened state. God can and will perfect that which concerns you, Psalm 138:8a, (NKJV paraphrased). and He gets to determine what that looks like! Just know that it will be greater! God is in the multiplication business and "His Word will not return void!" Isaiah 55:11, (NKJV paraphrased). So, get up and move past the lack to the increase that is coming and look for greater!! Be encouraged, there's power in relationship.

Blessings, Rupert & Red.

OCTOBER 3

Cancel That Appointment!

Meditation Verse: 1 Thessalonians 5:9 HCSB

For God did not appoint us to wrath, but to obtain salvation through our Lord Jesus Christ.

Scripture Reading: 1 Thessalonians 5:1-11

Initially we had an appointment to wrath. We were born in sin, shaped in iniquity and bound for hell. Because of Adam we inherited a rebellious spirit, our fate sealed. But thank God for the ability to receive salvation! He made a way for that appointment to be cancelled! Because of the second Adam, we inherited a new spirit, reborn and shaped through grace and mercy, and sealed by faith in Jesus Christ! That is exciting news, because it is far more than we deserve and could have ever hoped for. Have you been born again? Have you received salvation and had your appointment to wrath cancelled? Do Not let this opportunity pass you by! Don't let your earthly independence rob you of your heavenly destination. Jesus will return and you will stand before God, and when that happens, you don't want to keep that appointment! It is not His will that any should perish, but that all should come to repentance, 2 Peter 3:9b (NKJV paraphrased). That salvation is available now! Procrastination is the thief of time, the devil's tool to change your mind. Don't delay, cancel that appointment today!!

Blessings, Rupert & Red.

OCTOBER 4

Let Go And Let God!

Meditation Verse: Psalms 55:22 NLT

Give your burdens to the Lord, and He will take care of you.
He will not permit the godly to slip and fall.

Scripture Reading: Psalms 55

"Let Go and Let God." A phrase that we hear often yet pay little attention to. It is human nature to hold on to the things that forfeit our peace and carry our pain. It is hard to let go of traumatic events, worrisome situations, job loss, losing a loved one, broken relationships, and financial matters. These days just trying to survive day by day is a challenge. We all suffer some form of "PTSD" (post-traumatic stress disorder), and it can wreak havoc in our memories and daily lives. It is all real and can lead to even more health problems, both mental and physical. We cannot deny these realities, but what we do need is relief and peace in the middle of it. God wants to carry your burdens, He wants to give you His peace, He longs to see you healthy and whole. He knows we all will cry sometimes; He knows the feelings of despair, sadness and shame. He desires to free you of those things that bind you so that you might experience His joy and comfort. Learning to cast your care is never easy but so necessary. We must remind ourselves every day to give it to God. Peace is not the absence of conflict, but a calm during it that will cause you not to lose your mind! He will keep you from falling and provide you His strength. So, remember, In your time of greatest weakness, in your time of greatest struggles, in your time of greatest trials, yes, even in your time of greatest service. Learn to cast your cares on the Lord, because He cares for you. 1Peter 5:7 (NKJV paraphrased).

Blessings, Rupert & Red.

OCTOBER 5

Praise Break!!

Meditation Verse: Psalms 147:1 HCSB

Hallelujah! How good it is to sing to our God, for praise is pleasant and lovely.

Scripture Reading: Psalms 147

Any and every day is a good time to praise the Lord!! Yes, because He is good, and yes because of His mercy, His loving kindness is better than life itself!! The Scriptures declares from Genesis to Revelation reason after reason to give praise to our God. He is our Creator, Sustainer, Giver of every good and perfect gift. Without Him there would be no life, breath or being. We praise because He is altogether lovely, and His love endures forever. The psalmist declares that it is fitting that we should praise Him, it is the least and the most that we can do. There is no wrong time, every time is the right time. No matter who you are, where you are, if you have breath, you ought to give God praise! We can go on and on about why we should praise God. Our best and biggest reason though, why we should give God praise is because no one deserves it more! Praise Him above all because He is Worthy!!

Blessings, Rupert & Red.

OCTOBER 6

Find Joy And Gladness In Him

Meditation Verse: Psalms 70:4 NLT

But may all who search for you be filled with joy and gladness in you. May those who love your salvation repeatedly shout, "God is great!"

Scripture Reading: Psalms 70

We love Psalm 70! It is one of what we call our go to psalms. It is a cry for God to help when everything and everyone seems to be against you. We all have experienced those days. The days that make you realize that your only choice is to depend on God. Your trust in any other is pointless. One of the best decisions you can ever make is to declare dependence on God. To be filled with joy and gladness in Him does not mean that you won't have struggles or persecution. Remember we live in a world that is under the sway of the evil one. Trouble has a way of finding everyone at times. But we truly must seek God continually to find relief. We don't know why all the time. There are circumstances that we face that are beyond our understanding. There are questions we won't know the answers to. But knowing that God is great and His purposes work for our good will have to be enough. Sometimes we want to understand it now, but we must let patience have its perfect work. Through it all every new day brings its challenges but also, its blessings, if you search for God, you will find Him, for joy and gladness in this earth you will find none better!!

Blessings, Rupert & Red.

OCTOBER 7

Indescribable Love

Meditation Verse: Ephesians 3:18 NLT

And may you have the power to understand, as all God's people should, how wide, how long, and how deep His love is.

Scripture Reading: Ephesians 3:14-21

To know the love of God in the way that Paul describes, requires a power that is beyond mere mortal understanding. It cannot be measured by deductive reasoning, mathematical equations, or chemical formulas. It is the love that Jesus referred to in the express commands of God, it is the love that Paul alluded to in 1Corinthians 13, it is the love that will be revealed in its fullness when that which is perfect has come. The power of salvation and faith in Christ brings us closer to that experience as we grow in relationship. May we all come to know the incalculable dimensions of God's love, as we live, grow and walk from this life into eternity.

Blessings, Rupert & Red.

OCTOBER 8

Purposeful Motivation

Meditation Verse: Matthew 6:3-4 NLT

But when you give to someone in need, don't let your left hand know what your right hand is doing. Give your gifts in private, and your Father who sees everything, will reward you.

Scripture Reading: Matthew 6:1-6

Everything that we do, whether selfless or selfish, carries the weight of motive. Why we do anything is almost as important as the deed itself. The motive determines the reward. If your desire is to be seen by men, then their applause will be your reward. There will be no reward in heaven or earth for the one whose motive is human recognition. They have received payment in full. Our generosity in time, talent, or money, should be selfless acts, that don't bring conditions of recognition attached. In fact, don't dwell on any indulgent self-congratulations. Treat it as though the deed never happened, the left hand being clueless about the right. Jesus pointed out the importance of doing good things to the glory of God. It is better to receive our return from God, who rewards us more openly and more generously than any mere man can! God does see in secret, and the strength of the promise is that things done the right way, for the right reasons will certainly be rewarded. God knows and remembers; nothing is hidden from Him. The eyes of the Lord are always upon us, and right now He sees not only what we do, but also every motive that is in our hearts, so seek to operate from the purest of motives, it is always the pleasure of the Lord to give you the Kingdom.

Blessings, Rupert & Red.

OCTOBER 9

Total Dependence

Meditation Verse: Psalms 18:1 NLT
I love you Lord; You are my strength.
Scripture Reading: Psalms 18

The fact that our lives are subject to the will of God, is a daily reality in our lives. True love for God comes first because of who He is. He is Creator God, the One who created us and sustains us. We love God because He is merciful and loving, kind and long suffering. We love Him because He gives more grace, even when we can't see it. We love Him because His will is perfect, and He protects our going out and our coming in. Even in sad times, tough days, tragic circumstances, we can lean, rest and abide in Him. Knowing God is knowing where your help comes from, understanding that His strength is made perfect in your weakness. That means you cannot be strong without Him. That means the world to us because we are totally dependent on Him. That is why we love God no matter the circumstance. We choose to, because through the joy and the tears, and the brevity and uncertainty of this life, there is no one and nothing that we can hold onto that will get us through the unknowable journey ahead. As they said back in the day; "We may not know what the future holds, but we know who holds the future." Trust the God who made you, there will never be a good time to take this journey on your own.

Blessings, Rupert & Red.

OCTOBER 10

Total Dependence: 2.0

Meditation Verse: Psalms 18:2 NLT

The Lord is my rock; my fortress, and my savior; my God is my rock, in whom I find protection. He is my shield, the power that saves me, and my place of safety.

Scripture Reading: Psalms 18

This is a dangerous world that we live in. Man's inhumanity to man is at an all-time high, and no amount of technical, economic, or social advancement or construct has improved man's humanitarian outlook. We have become a wicked society, whose only concern is to subjugate the people, who they then force to carry out their selfish and self-serving agenda. As a result, there are not many places we can go to feel safe. Everything seems to be a scam of some sort and we are left feeling threatened. Our jobs, our homes, places of worship and our physical persons are under constant attack, leaving us exposed, helpless and hopeless. Life is often lived these days between a rock and a hard place. As we have said before, when you find yourself in this dilemma, choose the Rock, Jesus is the only One who can give you real peace, the constancy and stability we seek can only be found in Him. Everything you need is found in Him. Rock, Fortress, Savior, Protection, Shield, Power, Healer, Deliverer, and Place of Safety, there is no liability in Him. Find yourself in the ark of safety, it is free, and Jesus is waiting for you with open arms.

Blessings, Rupert & Red.

OCTOBER 11

Don't You Get Weary

Meditation Verse: 1 Kings 19:4 NLT

Then he went on alone into the wilderness, traveling all day. He sat down under a solitary broom tree and prayed that he might die. "I have had enough Lord," he said. "Take my life, for I am no better than my ancestors who have already died."

Scripture Reading: 1 Kings 19:1-9

In 1 Kings 18, Elijah had performed one of the greatest miracles of the Old Testament! Instead of being held in high esteem, he was threatened with death. Queen Jezebel was humiliated and wanted revenge. Elijah ran for his life! He fell into fear and worry. This was the man whom God had allowed to shut up the heavens from rain for three and a half years and had proved to the priests and prophets of the god Baal, that Yahweh was the One True God! Yet he was so afraid, that he begged God to take his life! To most of us who have read this passage of scripture, this is mind boggling! Thankfully, God did not answer his prayer. In fact, Elijah was one of the few men in the Bible that did not see death! You are and have been working for the Kingdom and in your natural eyes you are seeing no rewards. Nobody notices you and you get no recognition despite the good work you have done to produce fruit. The truth is there are people who will reject God regardless of the evidence. Always remember who you work for and who sees you. There will be times when you are exhausted, stressed, and feel that your work is accomplishing nothing. Don't give up or get weary in well doing! God knows more than you and is already working out everything for your good. He will provide you with everything that you need.

Blessings, Rupert & Red.

OCTOBER 12

Have A Talk With God

Meditation Verse: Psalms 27:8 NLT

My heart has heard You say, "Come and talk with me."
And my heart responds, "Lord, I am coming."

Scripture Reading: Psalms 27

One of the foundations of any relationship is communication. We seek dialogue with one another for many reasons; to voice our desires, wants, complaints, expectations, excitement, etc. We also seek clarity and understanding. This is true in the natural, it is also true in the spiritual. God has whispered in our hearts the desire for communication with us. Even more reason to respond to His voice, not only out of obedience, but to begin to cultivate relationship. We need to discern the voice of God and be quick to respond; the psalmist said eagerly, "Lord I am coming! The voice of God is always present where all others fail. We believe that our direction would be clearer, our lives more peaceful and our communication more certain, when we first talk with God. He longs to be in relationship with you, get with God, He will show you great and mighty things, that you would not otherwise know.

Blessings, Rupert & Red.

OCTOBER 13

God Deserves First Place

Meditation Verse: Colossians 3:2 NLT
Think about the things of heaven, not the things of earth.
Scripture Reading: Colossians 3:1-11

In the hustle and busyness of everyday life, it is easy to get distracted from what is important. You were not designed to be a slave to the system. We say that the struggle is real and that is the truth. Our priority, however, should be to put God first. There is a reason for this; 100% valid; Since everything you have comes from God, and you were also created by Him for His purpose, don't you think that He should get preeminence in your life? Your life ought to reflect His purpose and values, because your place in eternity will reflect the same. While you contemplate your weekend plans, vacation time, alone time or me time, think about the One who has enabled you to do so. Place your priorities with the God who made you, it will give you the fuel you need for this temporal life and the life you will need for forever.

Blessings, Rupert & Red.

OCTOBER 14

The Best Place To Be!!

Meditation Verse: Psalms 84:10 NKJV

For a day in Your courts is better than a thousand. I would rather be a doorkeeper in the house of my God than dwell in the tents of wickedness.

Scripture Reading: Psalms 84

The psalmist says, one day is better than a thousand elsewhere. There is no place comparable to the presence of the Lord. There is nowhere you can take us that will give us the sense of peace and worship like His House! Our burdened souls are at rest, and we have the truest sense of His presence, mercy and love. To rejoice in the presence of the Savior, to read His promises and feel the power of the Holy Spirit, is something that the world will never understand. The lowest station in His kingdom is better by far to the highest elevation in the world's palaces and halls of power. To share burdens and open doors for the Lord is better than to reign among the wicked. Spurgeon the commentator said, "Every man has his choice, and this is ours, God's worst is better than the devil's best." (Source: Blue letter Bible blueletterbible.org). If Jehovah is truly our God, then His house, altars, His doorstep all become precious to us. Wherever Jesus is, that is where we want to be, because relationship between us and the Savior, is more comparable to any place, no matter how noble and grand it may seem. We encourage you to get into His presence, don't delay, do it today, there is no better place to be!!

Blessings, Rupert & Red.

OCTOBER 15

From Death To Life

Meditation Verse: Ephesians 2:1 NKJV
And you He made alive, who were dead in trespasses and sins.
Scripture Reading: Ephesians 2:1-10

Though Christians have been made alive through Christ, we ought not forget, that we came to God dead in trespasses and sin. There are many kinds of life, vegetable life, animal life, mental life, moral life, physical life and spiritual life. To be spiritually dead does not mean you are dead physically, socially, or psychologically. Yet it is a real death. The most vital part of a person's personality, the spirit, is dead to the most important factor in life, God. We were born in this state. When you trespass, you cross the line, challenging God's boundaries, and to sin is to miss the mark, the perfect standard of God. This was the state of our lives before the grace of God and the blood of Jesus met us. Thank God for the blood and the regeneration of our spirit man to new life!! If you have not experienced the new birth, God is waiting, it is joy unspeakable and a blessing to know that your future is assured. God loves you and wants to give you a new life in glory! And the premium has already been paid! A new life and relationship in Jesus Christ, No Charge!! Who doesn't love Free?!!

Blessings, Rupert & Red.

OCTOBER 16

A Worthy Call

Meditation Verse: Ephesians 4:1 NLT

Therefore I, a prisoner for serving the Lord, beg you to lead a life worthy of your calling, for you have been called by God.

Scripture Reading: Ephesians 4:1-10

When we truly understand what God did for us, then we will want to serve and obey Him out of gratitude. We must know who we are In Christ, that is the foundation of this worthy walk. We don't walk worthy so that God will love us, we walk worthy because God loves us. And as we walk our declaration that we are Christians should be put in front of every temptation along the way. We walk worthy because He is worthy, our lives make a difference to all whom we encounter, simply because of our love and treatment of people. We don't walk with arrogance or pride, but with confidence and humility, which is grace under pressure, knowing what God has done for us did not result out of anything we could have done on our own, but His benevolence has brought us to freedom. To walk worthy is not just a request but a mandate that we must live out every day, sharing the love of Christ with those who we meet along the way. Our priority now is to share Jesus as we walk so that others will join us on that journey, to form the relationships that will encourage growth and build the kingdom of God! So, put on your walking shoes and get to stepping!!

Blessings, Rupert & Red.

OCTOBER 17

Amazing Grace!

Meditation Verse: Galatians 1:15a NLT
But even before I was born, God chose me and called me by His marvelous grace.
Scripture Reading: Galatians 1:11-15

That same grace, that caused Paul to see his purpose in being called by God, is the same grace that calls to you and I. We were chosen from the foundation of the world by God to fulfill His purpose in the earth. To us he gave the ability to choose or refuse. It has been said before that God's purpose and will does not have to include us for it to be manifested, but He desires us to participate by being co-workers with Him. 1Corinthians 3:9a, (HCSB). Do we have the ears to hear the sound of God calling us to His amazing grace? He will give us everything that we need, sparing no good thing. Every day that we wake up is an opportunity to take advantage of this awesome gift. The sobering thought is that every day is not promised. So, while you are thinking you have time, you have none to waste. Today is your day to hear the sound, don't close your ears to the sweet sound of God's amazing grace. Believe me it will eternally satisfy, in Paul's words, "It's Marvelous!!

Blessings, Rupert & Red.

OCTOBER 18

Truth Needs No Validation

Meditation Verse: Jeremiah 26:15 HCSB

But know for certain that if you put me to death, you will bring innocent blood on yourselves, on this city, and on its residents, for it is for certain the Lord has sent me to speak all these things directly to you.

Scripture Reading: Jeremiah 26:12-15

There will always be those who are in opposition of one taking a stand for what is right. All throughout the word of God are examples of men and women who have put their lives on the line in the name of truth. Such was Jeremiah, a prophet of God who even though on trial for his life, refused to compromise the message he was appointed to deliver. It was more important that he obey God, than to give in to the fear of what man might do to him. Our attitude should be the same. When faced with the decision of truth or consequences, we ought always to stand on the side of truth. The approval of man means nothing in comparison to Almighty God. That is a relationship where there can be no compromise. We live in a world where the truth is not always popular, even so, live in such a way where your message brings conviction to those who would ignore truth. Your message may not only be in words, but in deed, and or lifestyle. In whatever form, if it is rooted in His truth, God will be pleased.

Blessings, Rupert & Red.

OCTOBER 19

Desire The Mind Of Christ

Meditation Verse: 2 Corinthians 10:5 HCSB

And every high-minded thing that is raised up against the knowledge of God, taking every thought captive to obey Christ.

Scripture Reading: 2 Corinthians 10:1-6

We have often said that one of the most challenging things in the life of the Christian is his or her thought life. Thoughts are a peculiar phenomenon, they can enter the mind at any time in random ways, often without warning or invitation. The subject matter is usually not necessarily something being contemplated, meditated on, or relative to what we were thinking about at the time. It becomes problematic however, when they go against Godly thinking or carnal in nature. Dwelling on thoughts like these can hinder your relationship with God. It becomes an argument of the mind that is rooted in selfish thinking. In the text Paul is talking to Christians, so this is not just a worldly issue. When the wisdom of the world exalts itself above and against the wisdom of God, and Christians embrace it, rebellion is often the result. So, how do we break down these strongholds? According to Scripture we must take these types of thoughts captive, prisoner, and claim authority over them in the name of Jesus. Thoughts that are not true, lovely, honest, or of good report, probably should not take up residence in our minds. Submitting them to Jesus takes strength not weakness. Now the world may say: "I don't want my thoughts to be captive by anyone, I have a right to think what I want." Well, you, Child of God don't. You have been bought with a price and you are not your own. You have a duty to glorify God in your body and your spirit. 1 Corinthians 6:19-20 (NKJV, paraphrased). So, capture those thoughts when they come through the mind gate. Don't dwell on the evil thing. Guard your thought life, develop the mind of Christ.

Blessings, Rupert & Red.

OCTOBER 20

Where Is Your Focus?

Meditation Verse: Acts 3:4-5 NKJV

And fixing his eyes on him, with John, Peter said, "Look at us." So he gave them his attention, expecting to receive something from them.

Scripture Reading: Acts 3:1-10

The passage of scripture that gives the lame man the ability to walk, in our opinion, is one of the most powerful images of the disciples after the resurrection of Jesus. We love that Peter treated the beggar with respect. He said, "Look at us." He wanted to make eye contact with a man that most people would pass by and ignore. His condition was not of his own making, he was lame from birth, useless in a selfish and self-centered society. That somebody wanted his attention was probably a big deal to him. So, he looked at Peter in expectation of maybe a large gift or donation. What he received though, was beyond his wildest dreams, the ability to walk! What a gift from God! Should we live in expectation of receiving from God? The answer is a resounding YES!! As Christians sometimes we settle for far less than God is willing to give. It is faith pure and simple, that pleases God and puts us in the position to receive the blessing. Whatever condition we find ourselves in, God can improve it if we are willing to keep our eyes on Him. Worth more than silver and gold is the transforming power of Jesus Christ. It gives us the ability to carry out the plan and purpose that He has for our lives. Once we enter into a relationship with Him, we have the expectation of His promises. So then, we must focus on Jesus as the author and finisher of our faith, and the One that can exceedingly, abundantly bless us beyond what we can think or imagine! Ephesians 3:20a (NKJV, paraphrased). Jesus is saying, "Look at me, rise up and walk!!

Blessings, Rupert & Red.

OCTOBER 21

God Is On Your Side!!

Meditation Verse: Romans 8:31 HCSB

What then are we to say about these things? If God is for us, who is against us?

Scripture Reading: Romans 8

The beginning of this 8th chapter of Romans states that: "There is therefore now no condemnation to those who are in Christ Jesus." Romans 8:1 (NKJV). Jesus has said before; "I and my Father are one." John 10:30 (NKJV). So, if we are in Christ, God will not condemn us. So, what does it mean to be "in Christ?" it means to be in spiritual union with Christ, the indwelling of the Holy Spirit bears witness that Christ is in us and we are justified by our faith. Those who are in Christ have the assurance of His promises. God is for us! He is for those who are in Christ. From Romans 8:1-39 (NKJV), we are reminded and affirmed of God's love and promises. Verse 31 says it like this: "If God be for us, who can be against us?" This is God's power a testament to His greatness! He has never lost a battle so let Him fight for you. As you go about your day, surrender your life and battles to God, don't bear your burdens alone. If God is for you, it does not matter who is against you. If you are in Christ, you have the victory. Together, you are more than the entire world against you. God is for you in your trials, for you in your tribulations, He is for you when you are tempted, and when you are weak. He will not leave you nor forsake you, Deuteronomy 31:8b(NKJV), and nothing will separate you from His love for you. What an incredible promise! We don't know about you, but that is the only way to live your best life, by giving Him yours today.

Blessings, Rupert & Red.

OCTOBER 22

Love Is All You Need

Meditation Verse: John 13:34-35 HCSB

I give you a new command: Love one another. Just as I have loved you, you must also love one another. By this all people will know that you are my disciples, if you have love one for another.

Scripture Reading: John 13:31-35

This is Jesus speaking, the word new in the Greek is "kainen," implies not so much a commandment that we have not heard before, but presented in a fresh, new way. Love one another, simple yet profound in its import, Jesus is saying that the body of Christ, or disciples should have a love for each other that is on the same level that He has shown us. The command was not new, but the level of love that Jesus was about to display was to lay down his life as our ransom was the ultimate sacrifice, and the true definition of agape love. This was the mark that defined us as His disciples, that we would love one another, so as the world measures love that is conditional, and sees that as a sacrifice, as Jesus' disciples, our hallmark is identifiable by our unconditional love for each other. How do you identify yourself? Can Jesus recognize you as His disciple? Can the world see us as His disciples by our love? If you operate in the command to love, you will see that everything works by the outpouring of love. Love is the character of God, He is Love, and if you have God, then love is all you need.

Blessings, Rupert & Red.

OCTOBER 23

Get To Class!!

Meditation Verse: 2 Timothy 3:16-17 NIV

All Scripture is God-breathed and is useful for teaching, correcting, and training in righteousness, so that the servant of God may be thoroughly equipped for every good work.

Scripture Reading: 2 Timothy 3:10-17

My Father was all things education when his children were going to school. As a former student teacher of Math, Algebra, and believe it or not Latin, he checked our homework, and held us to the highest standards of academia, and there were consequences for not toeing the line. There was no excuse for failing a test, he used to say," you can read, and you have the book, so what's the problem?" The pressure was on for sure, but Dad was also an encourager even though he expected results. Paul likewise was encouraging his son in the gospel, Timothy, he knew that Timothy was going to face great opposition in his ministry, and the only thing that was going to get him through was the reading and studying of the word of God. All scripture is God breathed, that means that the scripture comes from God not man. The words that man wrote were breathed by God. The truth is that the scripture has been tested and held up over the centuries, it has stayed relevant, and current and all who have tried to discount or disprove the word of God have failed. There is no other book that has given more inspiration, has more honesty, influence, accurate predictions, life affirming and life changing power. It is more than a book of stories; it is the very recipe for life. It is the only book that when you read it, study it, practice and believe it, results in an eternal reward. Compare the Bible to any book that you have read and or written, that can thoroughly equip you for every good work. You can't, it does not exist. Want to be taught, advised, corrected, trained in what is right, equipped thoroughly for every good work? God has given you, His word. You can read, you have the book, there should be no problem!

Blessings, Rupert & Red.

OCTOBER 24

Live For The One Who Died For You

Meditation Verse: Galatians 2:20 NIV

I have been crucified with Christ and I no longer live, but Christ lives in me. The life I now live in the body, I live by faith in the Son of God, who loved me and gave himself for me.

Scripture Reading: Galatians 2:17-21

The justification of salvation by faith in Christ is not as complicated as it seems. Many have over-explained salvation to the point that some become confused. Well God is not the author of confusion, and He wants you to understand His love for you and the plan for your life. When Jesus died on the cross, an exchange happened. He took our place. Everything that we had done that would have led to a sentence of death for us, was taken away, so that we could be free to live the lives that God intended for us to live. Our debt was paid in full, and we believe it by faith. This faith connects us to Christ so that He takes up residence inside of us, and we live our lives through Him. This faith gives us the confidence that we are saved and that our future is eternally secured. Because Jesus loved you and gave himself for you. He. Loved. You. There was never a time when he didn't. Jesus loved you then and he loves you still. Receive his love today, He did the dying for you, now you do the living…for Him.

Blessings, Rupert & Red.

OCTOBER 25

Watch Your Mouth!

> Meditation Verse: Proverbs 13:3 HCSB
> *The one who guards his mouth protects his life; the one who opens his lips invites his own ruin.*
> Scripture Reading: Proverbs 13

There is a saying, that God has given us two eyes that we may see much, two ears that we may hear much, but has given us one tongue, and that fenced in with teeth, to indicate that though we hear and see much, we should speak but little. That my friends, is wise counsel! All of us can relate to the times when we, or someone we know has said too much. There are 30 or more bible references about the tongue in reference to its capabilities to tear down or build up. More than enough to let you know that it is important to God how we should monitor our words. Proverbs 18:21 (HCSB), puts it this way: "Life and death are in the power of the tongue." That says that your words can speak life, or your words can speak death. We ought to choose our words carefully and remind ourselves constantly about the power of our words. Our tongue is one of our most dangerous weapons, and often reveals our heart and character. Your words can leave scars that can destroy a person for life! Who really wants that on their conscience? Let us as the body of Christ, be intentional about our words, to bring life, light and healing to others. In fact, God commands it. He wants us to use our tongue to bring Him glory, and to edify His people. If we fill our hearts with the love and word of God, then the words that we speak will reflect the same. "For out of the abundance of the heart, the mouth speaks." Luke 6:45. (NKJV). Let your abundance be that of the fruit of the spirit, God will honor you for it.

Blessings, Rupert & Red.

OCTOBER 26

Grace, Grace, God's Grace!!

Meditation Verse: Titus 2:11-12 HCSB

For the grace of God has appeared with salvation for all people, instructing us to deny godlessness and worldly lusts and to live in a sensible, righteous, and godly way in the present age.

Scripture Reading: Titus 2:1-15

Thank God for GRACE!! Grace has found a place in every Christian's life. It is by grace we are saved, there is nothing that we can do to earn it. It has appeared to all men, and we can choose to accept or reject it. God's grace keeps us, sustains us, prepares us, develops us, and teaches us. It also empowers us to live godly lives, resisting temptation and worldly lusts. It is the way that God wants us to live, and His grace makes it possible. We have a future to look forward to, a life that is to be lived soberly and righteously, a life that takes salvation and the gift of God seriously in this present age. Ephesians 2:8-9 (NKJV), says: "For by grace you have been saved through faith, and not that of yourselves; it is the gift of God, not of works, lest anyone should boast." It goes on to say that we were created for good works, which God had prepared beforehand. God has a plan for your life, He always has had a plan, before we were born. And to offer you grace was a part of it. God knew that we would need grace to live this life with all of its craziness, debauchery, and wickedness everywhere you look. It is grace that will set you apart, and cause you to live a life of victory, a life that will give God glory. That's really what you were created for; to give Him glory, and to accomplish all that God has set for you to do. And we can do it… because His grace is sufficient.

Blessings, Rupert & Red.

OCTOBER 27

He's Got Your Back

Meditation Verse: Psalms 3:3 HCSB

But You, O Lord, are a shield around me, my glory, and the One who lifts up my head.

Scripture Reading: Psalms 3

David, the author of many of the psalms we read today, was an encourager not only to the people of whom he was King, but also to himself. He had a relationship with God that was like no other, even God spoke of him as "a man after His own heart." 1 Samuel 13:14a (NKJV). As believers, we who read the psalms and have known the comfort and strength that they have been in our own lives, should desire the type of intimate relationship that David had with God. In times of trouble, David called on God with the assurance that He would deliver him. We know that trouble will come our way sooner or later, and there will be times when we will need that same assurance. There is no such thing as a dead end for the believer. Jesus said that in this life we will have trouble, but we must believe not withstanding what we see that God will make a way! He will be our shield to protect us from the fiery darts of the enemy. During these troubled times find rest in Christ. God is the only One who can shield, sustain, strengthen and save us. We make it through because everything is intended to bring us through and give God glory. You are elevated to a place of safety and can hold your head high as you watch your enemies scatter. God will save the day; He will come through. No weapon formed against you will prosper, Isaiah 54:17a (NKJV), so even when it looks like the enemy has the upper-hand, God will place a shield around you, give you the victory, He gets the glory, and elevates you in front of your foes. Remember, David's troubles manifested a Kingdom, you never know what God has in store for you! Trust Him to have your back! There is power in relationship!

Blessings, Rupert & Red.

OCTOBER 28

Gratefulness!

Meditation Verse: Psalms 9:1 HCSB

I will thank Yahweh with all my heart; I will declare all Your wonderful works.

Scripture Reading: Psalms 9

Praise Break!! Did you know that we were created to praise God? Every culture and every tribe has the innate desire to worship! Even though sometimes that worship is misplaced, man inherently knows that he ought to worship. It is to be what we live, breathe and move for! Every breath is a thank you to God. It is because of Him that we are yet alive. So, with our whole heart we should show gratitude. A half-hearted effort is no effort at all. God deserves our most enthusiastic praise. If you stop and take the time to think of all that He has done for you, the ways He has made, the danger He has kept you from, you should have a spirit filled with gratitude and a mouth that will speak of all His wonderful works. Giving thanks is commanded in scripture again and again. So, we give thanks out of love and obedience, to elevate God above whatever it is we are going through. To declare His works is another way of praising God. Tell others of what He has done for you in your life, it is an act of worship, and may encourage others to receive what you have already! Our gratitude is necessary for our relationship with God to grow. Today, and everyday take the time to praise God, it is a habit that you need to develop. Besides, He. Is. Worthy!!

Blessings, Rupert & Red.

OCTOBER 29

Protection And Presence

Meditation Verse: Isaiah 43:2 HCSB

I will be with you when you pass through the waters, and when you pass through the rivers, they will not overwhelm you. You will not be scorched when you walk through the fire, and the flame will not burn you.

Scripture Reading: Isaiah 43:1-10

The protection and presence of a father is a very comforting and at the same time an empowering feeling. When he is around fear and trepidation are significantly lessened, and you feel like you can conquer the world. Why? Because a father is larger than life to a kid. He makes you feel safe. It is like that with your heavenly Father if you would develop a relationship with Him. God has promised to be with you in whatever circumstance and situation you might be facing. Trials and tribulations will come, just like the waters, rivers, and fires. We all must face it at some time or other. Isn't it assuring to know that whatever crisis you are facing the promise of God is to be with you, and to make sure that you come out on the other side. Cultivate, build, develop a relationship with Jesus, His promises are true, and you will be on the winning side. There is nothing like living daily with the protection and presence of God. Let your prayer today be to seek God, give Him your whole heart, you will be safe and the waters, and rivers and fires will not overwhelm, overtake, or consume you. Remember, there's power in relationship!

Blessings, Rupert & Red.

OCTOBER 30

Ready, Faith, Action!!

Meditation Verse: James 2:17 HCSB

In the same way faith, if it doesn't have works, is dead by itself.

Scripture Reading: James 2:14-26

We need to determine the difference between a dead faith and a living faith so that this verse by itself is given context. According to James 2:15 (paraphrased) if you fail to provide food and clothing toward a brother or sister in need, you demonstrate a dead faith. Knowing their need, you offer nothing but empty religious rhetoric; dead faith. A living faith is real faith. What you believe in you will act on. A real living genuine faith will be known by its works. That is how important a live faith is to the believer and God. It is what is in front of us as we "press toward the goal." Philippians 3:14a, (NKJV). That is why it is called the shield of faith; it is the tool that defeats unbelief. It is why Jesus said, "your faith has healed you." Luke 18:42b (NIV). The word faith is an action word, it must produce for the fruit to remain. A tree with no fruit may as well be a dead tree! So, develop your faith, grow it, water it, cultivate it, mature it, then act on it. Make a live and active faith your goal, don't be a fruitless tree!

Blessings, Rupert & Red.

OCTOBER 31

The Spirit Walk

> Meditation Verse: Galatians 5:16 NLT
>
> *So, I say, let the Holy Spirit guide your lives. Then you won't be doing what your sinful nature craves.*
>
> Scripture Reading: Galatians 5:16-26

We have spoken of this before, but like most of this devotional, we emphasize the key parts of righteous living and relationship, repeatedly. There is a war going on inside of the Christian. It is the war between the spirit and the flesh. This war is real and will continue until we receive our new bodies. The only remedy for this is to walk in the promise that Jesus said he would fulfill when He left this earth. He said that He would send a comforter, One who would speak of and emulate Him on the inside of us. That person is the Holy Spirit. If we walk in the Spirit, it becomes easier to deny our flesh. Winning this battle frees us from legalism and bondage under the law. It is a tough fight, but it is not a losing cause. Our goal is to be like Jesus, so walking in the Spirit means that you have greater living inside of you. You will always hear two voices; the key is to discern which voice you give heed to. When you listen to the Holy Spirit, He will guide you and lead you to live and walk like Jesus. While we cannot deny the existence of our carnal nature, we can choose not to give it any place. When we feel that "old man" rising up inside of us we can extinguish it with the Spirit and the word of God. Today, be intentional about walking in the Spirit. The result is love, joy, peace, longsuffering, kindness, goodness, faithfulness, gentleness and self-control. Galatians 5:22-23 (NKJV). With an arsenal like that, we will look a lot like Jesus and make the devil mad!

Blessings, Rupert & Red.

NOVEMBER 1

God's Choice, Not Ours

Meditation Verse: Romans 9:16 NLT

So, it is God who decides to show mercy. We can neither choose it nor work for it.

Scripture Reading: Romans 9:1-18

The children of promise in chapter 9 of Romans, are connected to God by the seed of Abraham. However, it is the ultimate seed that brings the redemption necessary to claim our inheritance. That seed is Christ, according to Galatians 3:16, (paraphrased). It is through that seed that all nations will be blessed. God has mercy on His children, but let's remember what mercy is: Mercy is not getting what we really deserve. We are children of promise, not by ethnicity, but by God's mercy. We are not saved because we live in a particular country or geographic location, but we are saved as we accept Christ as our personal Lord and Savior. Our inheritance is assured by Christ's finished work on the cross. God, however, calls for faith on our part, we have a part to play in how we live our lives before God. Trusting in His word, His sovereignty, and His calling in and on our lives. No one is beyond the reach of God's mercy, but our job is not to decide who is or who is not fit to be saved. Our job is to plant the seed and let God give the increase.

Blessings, Rupert & Red.

NOVEMBER 2

Let's Shine And Not Hide

Meditation Verse: Matthew 5:16 NLT

In the same way, let your good deeds shine out for all to see, so that everyone will praise your heavenly Father.

Scripture Reading Matthew 5:1-15

How do people know that you are a Christian? Is it obvious that you are an ambassador for Christ or is it just lip service? The word of God says that we are like "Living epistles, known and read by all men." 2Corinthians 3:2 (paraphrased). In other words, you are the only Bible some will ever see! Our lives should be a living example of what we believe, and our actions should reflect the same. What is the best way to be a witness for the gospel? Tell what you know! What has God done for you? How did you come to the saving grace and knowledge of God? Everyone can give their individual testimony as to why they became a follower of Christ. Allow the Holy Spirit to guide you and pray for boldness to speak. And then purpose in your heart to back your words with action! Let people see Christ in you! You may never know how you have helped, inspired, cheered, or encouraged the kingdom. If you just plant the seed, God will bring the increase, and fruit will result.

Blessings, Rupert & Red.

NOVEMBER 3

Doer or Just Hearer?

Meditation Verse: Romans 2:13 NLT

For merely listening to the law doesn't make us right with God. It is obeying the law that makes us right in His sight.

Scripture Reading: Romans 2:1-14

The application of scripture to our lives is a big part of being doers and not hearers only. Obedience is the required criteria for a healthy spiritual life. We need to search our hearts daily; it helps to purge us if you will of the wicked things. The word of God confirms; "The heart is deceitful above all things and desperately wicked; who can know it?" Jeremiah 17:9, (NKJV). It becomes a sounding gong in our ears that can pull us in either direction. We must realize that we are prone to wander, and that, "in our flesh dwells no good thing." Romans 7:18, (paraphrased). However, one thing is crystal clear: When the word of God is written in our hearts, it becomes harder to ignore the truth. Don't be a disciple in name only, live up to the deeds and actions so that talking is not all you do. The lost need to see your light, that is how we glorify God, with our bodies, souls, and spirits. By lighting up the dark places you will not only become a doer of the word, but your talk will be with the tongue of the wise, and your walk will not be towards death but towards life.

Blessings, Rupert & Red.

NOVEMBER 4

Jesus; The Greatest Gift

Meditation Verse: Matthew 2:11 NLT

They entered the house and saw the child with his mother, Mary, and they bowed down and worshipped Him. Then they opened up their treasure chests and gave him gifts of gold, frankincense, and myrrh.

Scripture Reading: Matthew 2:1-12

There are many lessons we can learn from the birth of Christ. Most important however, is our response to Him. David Guzik, commentator, said that all people respond in one of three ways:

1. "Like Herod, display an open hatred and hostility toward Jesus.
2. Like the chief priests and scribes, display indifference, all the while retaining their religious respectability.
3. Like the wise men, seek out Jesus and worship Him, even at a great cost!" Source: (Blue letter Bible, blueletterbible.org)

To learn from the wisdom of the wise men, those who look for Jesus will see Him, those who truly see Him will worship Him, and those who worship Him will honor Him with their time, talent, and treasure. God has given us an incredible gift! Let's not wait until the Christmas season to bring a deeper understanding of who Jesus is and determine our lives will bring Him the glory He deserves. He laid down His life so that we may be set free. Jesus said: "the hour is coming, when we will worship the Father in spirit and truth." John 4:23a (NKJV). The life we now live in Him will be made manifest in His kingdom. The wise men brought gifts, but the greatest gift, was right in front of them, the King of Kings, and Lord of Lord's! This is a story for the ages!! The truth of why we are so excited about Jesus, born to die that we might live!! Praises be to God who made it all possible!!

Blessings, Rupert & Red.

NOVEMBER 5

God's Not Through With You Yet

Meditation verse: Philippians 1:6 NKJV

Being confident of this very thing, that He who has begun a good work in you will complete it until the day of Jesus Christ.

Scripture Reading: Philippians 1:3-11

The old saints used to say, "I don't believe He brought me this far to leave me." If you truly belong to God, then you must be confident that God is working on your behalf. Paul was clear on the completion of this work; it was always for our own good. God has promised never to leave or forsake us. From now until the day Christ returns, God is working on the saint's behalf and planning our perfected good. He never starts something without finishing it. His track record is spotless!! Yield to His plan and trust the process. You are a work in progress, don't you give up! God is not through with you yet, so let the change begin!!

Blessings, Rupert & Red.

NOVEMBER 6

Love: It's Where We Belong

Meditation Verse: Jude 1:21 HCSB

Keep yourselves in the love of God, expecting the mercy of our Lord Jesus Christ for eternal life.

Scripture Reading: Jude 1

We have always said, "Love is all you need." For the believer, committing to a life where love is your seed brings a harvest of fruit and expectancy. To stay in the love of God, means to be in His will. While God loves everyone, everyone does not love God, so the benefits of His love are minimal. It's like the sun is shining, everybody seems to be warm, but I still feel cold!! Don't deny yourself the benefits of God's love and mercy, not only are they worth it, but they are crucial to our destiny. It is so easy to display mercy, when love is at the core. All your good deeds will not get you into heaven. The true deciding factors will be, how you treat Jesus and your neighbors. Once you get there, however, love will be the only currency you will need.

Blessings, Rupert & Red.

NOVEMBER 7

It's All Or Nothing!

Meditation Verse: Zechariah 7:9 NKJV

Thus says the Lord of hosts: "Execute true justice, show mercy and compassion Everyone to his brother."

Scripture Reading: Zechariah 7:8-14

The people of Israel were performing their rituals and festivals with their hearts far from God. Their religion was full of hypocrisy. When you are not right with God, your rituals before God will not, please Him. God does not care for empty rituals performed out of man-made traditions, God desires people who will listen and obey. In verse nine God commanded EVERYONE to execute true justice, show mercy, and compassion. Everyone means no one left out, so no one is exempt from this command. True justice, mercy and compassion are the pre-requisites for equality. You cannot make this about anything or anyone else. God rebuked the people through the prophet Zechariah for not being obedient to His word. The proper treatment of people has always been and still is important to God. Your relationship with people is in direct correlation to your relationship with God.

1 John 4:20b (NKJV) says: "for he who does not love his brother whom he has seen, how can he love God whom he can't see?" Your life will reflect your relationship. This command begins with you, no excuses, we all must examine our hearts and purpose to perfect this trifecta, Justice. Mercy. Compassion. God demands it! It is All or Nothing!!

Blessings, Rupert & Red.

NOVEMBER 8

How Real Is God To You?

Meditation Verse: Daniel 3:17-18 NKJV

If that is the case, our God whom we serve is able to deliver us from the burning fiery furnace, and he will deliver us from your hand, O king. But if not, let it be known to you, O king, that we do not serve your gods, nor will we worship the gold image which you have set up.

Scripture Reading: Daniel 3:9-18

We say that God is able, but do we believe it whatever the situation? Do you have the courage to stand, and having done all, still stand? The three Hebrew men did not consider their situation a dilemma. They were going to do what was right because it was the right thing to do. Their very speech said we are not afraid of you. God was able to deliver them, but even if He didn't, they were not going to bow to the king's idol. Do we have the "If not" kind of faith? The faith that says come what may, I am going to trust God! What if He does not answer our prayers the way we want? Can you deal with the fact that God's plans may be different from our desires? We must come to the realization that even if things don't turn out the way that we expect, God is still Sovereign. It takes courage to live out your faith during stressful and scary conditions. Doing the right thing may not always be popular, but it is always best to do the right thing and leave the results to God. God is well able to deliver us out of any situation. How, we don't always get to decide. Just know and believe that His way is best.

Blessings, Rupert & Red.

NOVEMBER 9

Basic Faith 101

Meditation Verse: Hebrews 11:6 NKJV

But without faith it is impossible to please Him, for he who comes to God must believe that He is, and that He is a rewarder of those who diligently seek Him.

Scripture Reading: Hebrews 11:1-39

This very well- known verse of Scripture is self-explanatory. This is the type of faith required of anyone who seeks God. You must believe first that He is, (exists), and you must believe that He rewards those who diligently seek Him. Nowhere else in the Bible is God and impossible mentioned in the same sentence, in this context. That is how important God regards faith. Faith is more important in this life than in the life to come. Our lives cannot be pleasing to God without it. It is one of the principal things which is the hallmark of our Christianity. It governs our walk and our talk. It is the sense that overrides all of the other senses. Faith characterizes us, justifies us, saves us and causes us to live by it. So, we must develop it, grow it, and mature in it. It is without a doubt essential to our relationship with Him. God will honor our diligence and eternity will be our reward.

Blessings, Rupert & Red.

NOVEMBER 10

Pass It Down!!

Meditation Verse: Psalms 145:4 NLT
Let each generation tell its children of Your mighty acts; let them proclaim Your power.
Scripture Reading: Psalms 145

Today we would rather text than talk. You can call someone on their cell, and they won't even answer their phone! Shoot them a text and an answer is almost immediate! No one seems to be bothered to really talk anymore. God has given us the awesome responsibility to communicate His love and goodness from generation to generation. Our children need to know that God blesses and upholds the righteous. How we live before our children and pour into their lives is a way to bring glory to God. They in turn must realize the importance of godly living and communicate that to their children. Put the phone down and talk to them. Let them hear and feel the passion and fervor in your voice. Let them know that our God is worthy of our praise and honor. When you speak the word into their lives, and read the Bible to them, it will build their faith. A faith that will be pleasing to God and will be a sign for generations to come. Just like the sower plants his seed and believes for a harvest, plant seeds of God's wisdom in their lives and watch the harvest of blessings that will increase and remain.

Blessings, Rupert & Red.

NOVEMBER 11

Leave Vengeance To God But Demand Justice!

Meditation Verse: Matthew 18:6 HCSB

But whoever causes the downfall of one of these little ones who believe in Me – it would be better for him if a heavy millstone were hung around his neck, and he were drowned in the depths of the sea!

Scripture Reading: Matthew 18:1-9

We have all been heartbroken by the horrific acts of violence that have been perpetrated on our schools and young people. There have been far too many of them in recent years, indeed one is too many! While we mourn the deaths of these precious lives and pray for their families, pray that our leaders will have the courage to do what is right to ban these assault weapons that no one should have. Jesus himself warned about the consequences to those who would cause children harm, and we should be angry enough to start building millstones and demand justice for the slaughter of innocent lives. Yes, we as Christians should address injustice when we see it and call out those who enable it. Jesus did all the time, and we are reminded in the word "woe to the man by whom the offense comes." Matthew 18:7b (NKJV). Vengeance belongs to God, but we have a responsibility before God to stand for a righteous cause. We cannot allow this scourge to persist. If we don't stand, who will? "God, we need You more than ever, help us to stand for justice and hold the offenders and enablers accountable. Our children depend on us, as well as those whose lives have been deemed worthless at the hands of the wicked with guns. We speak peace in our homes, schools, neighborhoods and communities, in Jesus' name, Amen."

Blessings, Rupert & Red.

NOVEMBER 12

It Is Important To God!

Meditation Verse: Isaiah 1:16-17 NLT

Wash yourselves and be clean! Get your sins out of my sight. Give up your evil ways. Learn to do good. Seek justice. Help the oppressed. Defend the cause of orphans. Fight for the rights of widows.

Scripture Reading: Isaiah 1:1-17

Many of you know by now that I am passionate about social justice! Why? Because it is important to God. I don't subscribe to the political terms and labels of the day. I am neither leftist nor right wing. In some things I am conservative, and in some liberal. Who I am first of all, however, is a Christian who has a radical love for God and a desire to see people saved and made whole. I also believe what is important to God should be important to me. God does not believe in oppression. You oppress people when you don't pay them a living wage. You oppress people when you offer them health insurance that is so expensive that they must decide between a premium or a grocery bill. You oppress people when you make poverty and lack a crime, and treat them as if it is their fault, because they cannot afford a decent quality of life. You oppress people when you deny them justice, harass, beat and yes kill them because their lives mean little to you. I realize there are evil people in this world and this world system is corrupt, because the powers of darkness control it. What angers God are so called Christians who support this system and are willing to stand behind men who perpetuate and sustain it. You cannot claim to be a follower of Christ and stand for what God is against. You can spin it anyway you want, but if it causes oppression you are fighting against God. If you will read it, the word of God says it, repeatedly. I will continue to speak out about the oppression of people, not because it is fashionable or fulfills any selfish desires, but because it is important to God!!

Blessings, Rupert & Red.

NOVEMBER 13

Conform To His Image

Meditation Verse: Psalms 89:14 NLT

Righteousness and justice are the foundation of your throne. Unfailing love and truth walk before you as attendants.

Scripture Reading: Psalms 89

Denying self in order to conform to the image of Christ should be every Christian's goal. This is a race not given to the swift. In order to walk with righteousness and justice as your companions, you must identify with Christ in the fellowship of His sufferings. In other words, the test is to endure to the end. If you practice Christianity without that foundation, then your relationship will be shallow. You cannot claim to love God and not love and practice justice and righteousness. How can we walk in love and yet not treat our brother fairly? John says in 1John 2:4 (NKJV), "He who says, "I know Him," and does not keep his commandments, is a liar, and the truth is not in him." That sounds harsh but God is serious about this. God will not operate in or bless hypocrisy. We need to bring Him glory in thought, word, and deed. The only way to become what God has called you to be is to have truth and unfailing love as your attendees. Want victory to be yours as you travail through this life? Do justice and righteousness for the sake of the kingdom and God will open doors that no man can shut. He has already seen to the outcome.

Blessings, Rupert & Red.

NOVEMBER 14

Be Sensitive To The Spirit

Meditation Verse: Acts 11:17 HCSB

Therefore, if God gave them the same gift that He also gave to us when we believed on the Lord Jesus Christ, how could I possibly hinder God?

Scripture Reading: Acts 11:1-18

While this text is primarily about the fact that salvation is for every man and woman, Peter also recognized the importance of sensing a move of God and following that leading. As the "body of Christ," are we allowing traditions and cultures to cloud our judgement? I have personally seen legalism and tradition kill a righteous cause. It is important to realize that we all suffer from some form of prejudice, but it is equally important to know that we should always let go of whatever is in the way of God's will. Whenever God reveals something to us, we should not hesitate to obey. "It is not His will that any should perish." 2Peter 3:9b (paraphrased). This is a desire that we should mirror. An acceptance of His will without selfish motive, our hearts should be pliable enough to be guided by God. Peter trusted the Spirit and moved, not doubting. Remaining open to change is one way to experience God's best. God has already determined your destination; LET HIM LEAD YOU!!

Blessings, Rupert & Red.

NOVEMBER 15

Corruption: It Is A People Thing

Meditation Verse: Micah 7:3 NLT

Both their hands are equally skilled at doing evil! Officials and Judges alike demand bribes. The people with influence get what they want, and together they scheme to twist justice.

Scripture Reading: Micah 7:1-7

We are more and more amazed at how timely God's word is! The fact that we are reading a book that was written thousands of years ago, and yet the relevance of each topic in our experiences is mind blowing! Solomon once said, "there is nothing new under the sun," Ecclesiastes 1:9b (NKJV), and the veracity of his words ring loud in light of today's shall we say postmodern society. This world is reeling under a cynicism that makes right wrong and wrong right. As we become more and more oblivious to the true nature of those in power, the system of checks and balances is slowly eroding before our eyes. Micah the prophet was confessing those very sins that are prevalent today on behalf of his people. What is almost disturbing as it is profound is the fact that any Pastor worthy of his calling could be echoing those exact same words today. The universality of corruption, bribes of people in high places, the very rich demanding their way, causing the justice of many to be denied. There must be a stand for righteousness in this wicked society. What is important to God cannot be buried under a web of deceit and complicit behavior. We need to stand and having done all we can, Still Stand!! Ephesians 6:13 (paraphrased). Pray that God will turn the hearts of leaders to what is right, but to hold people accountable for their actions or lack thereof. Micah spoke for the defenseless, we have the same duty.

Blessings, Rupert & Red.

NOVEMBER 16

Just Trust God!!

Meditational Verse: Psalms 84:12 NLT
O Lord of Heaven's Armies, what joy for those who trust in You.
Scripture Reading: Psalms 84

Trust in God is more than necessary, it is paramount! There is not a soul on earth that has not experienced dark days, sooner or later the rain is going to fall. We already know that we live under a world system that is sin ridden and wicked. However, we need to encourage ourselves and one another that God is greater than our circumstances and he is willing to trade our pain and sorrows for joy. We may not understand everything, and we may not get all the answers that we seek, but trust in God will give us the hope that will not disappoint. We need to decide every day to put our trust in God. Somebody needs to hear this today life has dealt you a cruel blow and you feel as if you will never recover. Wounds are not always physical or visible. You must trust that God has healing for you. It is possible to trust God in the middle of uncertainty. It is possible to feel peace in the middle of the crisis. It is possible to have joy in the morning. We all will have a time to mourn and a time to cry, when that time comes your daily declaration of trust in God will see you through. He is more than able. Our. God. Never. Fails.

Blessings, Rupert & Red.

NOVEMBER 17

God Is Not Lost; You Are!

Meditation Verse: Romans 3:11 NKJV
There is none who understands; There is none who seeks after God.
Scripture Reading: Romans 3:9-20

When something is lost, it is usually because it is obstructed from our view. We must look and try to uncover the place where that lost item is. Car keys and the television remote come to mind as those always seem to go missing! But with God He is always in plain sight! Romans 1:20 (NLT), says; "for ever since the world was created, people have seen the earth and the sky. Through everything God made, they can clearly see His invisible qualities, His eternal power and His divine nature. So, they have no excuse for not knowing God." All we need to do is open our eyes!! Why is it that we seek all the things that only satisfy temporarily, before we decide to seek what we have been seeing all along? Why go through this form of empty living, but not seek after God? Forget about religion! We see it everywhere it is not getting to God; you cannot inject God into religious forums! If it is not working by true agape love then there is no relationship, because everything works by love! No, we are not talking about church and the gathering of the saints for corporate worship. We are talking about the empty rituals for acceptance to find God. That is seeking an idol of your own making. God knows where you are, He is not lost. He is just waiting for you to yield. We all have a hole in our hearts that only God can fill. Trying to fill it with anything else is a lost cause and wasted effort. Yield to the one relationship that will truly satisfy. Open your eyes!! The rewards are inestimable and eternal.

Blessings, Rupert & Red.

NOVEMBER 18

Pray For The Working Man/Woman

Meditation Verse: James 5:4 HCSB

Look! The pay that you withheld from the workers who reaped your fields cries out, and the outcry of the harvesters has reached the ears of the Lord of Hosts.

Scripture Reading James 5:1-11

Again, we are talking about social justice. We thank God for all who work hard for a living, and struggle to make ends meet. In this day of unfriendly corporate culture (the nicest way I could put it), the people who make wealthy people possible could not be more disrespected and disenfranchised. More and more we see a regression of human dignity and respect that we fought for years to achieve. It is astounding to us the evil and cruelty that certain corporations and individuals foster on those who just want to take care of themselves and their families. The rollback of wages and benefits that helped to create a better quality of life for so many has fallen to such alarming levels that most cannot even feed their families adequately. We could go on and on about the horror of corporate greed but thank God for those that continue to fight for the workers welfare. God has something to say about this corporate culture which has become a stain on the fabric of society. We remind you in all fairness we said certain corporations and individuals! Woe to those who use their wealth and power to tear workers down instead of lifting them up. Who treat them as slaves and property instead of people of dignity and worth. Your day is coming, and it can't be soon enough. However, our trust is in God and not man and we defer to His timing. Our prayer should be that the wicked see the error of their ways before it is eternally too late. Until then we should stay in the fight for the working man/woman. Jesus said it simply and truthfully; "The laborer is worthy of his hire." Luke10:7b (NKJ).

Blessings, Rupert & Red.

NOVEMBER 19

Teach Them, Eternity Is Forever!

Meditation Verse: Deuteronomy 6:7 NKJV

You shall teach them diligently to your children and shall talk of them when you sit in your house, when you walk by the way, when you lie down, and when you rise up.

Scripture Reading: Deuteronomy 6:1-9

We know we are not alone when we say we did not always heed our parents' advice or rules when we were growing up. We were not full out rebellious kids, we were just like most kids, stubborn and selfish, thinking we knew better. The consequences we experienced as a result was not just the humiliation of a sore backside, but it helped to shape us in the raising of our own kids, and we see that pattern concerning our grandchildren. We required obedience and did not like to talk more than once. Why? Because our parents expected that of us and so it was passed down from one generation to the next. God expects obedience from us. The Hebrew word for hear and obey is "Shema," it is the word that Jesus used to say, "you who have ears to hear, let him hear." It is important to know and teach your children and your children's children your history and the heritage it represents. Likewise, we have an obligation to teach our children the word of God. To expose them to life affirming truths, that will prepare them for life and the future with God as their guide. It is more important than any level of education they can achieve, the amount of money they are able to make, or how popular and successful they may think they are. All those things will pass away. God wants you and your descendants to prepare for eternity that is true life. The best way to honor God is to obey Him. That brings the ultimate reward! So, Shema and give God the glory!!

Blessings, Rupert & Red.

NOVEMBER 20

Put God First!

Meditation Verse: Exodus 20:3 NKJV

You shall have no other gods before Me.

Scripture Reading: Exodus 3:1-6

While we have a God who is rich in love and mercy, desires relationship, and offers salvation and forgiveness, He demands to be put first. When we surrender our lives the promises of God are ours. We must, however, meet the conditions. Relationship is key because it establishes the boundaries of our hearts. God will grow us in the direction of His will for our lives. As we mature in His word, our desires conform to His will. It is a change of heart and a shift in our thinking. Once you understand that God is Sovereign, you will know why He must come first. You cannot allow anything to have preeminence over God. His word says that he is a jealous God and will not tolerate unfaithfulness. He will not share His glory. It does not mean that you are not to have a life aside from your relationship with God, we all have friends, some of us are married, have children, work and responsibilities. It is acknowledging that everything we enjoy in life is by the grace of God. To Him be all the praise and glory! He not only demands first place in our lives, He deserves it!! God is worthy of all the honor, all the praise, and all the glory! There should be no hesitation in putting God first in our lives, our gratitude and love should be reflected in all that we do, it will never come close to what He has done for us.

Blessings, Rupert & Red.

NOVEMBER 21

He Cares!

Meditation Verse: 1 Peter 5:7 HCSB

Casting all your care on Him, because He cares about you.

Scripture Reading: 1 Peter 5:1-11

We know that it looks hopeless, and you just don't know how you are going to make it through. We understand you are at the end of your rope and feel powerless to do anything about it. We are not going to pretend that there is an easy answer or solution that will absolve you of the pain that you feel. So many things happen that are beyond our control and there are those who empathize, but can't help, and those who can, won't. Discouragement, disillusionment, helplessness, fear, all these negative emotions are real and as much as you want to avoid them, they creep into your thoughts during the day, and into your dreams at night. We paint this dismal picture because everyone has or will experience this. Maybe for you it is right now! As cliché as it sounds; Don't Give Up!! Believe it or not this too shall pass. You have been down before, and you are still here. You may not want to hear it but, cast your care! That means throw it away from you. If it has happened, you have to get through it. Give it to God!! It is always good to have someone share the burden, but it is even better to let God carry it! We say this to encourage not just you but ourselves. No matter what we go through we have a God who not only cares but is able to see us through! If we did not believe it, we would have given up long ago! Not an option for us and should not be for you! Cast your care! He cares, God cares for you! Let's all talk about victory on the other side!!

Blessings, Rupert & Red.

NOVEMBER 22

It Is All His!!

Meditation Verse: 1 Chronicles 29:11 NLT

Yours, O lord, is the greatness, the power, the glory, the victory, and the majesty. Everything in the heavens and on earth is yours, O Lord, and this is your kingdom. We adore You as the One who is over all things.

Scripture Reading: 1 Chronicles 29:10-20

This prayer of praise from David really emphasizes the truth that all things come from God, and everything belongs to God. The staggering amount of giving that came from the people for the building of the Temple, was just giving back to God what was already His. He says in verse 12, "Wealth and power come from You alone, for You rule over everything. Power and might are in your hand and at Your discretion people are made great and given strength." 1Chronicles 29:12 (NLT). David knew that he was made great and powerful only because of the favor of God, and he understood the purpose for his great personal wealth. We, too, would do well to recognize; Everything belongs to God, He owns it all we own nothing, we are mere stewards over what we possess. He gets the glory, the honor and the praise, and whether you give it to Him or not, does not change a thing. Sooner or later, we are all going to kneel at his name, and confess Him as Lord, so you decide, but choose wisely, because remember, He owns everything even life and conquered death! All power belongs to God....and so do you!

Blessings, Rupert & Red.

NOVEMBER 23

What Are You Looking At?

Meditation Verse: 2 Corinthians: 4:18 NKJV

While we look not at the things which are seen, but at the things which are not seen: for the things which are seen are temporal; but the things which are not seen are eternal.

Scripture Reading: 2 Corinthians: 4

Everything that you see around you is temporary. Your house, the phone or computer that you are staring at, the money, the fame, the fortune. Even our bodies will one day disappear from existence. It is what you cannot see that will last forever. We have said before that spiritual realities are more real than the physical. We want to share five realities with you that we read by Rick Warren, a Pastor and author of, "The Purpose Driven Life."

1. God made you to love you and He wants you to learn to love Him back. (Jeremiah 31:3). That is the most important reality in life.
2. God made you to last forever, one day your heart will stop beating and that will be the end of your body, but that won't be the end of you. (Ecclesiastes 3:13).
3. God has prepared 2 eternal places, Heaven and Hell, they are literal places and not a state of being.
4. God has given you a choice as to where you want to spend eternity. You won't accidentally end up in hell, you will be there because you chose it or refused to choose Jesus.
5. You get no second chances to make your choice, your choice has a time limit. You have your entire life to make your decision, but you can't change your mind after death. Nothing matters more than eternal realities, what you do with these five sobering truths, will not only alter your eternal destiny but will transform the way you live on this side of

eternity. We love you and our prayer is that you make right decisions, you cannot just believe that God is love, if that belief does not cause you to choose Him! There's power in relationship.

Blessings, Rupert & Red.

NOVEMBER 24

Speak Now And Forever Live..

Meditation Verse: Luke 16:31 NLT

"But Abraham said, if they won't listen to Moses and the prophets, they won't be persuaded even if someone rises from the dead."

Scripture Reading: Luke 16:19-31

Another perspective: can we share with you that you are only one decision away from life or death? It is said that our lives now are the result of the decisions that we have made. Here is an amazing thought; You have to make so many decisions in this short life, yet only one for eternity. And for this one decision most need all sorts of signs and confirmation before they can make it. The decision is not based on what miracle you see to convince you, the miracle is that you make the decision without the sign. When the rich man tried to convince Abraham to send word to his brothers so they would not end up in a place of torment, Abraham said they have the word. A sign will not make them believe. Why? Because it is a heart issue, people can't and don't make a decision because their hearts need to change and only the Word can do that. It is based on faith and not the five senses. Faith comes by hearing the word. Romans 10:17 (paraphrased) Faith leads to belief and salvation. Speak the word in our everyday life, and that life will be an example that faith works and encourage others to make that decision. Again, Speak the Word! You never know who's listening.

Blessings, Rupert & Red.

NOVEMBER 25

God Hates Evil, So Should We

Meditation Verse: Proverbs 17:13 NLT
If you repay good with evil, evil will never leave your house.
Scripture Reading: Proverbs 17

We have heard it said, to repay evil with good is divine, to repay good with good human, and to repay good with evil devilish. The latter seems to be the order of the day, and the selfishness of man has taken on a devilish taint. The saying, "no good deed goes unpunished," loses its sarcasm and becomes reality in our everyday lives. It is a slap in God's face to punish good. Nothing discourages a person more than to see their hard work and efforts rewarded with pain. In our world, the milk of human kindness has turned sour. Just turn on the news and we see senseless attacks on people that were just going about their day. There seems to be an unprecedented level of hate, that has permeated society, to a point to where it has become expected, and no one should be surprised at these horrific behaviors. When God sees His moral order offended, he will answer, and evil will not leave the perpetrator's house. The ingratitude of man has led to the wretchedness of man, which leads to the perpetuity of evil. The answer is to restore God's moral order, treat people who mean you no harm with love and compassion, the love of God can change men's hearts. Aren't you exhausted by the weight of misdirected anger and hate? We are. Let's remove evil from our houses, show God's love, and watch lives change.

Blessings, Rupert & Red.

NOVEMBER 26

The Lord Is Coming Soon!

Meditation Verse: Malachi 3:5b NLT

"At that time, I will speak against those who cheat employees of their wages, who oppress widows and orphans, or who deprive the foreigners living among you of justice, for these people do not fear me," says the Lord of Heaven's Armies.

Scripture Reading: Malachi 3:1-5

Once again social justice matters to God. In light of all that is going on today, the mistreatment of people of color and immigrants, they seem to be one in the same, this is something that God hates. The ramping up of the vitriol is real and the ones responsible will answer to a righteous God. God has admonished us, no commanded us to treat the foreigner and the stranger, with love, respect, and equality. Everyone should have the dignity of fair treatment and be allowed to go through the legal and vetting process. There are some who believe that God's love is only for a certain demographic, the truth is God made man and woman in His image and likeness. All have the capacity to praise, all have the freedom to worship, and can have relationship with Him. God is no respecter of persons; we are because He is! There is no division in Christ, no room for discrimination, placing certain people in categories, promoting dissension violence and separation. We need to pray because prayer does change things. Then we need to be active in our communities and stand against wrongful unjust treatment of our fellow man. As Christians, that is disciples of Jesus Christ, it is demanded of us that we show love, and to conform to His image. We must allow the love of God to transform us, so that the things that are important to Him, become important to us, in this way, and only in this way will we fulfill the law of Christ.

Blessings, Rupert & Red.

NOVEMBER 27

Praise Until We See Victory!

Meditation Verse: Psalms 18:2 NLT

The Lord is my rock, my fortress, and my Savior; my God is my rock, in whom I find protection. He is my shield, the power that saves me, and my place of safety.

Scripture Reading: Psalms 18

This psalm, like many psalms, is a song of praise! David has been delivered from Saul and all his enemies and he was rejoicing in the God of his salvation. As we read this, we thought of all the times that David was running from Saul and all who sought to end his life, and all his psalms ended the same way, with affirmation and praise. Our takeaway was this; Praise your way through!! Are you still in the tunnel of despair and you can't see your way out? Are the circumstances of your situation so dire that only the miraculous seems to be the answer? The plan of God is sometimes hard to see in the mess we seem to find ourselves in, but when you can't trace Him, praise Him anyhow!! It may not make sense, but faith is not about sense or how you may feel! It is about the belief that God can do the impossible! Purpose still works as long as you are breathing!! We encourage you and ourselves today, Praise God for His mercy and His benefits, there is victory on the other side!!

Blessings, Rupert & Red.

NOVEMBER 28

Lord, Be It Unto Me According To Thy Word.

Meditation Verse: Luke 2:19 NKJV
But Mary kept all these things and pondered them in her heart.
Scripture Reading: Luke 2:8-20

Sometimes the complexities of life can cause great concern, resulting in deep reflection. Why do certain things happen in the way that they do, and what does it really mean? What is God up to? It really comes down to a specific level of trust because from second to second we don't know what the future holds. We go about our lives, making our own plans often oblivious to the fact that these plans are subject to the will of God. Those plans can be altered in a nanosecond. We are sure that Mary's plans did not include a virgin birth! We think of her excitement to be wed and start a new chapter in her life. But instead, her plans were interrupted, and she became the subject of a scandal. Oh, you know they talked about her that's what we do. But even in her willingness to make herself available despite the consequences, even after everything happened just as the angel of the Lord had said, she wondered, what did it all really mean? What was the end game? What was God really doing? One of the many lessons here is that Mary's obedience preceded her own uncertainty. Her level of trust gained her great reward. The countless lives that were changed for the better was an unknown quantity to her. Sometimes our obedience will require a leap of faith, not knowing does not have to mean not doing. Like Mary, it will bring questions and uncertainty, but we may never know the impact our obedience will have on future generations. Is there something that you know the Lord is requiring of you? Your response should be: "Be it unto me according to THY WORD!!" Luke 1:38b (KJV emphasis mine).

Blessings, Rupert & Red.

NOVEMBER 29

A Prayer To Encourage The Saints!

Meditation Verse: James 5:16 MSG

Make this your common practice: Confess your sins to each other and pray for each other so that you can live together whole and healed. The prayer of a person living right with God is something powerful to be reckoned with!

Scripture Reading: James 5:13-18

We just want to let you all know! We are not ashamed of the gospel of Jesus Christ! Our desire is to share the amazing love of God with everyone. Know that we will pray for you and with you. We will rejoice with you and cry with you. We want to encourage you and bless you with our words, thoughts, and deeds. May the peace and wisdom of Almighty God surround you, guide you, and keep you safe from all harm and danger seen and unseen. May His love envelop you and grow you into sharing it and showing it to others, May His light shine on you and through you, to order your steps, and cause you not to stumble, so that those whom you come into contact with will seek the same path. May His grace and favor be upon you in every area of your life. So that you will live a healthy, safe and prosperous life today and beyond. "May Yahweh bless you and protect you; may Yahweh make His face shine on you and be gracious to you; may Yahweh look with favor on you and give you peace." Numbers 6:24-26 (HCSB). We love you all and there is nothing that you can do about it!! We decree and declare that the best is yet to come!!

Blessings, Rupert & Red.

NOVEMBER 30

He Is The God Of The Second Chance

Meditation Verse: Luke 13:6-9 HCSB

A man had a fig tree that was planted in his vineyard. He came looking for fruit on it and found none. He told the vineyard worker, "Listen, for three years I have come looking for fruit on this fig tree and haven't found any. Cut it down! Why should it even waste the soil?" But he replied to him, Sir, leave it this year also, until I dig around it and fertilize it. Perhaps it will bear fruit next year, but if not, you can cut it down.

Scripture Reading: Luke 13:1-9

This parable is about the God of a second chance. If nothing else God's love for us is also shown in His patience with us. However, this parable also shows the principles of God's judgement. The first principal is, God looks for fruit. The fruit in your life or lack thereof determines the type of person or soil you are. If Christ has touched your life in a meaningful way, then it should show in the fruit we bear. The first fruit that we should cultivate is the fruit of the Spirit; love, joy, peace, long suffering, kindness, goodness, faithfulness, gentleness and self-control. Galatians 5:22-23, (NKJV). God gives us special care, even though the pruning sometimes can be painful, He is nourishing us for growth. Growth can be useful for much fruit. On the other hand, a tree can be pruned and pruned and found to be useless for fruit bearing. In the parable the owner waited for three years to see some fruit, but the farmer begged for another chance to see if the tree would finally bear fruit. Are you useful or useless? Are you pouring into the kingdom or just taking? Uselessness invites disaster, anything that just takes cannot survive, but God gives second chances, if you are reading this you have been given another chance. Let's cultivate our lives and bear the type of fruit that God is longing to see. The fruit that will multiply and remain.

Blessings, Rupert & Red.

DECEMBER 1

It Is Finished, The Cry Of Victory!!

Meditation Verse: John 19:30 NLT
When Jesus had tasted it, he said, "It is finished!" Then He bowed His head and gave up His spirit.
Scripture Reading: John 19:16b-30

Jesus' final words, "it is finished," (Tetelestai in the Greek), was a cry of Victory! Jesus had finished the eternal purpose of the cross. It stands today as the foundation to all Christian faith, paying in full the debt we rightfully owed to God, and saving us from the wrath of God toward man. Hallelujah!! It has been said that a few words can change everything, "Not guilty" in a court of law can change everything, "Yes" or even "No" to a marriage proposal can change everything, "Goodbye" can change everything. But no words have had more impact on history, than the last words of Jesus in John 19:30. His perfect obedience was finished, the satisfaction of God's justice was finished, the power of Satan over sin and death was finished. He bowed His head in voluntary surrender, He gave up His Spirit because He had the authority, only Jesus could lay down His life and then take it up again. Has Jesus finished His work for you? Then you must finish your work for Him. We must persevere in love to fulfill His purpose in our lives. On this day and every day, we ought to reflect on all that Jesus has been through in order that we may have a right to the tree of life. He suffered unbelievably, bled and died for you; the very least you can do is live for Him…

Blessings, Rupert & Red.

DECEMBER 2

What Say Your Heart?

Meditation Verse: Jeremiah 17:10 HCSB

I, Yahweh, examine the mind, I test the heart to give to each according to his way, according to what his actions deserve.

Scripture Reading: Jeremiah 17:1-13

When it comes to matters of the heart, there are countless, books, gurus, both medical and psychiatric, physical, and even spiritual schemes, full of advice that some claim to be expert in. There are so many ways and directions that people can be swayed and pulled, causing countless damage to the very people that were supposed to be helped. The truth is that no one is capable of examining their own heart, much less the hearts of others, we just don't have the ability to see that deep. That is the reason for mega-heart break, deception, and even self-deception! We don't know what we need so we feed our fleshly desires, always falling short of the goals set. In verse 9 of Jeremiah 17, (NKJV), it states, "The heart is deceitful above all things, and is desperately wicked, who can know it?" If you have a car of a particular make or model, when some part of it fails, the best place to take it for repair is the place that made or manufactured it. They can examine it and make an accurate assessment of what is needed and the level of repair. So, who better to examine our hearts than the God who made us? You do know that is a process that will take place with or without our consent. David understood that process which is why he said in Psalm 139:23 (HCSB), "Search me, God and know my heart, test me and know my concerns." God and God alone is capable of examining your heart, allow Him full access today, grow in relationship with the One who made you, He will test your heart, and lead you on the path that you should take, the one that leads to everlasting life.

Blessings, Rupert & Red.

DECEMBER 3

The Time Is Now!

Meditation Verse: 2 Peter 3:9 HCSB

The Lord does not delay His promise, as some understand delay, but is patient with you, not wanting any to perish but all to come to repentance.

Scripture Reading: 2 Peter 3:1-13

Impatience to a child depending on what their desire is can seem adorable, irritating, or downright annoying. Impatience for an adult, however, depending on their circumstances can seem excruciating. Waiting was never the forte of the human experience. In the moment of any intense want or desire we often fail to see any benefit for patience. Thankfully and mercifully, God, for our sake, knows the wisdom in patience. This verse is not just about patience, but about God's love and long suffering for us. He desires relationship rather than estrangement, repentance rather than punishment, life rather than perishing. Every day that the Lord tarries is a day for you to get it together. Most of us, Christians included, if we are honest, are grateful that Jesus did not return last year, or even last night! Your life on earth means nothing if you are not in preparation mode for eternity. This is not a futile exercise, Jesus will return!! He is waiting on you to see the value of relationship with Him and have the assurance of a forever life in His presence. Don't procrastinate, even patience has an expiration date!

Blessings, Rupert & Red.

DECEMBER 4

Unashamed!!

Meditation Verse: Romans 1:16 HCSB

For I am not ashamed of the gospel of Jesus Christ, because it is God's power for salvation to everyone who believes, first to the Jew, and also to the Greek.

Scripture Reading: Romans 1:8-17

Where are you on the spectrum as it relates to the gospel of Jesus Christ? Do people know that you are a Christian? Do you boldly declare yourself as belonging to Christ or is there something that is holding you back from that acknowledgement to others? Is it fear or shame that has you hesitant to share the gospel when it comes to your relationship with Christ? Jesus left us with very specific instructions to go into all the world and make disciples. No, it was not just the disciples that received that mandate. The church of Jesus Christ has that same responsibility. Now not everybody is called to be a pastor, teacher, or evangelist, or even a missionary but everyone is called to serve. We can witness to people in many ways, through our attitudes, our speech, our kindness, and most importantly our love. God is looking for those who will stand unashamed and promote His kingdom. Realize that the gospel has real power and that planting of seed is all that God requires of you. He has promised the increase! That is a great partnership! And yes, representing Jesus will come with its persecution, but the final victory is ours! We encourage you to let your light shine, so that others may see your ministry and in turn glorify God. That's how powerful the gospel is, it is not just a game changer, but a life changer, and helping to change lives is nothing to be ashamed of!!

Blessings, Rupert & Red.

DECEMBER 5

Obtain Mercy And Find Grace

Meditation Verse: Hebrews 4:16 NKJV
Let us therefore come boldly to the throne of grace, that we may obtain mercy and find grace to help in time of need.
Scripture Reading: Hebrews 4:14-16

We like to call this verse the great invitation! Have you ever known about a function or an event that everyone you knew seemed to be attending but you did not have an invitation? It would make you feel pretty small and unpopular right? We are sure you would be hesitant to show up for fear of being turned away. Because now days people are not overly concerned about your feelings, without an invitation there is no access. Jesus doesn't play that! Verse 15a of that same chapter in Hebrews states: "For we do not have a High Priest who cannot sympathize with our weaknesses." (NKJV). In other words, He knows and cares about what we are going through, what our concerns are, and the ability to change the situation. He has given you an open invitation to approach the throne of grace, not arrogantly, but not timidly either, He says boldly, with confidence and assurance that you will be granted access! So that we may obtain mercy, (not getting what we deserve) and find grace, (getting what we do not deserve) just at the time that we need it. Jesus has given us the invitation, it is up to us to walk through that door and approach the throne, He loves you, He's waiting, and will under no circumstance cast you out. Access Granted!!

Blessings, Rupert & Red.

DECEMBER 6

Courage + Obedience = Success!

Meditation Verse: Joshua 1:7 HCSB

Above all, be strong and very courageous to carefully observe the whole instruction My servant Moses commanded you. Do not turn from it to the right or the left, so that you will have success wherever you go.

Scripture Reading: Joshua 1:1-9

Here God is commissioning Joshua to not only take over from Moses to lead the children of Israel into the promised land, but also to divide the land between the tribes. In order to successfully do that Joshua will have to be a fierce warrior and lead the cause to drive the current inhabitants from the land. He will need to be steady, strong, courageous and focused. God is saying to Joshua, if you will listen and obey Me, then your confidence and courage will also be in Me. It is important to remember in relationship with God, our weakness is made strong in Him. Without your trust and faith in God, you will not be able to accomplish your purpose. So, whatever you do in life is dependent, on what you do in God. Like God told Joshua, "Be strong and very courageous" our mandate is the same. It is what God has told us to be. Courage is not the absence of fear, it is the ability to press on in spite of what or how you feel. God will never tell you to be something you can't, so, like Joshua step out in faith and "be" whatever God is calling you to be. Don't place your confidence in self, place it in God, do what He says, and your success will be the result.

Blessings, Rupert & Red.

DECEMBER 7

He Is Worthy!

Meditation Verse: Psalms 100:4 HCSB

Enter His gates with thanksgiving and His courts with praise. Give thanks to Him and praise His name.

Scripture Reading: Psalms 100

Praise Break!! This morning or at whatever time the day starts for you, pause and thank God for His goodness toward you. Relationship demands that we show our love and appreciation to the One who made us. Praise was not just made for Sunday morning. There should be a ready praise for God at any moment through the day. Listen, every breath that you take is not dependent on you but on God. So, we would suggest to you that every breath is a testament to His sovereignty, grace and mercy. Although the verse would suggest that this praise should take place inside of some building or court, however, I would like to think that when you walk anywhere inside or out you are walking or entering the presence of God. You cannot be where He is not. So, you can praise Him where you are, God is there. In fact, the word says that God inhabits the praises of His people, therefore the praise on your lips already has God in it, you just have to express it! The God we serve is worthy!!

Blessings, Rupert & Red.

DECEMBER 8

Give Me A Clean Heart

Meditation Verse: Psalms 51:10 KJV

Create in me a clean heart, O God, and renew a right spirit within me.

Scripture Reading: Psalms 51

The word create gives this verse an exclusive benefactor. For who can create a heart but God? David's cry I suspect is one of anguish after being convicted of his sin with Bathsheba. In his plea for forgiveness, he wants to start afresh, so he asks for a clean heart and renewed spirit. Change this feeble weak and useless human for a contrite and repentant one. Missing the mark can cause untold grief and regret in our lives as well. Fortunately for us as in David's case, God is merciful. "If we confess our sins, He is faithful and just to forgive us our sins and to cleanse us from all unrighteousness." 1 John 1:9, (NKJV). It does not matter what you have done, God is faithful and just where we are not, and He has promised to throw our sins into the sea of forgetfulness. Because we were born in sin, we have an issue that will not go away on its own. It takes the cleansing of our hearts with the blood of Jesus that renews the right spirit in us. It is the new birth that signifies that new beginning. Want a clean heart and a right spirit? Get born again, start over in a brand-new relationship with Christ, He will exchange your old life for a new one, one that will last forever, it will be by far the best decision you ever made!

Blessings, Rupert & Red.

DECEMBER 9

The Pursuit Of True Happiness.

Meditation Verse: Proverbs 21:21 HCSB
The one who pursues righteousness and faithful love, will find life, righteousness and honor.
Scripture Reading: Proverbs 21

There are many paths that one can choose in life. It is said that your choices will define the type of life you will have. And that makes sense. So, if that is a given, common sense would be to choose wisely. Proverbs 21:21 gives us the wisdom to make right choices. To pursue righteousness is seeking to be in right standing with God. "So are My ways higher than your ways, and My thoughts than your thoughts." Isaiah 55:9b (NKJV). So, to pursue a righteous way of life is a Godly attribute. Faithful love will provide stability and prevent distraction from the goals in your life. These two qualities add up to the God kind of life. That is a life that knows no equal! What makes it more exciting is the promise that God gives. As God is faithful and righteous, and you emulate these attributes, you will find the life and right living that God will not only bless but honor. Sounds like a worthy pursuit to us! Get on the path that emulates the Father! Start living the God kind of Life!!

Blessings, Rupert & Red.

DECEMBER 10

Standing On The Promises!

Meditation Verse: Isaiah 41:10 HCSB

Do not fear, for I am with you; do not be afraid, for I am your God. I will strengthen you; I will help you; I will hold on to you with My righteous right hand.

Scripture Reading: Isaiah 41:1-13

I remember fondly that whenever we would ask my mom how she was doing she would always answer, "Oh, I'm just standing on the promises." This verse in Isaiah reminds me of my mom because it is one of the many great and precious promises that she stood on. Fear, they say, is an emotion experienced when encountered with a threat. Our brains are wired to feel fear so when God says, "fear not," it is because fear is real. The presence of God however calms all fears. He has promised to be with us, so there is no need to be afraid. God plus you will always be a majority. With God you are never alone. He will help us, because He loves us! We can't think of anyone that we would rather have on our side than God! Can you claim these promises? Can you say that God is my God? Can you use strength, help and a powerful hand in your life? Relationship with God can change everything! Then when someone asks you how you are doing, you can say; "I am standing on the promises!!"

Blessings, Rupert & Red.

DECEMBER 11

Where Is Your Hope?

Meditation Verse: Psalms 119:114 HCSB
You are my shelter and my shield; I put my hope in Your word.
Scripture Reading: Psalms 119:114-120

David was the target of a relentless manhunt, conducted and sanctioned by King Saul. If anyone ever needed protection it was David! His very life was in constant danger. God's protection was a great comfort to David and throughout the Psalms you read of David's praise and gratitude for God being His defense and hiding place. David's relationship with God was not just based on his dependence on God or the intimacy that he shared in his vulnerability, but also on his purpose. God had spoken into David's life and told him that he was to be the next king of Israel. His hope and trust is in the word of God. God has a purpose for each and every one of our lives. Like David, we must trust in God's word. And believe that God will shelter us and protect us until everything that concerns us is perfected. That takes a relationship that is built on the hope that God keeps His promises, and His purpose for our lives is in His hands. Surrender your will to God. Submit to His plan for your life. It is the only surrender that will guarantee victory and not defeat, hope in God will never disappoint.

Blessings, Rupert & Red.

DECEMBER 12

Wait Patiently On God

Meditation Verse: Psalms 37:7 NLT

Be still in the presence of the Lord and wait patiently for Him to act. Don't worry about evil people who prosper or fret about their wicked schemes.

Scripture Reading: Psalms 37

The 37th Psalm is a teaching moment! It is both encouraging and admonishing. It expresses, both the wisdom of God and the folly of the ungodly. It is a lesson in discipline and extols the benefits of waiting. In this microwave society, waiting seems to be a thing of the past. Nobody wants to wait for anything! We want everything fast, quick, and in a hurry! Even traffic lights try our patience! Our expectation is based on how we can track our purchases if they are sent in the mail, and how long we have to wait for an oil change. Man!! This is so hard to do!! Especially when it seems as if people are just enjoying all the luxuries and amenities that this world has to offer. But maturity dictates that we must declare dependence on God, rather than independence from God. God says to wait patiently for Him to act. We will get a chance to do our part, but you will mess it up every time if you feel that you need to "help God out." Leave it to God, let patience have its perfect work, the wicked will only prosper in their temporary lifetime. We will have eternity! Don't fret, believe He is the ultimate way maker! After all He has been doing this a lot longer than you!!

Blessings, Rupert & Red.

DECEMBER 13

Know Your Enemy

Meditation Verse: Ephesians 6:12 NLT

For we are not fighting against flesh-and-blood enemies but against evil rulers and authorities of the unseen world, against mighty powers in this dark world, and against evil spirits in the heavenly places.

Scripture Reading: Ephesians 6: 1-20

Face it!! You are in a spiritual battle. That is not an idea, it is a fact. Spiritual warfare is real. Principalities and powers do exist. Look there always seems to be contention and division everywhere. You never have to look far for a fight or confrontation even when you are minding your own business! People today seem to be meaner and more selfish than ever, and therein lies the real issue. People in the natural are not really your problem, it is the spirit that they emulate. Sometimes willingly and sometimes unwillingly. Oh yes, there are those who choose to emulate and entertain an evil spirit, and those who don't understand why they do the things they do. If we don't recognize that there is a spirit world that is more real than this three-dimensional physical world, we will always feel like we are in a fight that we cannot win. But once you know your enemy, a new strategy is needed, and the demons need to flee, how you ask? By putting on the whole armor of God, Ephesians 6: 14-17 (NKJV), when you have God on you, the only result is Victory!!

Blessings, Rupert & Red.

DECEMBER 14

Lifetime Security

Meditation Verse: Proverbs 18:10 HCSB
The name of Yahweh is a strong tower; the righteous run to it and are protected.
Scripture reading: Proverbs 18

We love the promises of God!! He has provided for His children in immeasurable ways! You can read them and meditate on them and memorize them. In this verse, God is offering His protection on His Name! There is sufficiency in just the name for everything and anything you may need and desire. However, as wonderful as this promise is and sounds, it is conditional. You have to meet the criteria. He protects the righteous!! No, he did not say the perfect, the poor the rich, the young or the old, but those who are in right standing with God. It is quite simple, if you want to enjoy the protection of God, get in right relationship with Him. He loves you and wants to protect you in ways that you cannot even imagine. He has given you today to make that important decision. So do it today and walk, no run into the strong tower, the ark of safety, you know that is where you belong!!

Blessings, Rupert & Red.

DECEMBER 15

Just Because God Is Good!

Meditation Verse: Psalms 107:1 NLT

Give thanks to the Lord, for He is good! His faithful love endures forever.

Scripture Reading: Psalms 107

We are feeling inspired this morning, and we just want to share with you a little encouragement, by praying a prayer for you today that God has laid on our hearts. Our prayer today is that you will see creation as it is meant to be seen, through the eyes of the Creator God, and that your day will be filled with the wonder of The One who is the giver of every good and perfect gift, one of them being your life. Praise God today for who he is, search for His heart, more than His hand. His loving mercy and kindness are everlasting. Love, because He first loved you. Seek to be a blessing, show kindness, replace your harsh words with soft ones, show justice and forgiveness so that you may live your lives in peace. Give thanks with a grateful heart, and NEVER forget where your help comes from. Be blessed in Jesus' name, Amen. Have an amazing day!

Blessings, Rupert & Red.

DECEMBER 16

A Change Of Heart

Meditation verse: 1 Corinthians 3:18 HCSB

No one should deceive himself. If anyone among you thinks he is wise in this age, he must become foolish so that he can become wise.

Scripture Reading: 1 Corinthians 3:1-20

At first glance this passage of scripture seems contradictory, oxymoronic, and cynical all at once! How in the world does someone have to become a fool in order to be wise? While Paul seems to be sarcastic in this text, he is speaking a profound truth. There needs to be a change of ideas. The wisdom of this world is foolishness to God. Our ideas and advancement in technology and science, have only increased wickedness and greed, in exchange for human kindness. We exploit the poor and the workers in exchange for an embarrassment of riches. We seek to gain the whole world in exchange for our very souls. In all our worldly wisdom we have not yet found the cure for the depraved human condition. When you think that something is just for you, then you become the definition of a fool, selfish and self-deceived. Our exchange needs to be a heart of flesh instead of a heart of stone. Selflessness instead of selfishness. Peace instead of conflict. Relationship instead of resentment. All the wisdom of this world can't compare to the love of God. Exchange everything you know for a relationship with Him, it will change all you thought you knew, and bring you to the wise realization that you made the best trade of your life!

Blessings, Rupert & Red.

DECEMBER 17

Prayer Changes Things

Meditation Verse: Philippians 4:6 NIV

Do not be anxious about anything, but in every situation, by prayer and petition, with thanksgiving, present your requests to God.

Scripture Reading: Philippians 4:4-9

I know that we have spoken of prayer a few times throughout this devotional. But it cannot be emphasized enough how important communication is in any relationship. Prayer is how we communicate with God. Jesus talks about prayer and demonstrates the importance of it in His own life on earth. Praying to God on a consistent basis shows Him your heart and you will begin to discern His. In this particular passage God is saying through Paul, don't be anxious about anything, but pray about everything. Prayer is powerful!! No matter the situation, bring it to God in prayer. He knows what you need before you ask, but your participation is needed in order for you to put your faith to work, for the circumstance you may find yourself in. God neither slumbers nor sleeps, He is more than able to hear you at any time of the day. The blessing is, God wants to hear from you. He is waiting, a surrendered life has the power to touch the throne of God. Be consistent in your prayer life and watch God change things. Relationship has its privileges.

Blessings, Rupert & Red.

DECEMBER 18

The Best Meal Ever!!

Meditation Verse: Revelation 3:20 HCSB

Listen! I stand at the door and knock. If anyone hears My voice and opens the door, I will come into Him and have dinner with him, and he with Me.

Scripture Reading: Revelation 3:19-22

Few things make me happier than to go out to a nice or favorite restaurant with my wife. I just love the intimacy that a candle lit table and a good meal can create! Communication increases and all things being equal, the relationship improves. Remember the Bible says, with all your getting, get understanding. Proverbs 4:7b (NKJV). Jesus understands the importance of relationship along with fellowship. His invitation is for anyone who can hear. It is for the increase of understanding, and the development of relationship and intimacy. It is essential, Jesus has a blessing that will blow your mind. His promises are true, and He is ever faithful. The joy that He gives the world cannot take away. He wants that for you. Get up! Get dressed! He is knocking on the door of your heart. Open the door! Let Him in! We guarantee you that it will be the most satisfying meal you ever had!

Blessings, Rupert & Red.

DECEMBER 19

In His Presence

Meditation Verse: Psalms 27:4 NIV

One thing I ask from the Lord, this only do I seek: that I may dwell in the house of the Lord all the days of my life, to gaze on the beauty of the Lord and to seek him in his temple.

Scripture Reading: Psalms 27

This psalm is about the confident, comforting, and caring relationship that David had with God. No matter what the situation or circumstance, David knew that he could always put his trust and faith in God. God would never fail him. Understand that if there ever was a person who would be stressed out and worried it would be David. His life was in constant danger, and he had the responsibility of his army and their families as well to keep them safe. He knew, however, where his help came from. His greatest desire, though, was to fellowship with the Lord, and bask in His presence. Not just on Sundays, but all the days of his life! Praise was his priority! I believe that praise should be the believers' priority as well. God has blessed you in ways that you have not even thought of. Because we take so much for granted, we don't even realize that God is still in the blessing business, even though sometimes it gets really tough, and you feel like it is all falling apart. That is the time to get your praise on. Praise will put things in proper perspective. Get in God's presence, meditate on His word, this psalm would be a good place to start. Develop a confident, comforting and caring relationship with God, and you will desire to be in His presence; All the days of your life!!

Blessings, Rupert & Red.

DECEMBER 20

For All That He Has Done!

Meditation Verse: Psalms 103:1-2 NKJV

Bless the Lord, O my soul; and all that is within me bless His holy name!
Bless the Lord, O my soul, and forget not all His benefits.

Scripture Reading: Psalms 103

Praise Break!! Do you know that feeling when you have been blessed, and you know that God has used people in your life to do it? Well, if you don't there is an overwhelming feeling of gratitude that swells up on the inside of you! When you serve God, He will bless you with people who not only talk the talk but walk the walk! You will be the recipient of His benefits! God will allow the seed of favor to be sown in your life, and the fruit of it will remain. Praising God with everything that is in you will; make you want to be better, live better, love better, and show and share the love that has been shared with you. When you bless Him for His benefits, it will; encourage your walk, strengthen your faith, deepen your relationship, and increase your capacity to give. You can't help it, God is so awesome, you can't begin to tell it all! It makes you want to shout: Praise God from Whom all blessings flow!!

Blessings, Rupert & Red.

DECEMBER 21

Always And Forever...

Meditation Verse: Hebrews 13:8 NKJV
Jesus Christ is the same yesterday, today, and forever.
Scripture Reading: Hebrews 13:1-19

The ten words of this verse are worth more than a picture said to be worth a thousand. The immutability of Jesus Christ is a constant from Genesis to Revelation. The magnificence that this verse implies is contrasted by its simplicity and comfort. We can rest in the fact that no matter what rocks our world or even sets it on end, we can depend on the stability and constancy of a Savior that is forever making intercession for us and working for our good. It is the example that we should aspire to in our Christian journey. To be steadfast and unmovable in our faith, because He is faithful, and His promise is to never leave nor forsake us. By faith we accept this truth and live out our lives with the knowledge that our future is secure. If you want to live your life with the assurance of forever, then connect with the one and only stabilizing force on the planet! Let me recommend Jesus, He is the only constant, the only steadfast, the only stable force that you need in your life. Don't delay, do it today! He has not changed, He's still waiting!

Blessings, Rupert & Red.

DECEMBER 22

His Word Never Fails

Meditation Verse: Isaiah 55:11 HCSB

So, My word that comes from My mouth will not return to me empty, but it will accomplish what I please and will prosper in what I send it to do.

Scripture Reading: Isaiah 55

This is my favorite chapter in Isaiah. It feels as if the Lord is talking directly to me. And He is!! And to you too. It is a reminder of God's compassion and grace, His desire to have a relationship with you, however, a reminder again that He is still Sovereign. The sobering truth is that while God is desirous of relationship with you, your decision to be in relationship or not, does not in any way thwart the purposes of God. God is and has always been intentional in His purpose. You can't change anything on His schedule or calendar. There are some people who have the reputation of being "all talk," never any follow through. Not true in God's case, he wants your participation, but He does not need it. The only thing that you can hold up is your own destiny. Procrastination does not live in the throne room! We move when God says move, or He will move without us! So, get on board with the program, you do not want to be left behind. God has too much in store for us in the kingdom, plans and purposes far beyond what we can even imagine! We cannot afford to delay; His word is going forth right now! It's going down, ready or not!!

Blessings, Rupert & Red

DECEMBER 23

Everlasting God!

Meditation Verse: Isaiah: 40:28 HCSB

Do you not know? Have you not heard? Yahweh is the everlasting God, the Creator of the whole earth. He never grows faint nor weary; there is no limit to His understanding.

Scripture Reading: Isaiah 40

We have always said that the natural beauty of this earth screams intelligent design! God has created this magnificent world without the help of any big bang! In verse 22 of this same chapter, Isaiah says, that it is God who sits above the circle of the earth, and that the majestic creation in that circle was His doing. This is the same God that neither slumbers nor sleeps, the same God that loves you and I, the same God that is desirous of a relationship with you! Got a problem, a situation, a circumstance that you just can't figure out? There is no limit to God's understanding. In fact, He understood what you needed before you did! I believe it was the commentator Herbert Wolf who said: "How easy is it to believe in the infinite power of God and at the same time feel that He is unable to meet our personal needs." Source: (Blue letter Bible, blueletterbible.org). Believers should live out these truths in a way that people will see that God is alive!! No one can compare to our God! As you go through this day, entering the holiday season, be mindful of the Great God you serve! To Him be all praise, worship, adoration and power!!

Blessings, Rupert & Red.

DECEMBER 24

God Is Close To The Brokenhearted

Meditation Verse: Psalms 82:3 NKJV

Defend the poor and fatherless; Do justice to the afflicted and needy.

Scripture Reading: Psalms 82

Enough of people using the word of God to justify wickedness. What is really infuriating is that there are members of the body of Christ that are not only condoning this but aiding and abetting in the practice. What practice you say? Treating the poor as criminals. Those who have little to no means are as important to God as you are. The bible says we are to defend the fatherless, and to treat immigrants with respect. I know we have talked about this before, but I want us on this Christmas Eve, to reflect on the goodness of God and all He has done for you. Did you not know that it wasn't all for you? God blessed you, so you can in turn be a blessing to someone else, we pass the bread around until everyone is fed. Our purpose is to make a difference. Let's show the love of Christ this Christmas and be a blessing to some one less fortunate than you. You may never know the joy that your deeds will bring, but God will, and He honors that.

Blessings, Rupert & Red.

DECEMBER 25

The Greatest Gift!!

Meditation verse: Isaiah 9:6 NKJV

For unto us a child is born, unto us a son is given: and the government will be upon his shoulder: and His name shall be called Wonderful, Counsellor, The mighty God, the everlasting Father, the Prince of Peace.

Scripture Reading: Isaiah 9: 1-7

Today is more than a "Holiday," It is a "Holy Day." The day that the Christian world celebrates the birth of the greatest gift ever to mankind. The day that Jesus Christ came into the world in human form. The Incarnate miracle, very man, yet very God, was born into the world, in a lowly state, in lowly surroundings, identifying not with the so-called hierarchy, but with the common man. Even though He was King of kings and Lord of lords, He came to die, to redeem us from the condemnation and punishment of our sins. This gift, which changes us from mortal to immortal, is the reason why we celebrate. Jesus is the reason for this blessed season, and if you are celebrating for any worldly reason you are celebrating in vain. Because before you can celebrate the Gift, you must receive it. Otherwise, there is no point. We pray that you move from holiday to Holy Day. This Gift is freely given! It is the reason we have life in the first place. Receive the Gift so that you can celebrate the true reason! Have a Blessed Christmas!!

Blessings, Rupert & Red.

DECEMBER 26

Spiritual Insight

Meditation Verse: Ephesians 1:17 HCSB

I pray that the God of our Lord Jesus Christ, the glorious Father, would give you a spirit of wisdom and revelation in the knowledge of Him.

Scripture Reading: Ephesians 1:15-19

Do you know who God is? I mean do you really have a relationship with God and can say I am in fellowship with The Almighty? God wants to grant you wisdom and give you a rhema word concerning the revealing of His plan for your life. And do you know what a major part of that plan is? To have a better understanding of who God is. Understanding that God is truth, and so is His word. Our ideas are flawed so we find ourselves with lives that become problematic All because we have a false idea of who God is. Most people want to get saved just enough to miss hell when they die. Life with God means so much more than that. We encourage you if you are not already doing so, read God's word, commune with Him in prayer, share what you have and know with others. You will grow in the spirit of wisdom and revelation as His plan unfolds in your life. It is why we live, and why we breathe... There's power in relationship.

Blessings, Rupert & Red.

DECEMBER 27

Improve Your Thought Life

Meditation Verse: Philippians 4:8 NIV

Finally, brothers and sisters, whatever is true, whatever is noble, whatever is right, whatever is pure, whatever is lovely, whatever is admirable; if anything is excellent and praiseworthy, think about such things.

Scripture Reading: Philippians 4:4-9

The majority of the battles that Christians face, are in the mind. Meditating or dwelling on the wrong things will often times invite the wrong type of spirit or temptation into your life. Paul knew about these distractions and puts a final note on how to keep peace and joy in the middle of trying circumstances. It requires a paradigm shift in our thinking or thought process. From mediocre and worldly, to excellent and praiseworthy. I bet if you think about things that are true, right, lovely, and noble, you quickly find a reason to rejoice! To dwell on the goodness of the Lord is to see everything in a different light. All of a sudden you realize that God is bigger than your problems! It does not mean that they won't come, you just now have the mindset to overcome. Your joy in the Lord becomes your strength. The peace of God is the cure for the imaginations that sometimes try to occupy our minds. Those things that need to be cast down in order to bring every thought into captivity that exalts itself against the knowledge of God. (2 Corinthians 10:5 paraphrased). The bottom line is if you want to improve your thought life, you must change the way that you think. Meditating on what is praiseworthy will build your faith and honor your Heavenly Father. So, develop the mind of Christ, and cast down those imaginations.

Blessings, Rupert & Red.

DECEMBER 28

The Spiritual Advocate

Meditation Verse: John 14:26 NLT

But when the Father sends the Advocate as my representative, that is, the Holy Spirit, He will teach you everything and will remind you of everything I have told you.

Scripture Reading: John 14:23-31

An advocate is one that pleads the cause of another, before a tribunal or judicial court. One that defends or maintains a cause or proposal. And my favorite; One who supports or promotes the interest of another. The Bible calls him The Holy Spirit! He is not your conscience! The Holy Spirit is unchangeable, your conscience is not, The Holy Spirit will lead you into all truth, your conscience will often mislead you. The Holy Spirit agrees with God, your conscience agrees with your flesh. Look, it is true that we are called, justified, sanctified and kept in the faith, through no effort of our own. We have that because of the Advocate. Most of what Jesus taught His disciples, were not necessarily the commandments they were responsible to obey, but the promises that He would fulfill on their behalf. At the center of His message of comfort was the fact that the Advocate would come. Don't let your conscience be your guide!! Follow the Advocate!

Blessings, Rupert & Red.

DECEMBER 29

From Generation To Generation

Meditation Verse: Psalms 72:1-2 NLT

Give your love of justice to the king, O God, and righteousness to the king's son. Help him judge your people in the right way; let the poor always be treated fairly.

Scripture Reading: Psalms 72

This was a psalm written by King David for Solomon as he was to be his heir to the throne. One of the lessons in this psalm is a prayer for leadership to continue under the next king with justice and fairness for the people. Not just under the next king but in the generations to come. True Christians should pray for their leaders to do what is right and fair in the eyes of God for the people that they serve. We seem to have forgotten that elected people are not celebrities, or leaders who have been elected to lord it over their constituents, but men and women who are servants of the people. The legacy that God intended was for servants to act judiciously, in fairness to all, especially the poor and vulnerable. We as the body of Christ owe it to God to hold these people accountable for; corruption, racism, police brutality, theft, sexual abuse, and too many other crimes to mention. It is not enough to just rally around one cause and ignore all the others. Remember that we all will stand before God one day to give an account for how we spent our lives here on earth. You need to learn what is important to God before it is too late. Teach your children and your children's children, from generation to generation to love justice and righteousness, so that we can raise true leaders that will serve people with dignity and fairness. As we move into a New Year, let's resolve within ourselves to let the love for justice and righteousness begin with the body of believers, and pass it down through the generations, so the legacy of what is important to God remains.

Blessings, Rupert & Red.

DECEMBER 30

A Forever Praise!!

Meditation Verse: Psalms 145:1-2 NLT

I will exalt you my God and King and praise your name forever and ever I will praise you every day; yes, I will praise you forever.

Scripture Reading: Psalms 145

Praise Break!! There is never a bad or wrong time to give praise! God is worthy of our constant praise!! David says that He is to be exalted as God and King. We can never give God too much praise! We don't give Him all that He deserves! If we pause and reflect on how good God has truly been, ten thousand tongues will not be sufficient to praise Him! Everyone has a story that shows the goodness of God in their lives, we need to share that story with everyone we know, God is no respecter of persons, and He is good to everyone! We all enjoy the benefits of the sun, moon and stars, the rain falls on the just and the unjust alike. His kingdom is an everlasting kingdom, that will never be shaken or taken. If you are reading this you are almost through another year, and regardless of the trials and tribulations you are still here! Give God your best praise, He is close to all who love Him, and He keeps His promises! Let us continually praise Him from now into the new Year, and into eternity! He is Worthy!!!

Blessings, Rupert & Red.

DECEMBER 31

No Never Alone!

Meditation verse: Isaiah 43:2-3 NLT

When you go through deep waters, I will be with you. When you go through rivers of difficulty you will not drown. When you walk through the fire of oppression, you will not be burned up; the flames will not consume you. For I am the Lord, your God, the Holy One of Israel, your Savior.

Scripture Reading: Isaiah 43:1-13

As we are about to embark upon a New Year, we want to encourage you, Trust in the Lord! There will be a host of challenges, some opportunities, some closed doors, there will be gain, and there will be loss, joyous times, sad times great memories, and painful ones. Do not be discouraged, do not give up! While life can be hard at times, there is nothing better than living, because it is all about helping to make this place better for someone else. Let your legacy be to encourage, lift up, inspire, raise standards and expectations, show up and show out every time, on time and never settle for less than you deserve. Serve God first and watch favor follow your efforts. Believe that no matter what you go through God will see you through. He will never leave you nor forsake you, but you must trust him and put Him first. Get up every day, thank God for life and then live it to the fullest. Give your plans and aspirations to Him and then work your plan. Pray every day all through the day over every decision and step you take. Allow His will to supersede yours and He will give you the desires of your heart. He has given you a passion and a gift. Create, Develop, Work, Succeed, and give Him all the glory!! Move with integrity, humility, forgiveness, and a sense of justice. Do not seek revenge against anyone, put them in God's hands, remember that you wrestle not against flesh and blood, so don't let flesh become your problem. Finally, stand on Christ the Solid Rock, God is not a man that He should lie, you can trust Him to keep His promises. All other ground is sinking sand.

A Happy and Blessed New Year!

Love and Blessings, Rupert & Red.

INDEX NOTES

1/1. Jeremiah 29:11 HCSB, Psalms 40:5 NKJV.

1/2. Psalms 71:15 NKJV

1/3. Proverbs 31:11 NLT. Statistics Quote: Rick Warren.

1/4. 2Peter 3:9 HCSB.

1/5. Romans 8:15 HCSB

1/6. Romans 5:8 KJV

1/9. Philippians 3:13 NLT

1/10. Proverbs 20:7 HCSB

1/11. Psalms 70:1 NKJV

1/12. Galatians 5:14 HCSB

1/13. 1Corinthians 10:13a HCSB

1/14. James 2:13 HCSB

1/15. Psalms 133:1 NKJV

1/16. Psalms 127:1 HCSB

1/17. Psalms 146:2 NLT

1/18. Joshua 6:2 NLT

1/19. 1Kings 8:49 MSG

1/20. Matthew 18:32-33 NLT

1/21. Isaiah 40:8 NLT

1/22. Galatians 5:22-23 KJV

1/23. Psalms 139:13 HCSB

1/24. Daniel 1:7 HCSB

1/25. Psalms 143:10 HCSB

1/26. Ezra 1:2 HCSB

1/27. 1Timothy 6:5 NLT

1/28. Psalms 146:3 NLT

1/29. Luke 22:32 HCSB

1/30. Luke 6:22 HCSB

1/31. Psalms 147:1 HCSB

2/1. Genesis 22:13 HCSB Quote: Myles Munroe

2/2. Genesis 12:1 HCSB

2/3. 1Timothy 6:12 HCSB Hebrews 11:6 HCSB

2/4. 1John 4:4 KJV

2/5. Psalms 33:20-21 NLT Isaiah 26:3 NKJV

2/6. Psalms 33:14-15 NLT

2/7. Jeremiah 29:7 HCSB

2/8. Ephesians 3:16 HCSB

2/9. Psalms 8:3-4 HCSB

2/10. Acts 20:35 HCSB

2/11. Deuteronomy 28:2 HCSB

2/12. Romans 12:2 HCSB

2/13. Psalms 90:2 HCSB Matthew 9:29 KJV

2/14. 1Corinthians 13:6-7 HCSB

2/15 Psalms 3:3 HCSB

2/16. Psalms 46:10 NKJV

2/17. Deuteronomy 8:18 HCSB

2/18. Ephesians 2:10 HCSB 2Corinthians 5:7 KJV

2/19. Psalms 91:1 KJV Hebrews 11:6b NKJV

2/20. Romans 15:4 HCSB

2/21. Deuteronomy 8:18 HCSB

2/22. Colossians1:16 CEB

2/23. Psalms27:8 NLT

2/24. Daniel 3:1 NLT

2/25. Psalms 37:4 NLT

2/26. Hebrews 1:2 HSCB

2/27. Revelation 22:1 HCSB, 1Corinthians 2:9 NKJV

2/28. Nehemiah 9:33 NLT

2/29. Hebrews 12:22 NLT

3/1. John 10:14-15 HCSB

3/2. Acts 3:16 NKJV

3/3. Psalms 53:2 NKJV

3/4. Psalms 16:11 NKJV

3/5. Colossians 4:6 HCSB, Proverbs 18:21 KJV, Psalms 19:14 KJV

3/6. Psalms 50:23 NLT, Psalms 113:3 KJV

3/7. James 2:13 NLT, 1Peter 3:16b NLT, Romans 12:20 NKJV

3/8. Matthew 7:24 NLT, John 13:17 NLT

3/9. Matthew 25:32 NLT, Matthew 25:35-36 NLT

3/10. Jeremiah 4:2 NLT

3/11. Matthew 11:28 HCSB

3/12. Psalms 45:4 NLT

3/13. Isaiah 59:14 NLT

3/14. 2Peter1:16 NKJV

3/15. Romans 7:24 NLT

3/16. Ephesians 2:9 NLT, Romans 10:9-10 NLT

3/17. 1Peter 4:8 NLT

3/18. Colossians 3:3 NLT

3/19. Psalms 5:3 NKJV

3/20. Psalms 77:8 HCSB

3/21. Psalms 75:9 NLT

3/22. Matthew 7:4 NLT, John 8:7 NKJV

3/23. Job 23:12 HCSB, John 6:63 HCSB, 1Peter 2:2 NIV

3/24. Luke 8:35 HCSB, Ephesians 6:12b NIV

3/25. Acts 15:8-9 KJV

3/26. Acts 5:29 NLT

3/27. Acts 9:15 NLT

3/28. James 5:16 NLT, Philippians 2:9 NIV, Foot Note: "Say The Name" – by Martha Munuzzi, Clint Brown.

3/29. 2 John 1:8 NLT

3/30. Zephaniah 3:7 NLT, James 4:17 NKJV

3/31. Mark 14:30 NLT, 1Peter 5:8 NKJV, 1Corinthians 10:12 NKJV

4/1. Luke 10:36-37 NLT

4/2. Psalms 24:1 NLT Quote: Commentator Matthew Henry, "My Father owns everything,"

4/3. 1Timothy 6:12 NLT, Romans 8:31b KJV

4/4. Amos 5:24 NKJV

4/5. Psalms 1:3 NKJV, Hebrews 6:1 NLT

4/6. Mark 11:9 NKJV

4/7. Jonah 1:3 NKJV

4/8. Psalms 23:1 NKJV

4/9. Romans 4:25 NLT, Revelation 1:18 NKJV, John 11:26 NKJV

4/10. Psalms 27:13 NKJV

4/11. 1Peter 5:7 NKJV

4/12. Deuteronomy 15:11 HCSB

4/13. 2Corinthians 5:14 NLT

4/14. 2 Corinthians 5:2 NLT.

4/15. 1Peter 5:10 HCSB, 2Corinthians 4:17 NLT

4/16. Matthew 5:16 HCSB, John 8:12 NKJV

4/17. Psalms 146:5 NLT

4/18. Colossians 2:8 HCSB

4/19. Nehemiah 6:3 NIV

4/20. Nehemiah 6:16 NIV

4/21. Romans 12:2 NKJV, Romans 12:2 J.B Phillips

4/22. Mark 7:15 NLT

4/23. Lamentations 3:22-23 HCSB

4/24. Isaiah 10:1-2 NLT

4/25. Proverbs 1:7 HCSB

4/26. Psalms 130:3 NLT, Psalms 103:12 NKJV. Quote: "No mortal man can answer for himself before a judge so perfect, concerning a law so divine." Matthew Henry, Commentator.

4/27. Psalms 137:4 KJV, John 4:13 NKJV

4/28. Mark 4:14 KJV

4/29. James 4:6 HCSB

4/30. James 1:5 HCSB

5/1. Genesis 2:7 KJV

5/2. Galatians 2:21 NLT. Analogy by Rick Warren.

5/3. Joshua 1:6 NLT

5/4. Psalms 71:14 NLT

5/5. Ecclesiastes 7:9 HCSB, Romans 12:19b HCSB

5/6. Ecclesiastes 12:13-14 HCSB, Matthew 6:33 HCSB. Quote: Seek not success but truth, and you will find both." John Mason Commentator.

5/7. Psalms 91:2 HCSB

5/8. 1Corinthians 2:14 NKJV

5/9. 1Peter 1:13 NLT

5/10. Luke 7:20 NLT

5/11. Luke 16:15 NLT, Romans 3:23 NLT

5/12. Psalms 27:13 HCSB, Galatians 6:9 KJV

5/13. James 3:6 HCSB

5/14. Ephesians 4:16 NLT. Quote: "A Church that is only united in itself, but not united to Christ, is no living church at all." Charles Spurgeon, Commentator.

5/15. Psalms 19:7-9 NKJV, 2Peter 1:3 NKJV

5/16. Psalms 19:7 NKJV. Quote: "While it does not give us all knowledge, all the knowledge that it gives is true and perfect." David Guzik, Commentator.

5/17. Psalms 19:8 NKJV

5/18. Psalms 19:9 NKJV. Quote: "David wrote this psalm with a fraction of what we have today as the word of God." David Guzik, Commentator.

5/19. Psalms 19:10 NKJV, Matthew 6:33 NLT

5/20. Romans 3:24 NKJV

5/21. John 8:7 ASV

5/22. John 20:31 ESV

5/23. Joshua 24:15 NKJ

5/24. Hosea 13:5 NKJV

5/25. Micah 6:8 NKJV

5/26. Lamentations 3:22-23 NKJV

5/27. Psalms 51:1 NKJV

5/28. Romans 2:11 ASV

5/29. Hebrews 8:6 NKJV

5/30. Psalms 24:2-3 NKJV

5/31. Colossians 3:1-2 HCSB

6/1. Romans 3:20 NLT, Romans 3:20 JB Phillips

6/2. Ephesians 2:10 NLT

6/3. James 2:13 HCSB, Matthew 7:2 NKJV

6/4. Ephesians 2:19 NKJV

6/5. Psalms 145:3 NLT

6/6. Joel 2:12 KJV

6/7. Psalms 17:8 KJV

6/8. Galatians 6:2 NLT

6/9. Proverbs 1:7a NKJV, Galatians 6:7 NKJV

6/10. Psalms 33:7a NLT

6/11. Proverbs 12:25 NKJV

6/12. Psalms 77:11 NLT

6/13. Romans 3:24 NLT. Quote: "All other religions are based on the word do, Christianity, however, is based on the word done." Pastor & Author Rick Warren.

6/14. Acts 18:9-10 NLT, Statistics: "Between 2-17% of Christians actively share their faith." Source: Blue Letter Bible.

6/15. 2Timothy 4:3 KJV

6/16. Jeremiah 26:13 KJV

6?17. Titus 1:16a NLT

6/18. James 4:17 NLT, Luke 12:48 KJV

6/19. John 3:16 NKJV

6/20. Luke 13:30 HCSB, Luke 16: 19-31 HCSB

6/21. James 4:6b NLT

6/22. Colossians 3:14 NLT

6/23. Psalms 12:5 NLT

6/24. Deuteronomy 4:29 NLT

6/25. Hosea 4:1b-2a NKJV

6/26. Hosea 4:6 NKJV, Psalm 138:2 NKJV

6/27. 1John 3:11 NKJV, Psalm 15:3 HCSB

6/29. Psalm 150:6 NLT

6/30. Job 13:15 NKJV

7/1. Psalm 121:1-2 NKJV, Jeremiah 3:23 NKJV

7/2. Philippians 4:7 NKJV

7/3. Matthew 23:4 NLT, Acts 5:10 NLT, Matthew 11:30 NLT

7/4. Romans 7:6 NLT, Galatians 3:24 NLT, Romans 7:18 NKJV

7/5. Proverbs 22:7 NKJV

7/6. 1Corinthians 15:58 NLT, Hebrews 6:10 NLT

7/7. Psalm 84:10 NKJV, Matthew 25:23 NKJV

7/8. Matthew 23:27 NKJV, Matthew 7:21 NKJV

7/9. Psalm 18:33 NLT

7/10. Psalm 86:15 NKJV

7/11. Habakkuk 3:17-18 NLT

7/12. Psalm 63:3 HSCB, Acts 17:28 NKJV

7/13. Genesis 1:1 HCSB

7/14. Luke 11:9 HCSB, Acts 17:11 HCSB

7/15. Nahum 1:7 NLT, Definition of trust, reference: Webster's Dictionary. Quote: God knows us, He knows our prayers, tears, wishes, etc. Charles Spurgeon, Commentator.

7/16. 1Thessalonians 5:16-18 NKJV

7/17. Psalms 77:11 HCSB

7/18. Titus 3:4-5 NLT

7/19. Proverbs 18:21 NKJV.

7/20. 1John 1:10 NLT, 1John1:9b NKJV

7/21. Proverbs 21:3 NLT, Matthew 23:39 NLT

7/22. Isaiah 6:3 NKJV

7/23. Psalm 90:12 NKJV

7/24. Luke 11:1 NKJV

7/25. Psalm 107:2 NKJV. Quote: "Ours is a particular redemption, so we must offer a particular praise." Charles Spurgeon, Commentator.

7/26. Matthew 6:33 NKJV

7/27. Ephesians 2:18 NLT

7/28. Psalm 9:10 NKJV

7/29. Psalm 14:1 NLT, Definition of a fool, Source: Webster's Dictionary.

7/30. Matthew 5:6 HCSB. Quote: "It is not enough to know that my sin is forgiven, oh that my nature could be changed etc. Charles Spurgeon, Commentator.

7/31. Psalm 23:6 NKJV

8/1. Philippians 3:13 NLT

8/2. Psalm 138:2 NKJV

8/3. Mark 10:21 NLT

8/4. Psalm 18:2 NKJV

8/5. Hebrews 2:1 HCSB

8/6. Romans 1:20 NLT

8/7. Psalm 37:25 NKJV

8/8. Matthew 11:15 NLT

8/9. 1Timothy 6:10 NKJV

8/10. Psalm 29:2 NKJV

8/11. Matthew 5:7 NKJV

8/12. Matthew 16:26 NKJV

8/13. James 1:27 CEB

8/14. Ephesians 6:12 NLT, 1John 5:19 NLT

8/15. Psalm 24:1 NLT

8/16. Mark 2:17 NLT, Romans 3:23 NKJV

8/17. Matthew 7:20 NLT

NKJV

8/19. 2Corinthians 6:2b NIV

8/20. Philippians 2:2 HCSB

8/21. James 3:13 NLT

8/22. Psalm 8:3 NLT

8/23. Hebrews 3:7-8 HCSB

8/24. Hebrews 4:12 NKJV

8/25. Proverbs 16:24 NLT

8/26. Proverbs 3:5-6 HCSB

8/27. Philippians 2:3 NKJV

8/28. 1Corinthians 13:7 NLT

8/29. John 10:14-15 NKJV

8/30. Psalms 46:10 NKJV

8/31. Proverbs 22:6 Amplified/Paraphrased

9/1. Galatians 6:9 NKJV

9/2. Psalm 63:3 NKJV

9/3. Mark 10:24b NKJV, Mark 8:36 NKJV, Matthew 6:20 NKJV

9/4. John 14:27 NKJV

9/5. Psalm 56:4 NLT

9/6. 2Corinthians 10:4 NLT, Proverbs 23:7a NLT

9/7. Proverbs 21:1 Amplified

9/8. Psalm 23:1 NLT, John 10:11 NKJV

9/9. Proverbs 21:2 Amplified

9/10. Proverbs 21:3 MSG

9/11. Proverbs 21:4 Amplified

9/12. Genesis 2:15 NLT

9/13. Genesis 3:6b-7a NLT

9/14. 1Peter 3:15-16a HCSB

9/15. Psalm 92:2 HCSB, Definitions, Declare, Emphatically, Source Webster's Dictionary.

9/16. 2Thessalonians 3:5 NLT

9/17. Psalm 20:7 NLT

9/18. Psalm 93:2 HCSB

9/19. Psalm 55:10 NLT

9/20. Jeremiah 1:5 NLT

9/21. Exodus 20:3 NLT

9/22. Luke 22:32 NLT

9/23. Luke 12:24 NLT

9/24. Luke 17:20 NKJV

9/25. Hebrews 2:1 NKJV, Story, Author Unknown.

9/26. 2Corinthians 4:8-9 HCSB

9/27. 2Corinthians 4:7 NKJV. Quote: "This treasure is the greatness of the gospel of Jesus Christ and the glory of God made evident through that gospel." David Guzik, Commentator.

9/28. Psalm 119:105 NKJV

9/29. Psalm 119:11 NKJV

9/30. 1Thessalonians 5:15 NKJV

10/1. Psalm 19:14 NKJV, Matthew 12:34 KJV

10/2. 1John 4:4 HCSB

10/3. 1Thessalonians 5:9 HCSB

10/4. Psalm 55:22 NLT

10/5. Psalm 147:1 HCSB

10/6. Psalm 70:4 NLT

10/7. Ephesians 3:18 NLT

10/8. Matthew 6:3-4 NLT

10/9. Psalm 18:1 NLT, Acts 17:28 KJV

10/10. Psalm 18:2 NLT

10/11. 1Kings 19:4 NLT

10/12. Psalm 27:8 NLT

10/13. Colossians 3:2 NLT

10/14. Psalm 84:10 NKJV. Quote: "Everyman has his choice, and this is ours, God's worst is better than the devil's best." Charles Spurgeon, Commentator.

10/15. Ephesians 2:1 NKJV

10/16. Ephesians 4:1 NLT

10/17. Galatians 1:15a NLT

10/18. Jeremiah 26:15 HCSB

10/19. 2Corinthians 10:5 HCSB, 1Corinthians 6:19-20 HCSB

10/20. Acts 3:4-5 NKJV

10/21. Romans 8:31 HCSB

10/22. John 13:34-35 HCSB

10/23. 2Timothy 3:16-17 NIV

10/24. Galatians 2:20 NIV

10/25. Proverbs 13:3 HCSB, Luke 6:45 HCSB. Quote: "God has given us two eyes that we may see much, two ears that we may hear much, but has given us one tongue, and that fenced in with teeth, to indicate that though we see and hear much, we should speak but little." Adam Clarke, Commentator.

10/26. Titus 2:11-12 HCSB, Ephesians 2:8-9 HCSB

10/27. Psalm 3:3 HSCB

10/28. Psalm 9:1 HCSB

10/29. Isaiah 43:2 HCSB

10/30. James 2:17 HCSB

10/31. Galatians 5:16 NLT

11/1. Romans 9:16 NLT, Galatians 3:16 NLT

11/2. Matthew 5:16 NLT, 2Corinthians 3:2 NLT

11/3. Romans 2:13 NLT

11/4. Matthew 2:11 NLT

11/5. Philippians 1:6 NKJV

11/6. Jude 1:21 HCSB

11/7. Zechariah 7:9 NKJV, 1John 4:20b NKJV

11/8. Daniel 3:17-18 NKJV

11/9. Hebrews 11:6 NKJV

11/10. Psalm 145:4 NLT

11/11. Matthew 18:6 HCSB

11/12. Isaiah 1:16-17 NLT

11/13. Psalm 89:14 NLT

11/14. Acts 11:17 HCSB

11/15. Micah 7:3 NLT

11/16. Psalm 84:12 NLT

11/17. Romans 3:11 NKJV, Romans 1:20 NKJV

11/18. James 5:4 HCSB

11/19. Deuteronomy 6:7 NKJV

11/20. Exodus 20:3 NKJV

11/21. 1Peter 5:7 HCSB

11/22. 1 Chronicles 29:11 NLT

11/23. 2Corinthians 4:18 NKJV. The Purpose Driven Life, Rick Warren, Author.

11/24. Luke 16:31 NLT

11/25. Proverbs 17:13 NLT

11/26. Malachi 3:5b NLT

11/27. Psalm 18:2 NLT

11/28. Luke 2:19 NKJV

11/29. James 5:16 MSG

11/30. Luke 13:6-9 HCSB

12/1. John 19:30 NLT

12/2. Jeremiah 17:10 HCSB, Psalm 139:23 HCSB

12/3. 2Peter 3:9 HCSB

12/4. Romans 1:16 HCSB

12/5. Hebrews 4:16 NKJV

12/6. Joshua 1:7 HCSB

12/7. Psalm 100:4 HCSB

12/8. Psalm 51:10 KJV, 1John1:9 KJV

12/9. Proverbs 21:21 HCSB

12/10. Isaiah 41:10 HCSB

12/11. Psalm 119:114 HCSB

12/12. Psalm 37:7 NLT

12/13. Ephesians 6:12 NLT

12/14. Proverbs 18:10 HCSB

12/15. Psalm 107:1 NLT

12/16. 1 Corinthians 3:18 HCSB

12/17. Philippians4:6 NIV

12/18. Revelation 3:20 HCSB

12/19. Psalm 27:4 NIV

12/20. Psalm 103:1-2 NKJV

12/21. Hebrews 3:8 NKJV

12/22. Isaiah 55:11 HCSB

12/23. Isaiah 40:28 HCSB. Quote: "How easy is it to believe in the infinite power of God, and at the same time feel that He is unable to meet our personal needs." Christian Wolf, Commentator.

12/24. Psalm 82:3 NKJV

12/25. Isaiah 9:6 NKJV

12/26. Ephesians 1:17 HCSB

12/27. Philippians 4:8 NIV

12/28. John 14:26 NLT

12/29. Psalm 72:1-2 NLT

12/30. Psalm 145:1-2 NLT 12/31. Isaiah 43:2-3 NLT.

www.ingramcontent.com/pod-product-compliance
Lightning Source LLC
Chambersburg PA
CBHW022047160426
43198CB00008B/146